Synchronizing Internet Protocol Security (SIPSec)

T0142954

Advances in Information Security

Sushil Jajodia
Consulting Editor
Center for Secure Information Systems
George Mason University
Fairfax, VA 22030-4444
email: jajodia@gmu.edu

The goals of the Springer International Series on ADVANCES IN INFORMATION SECURITY are, one, to establish the state of the art of, and set the course for future research in information security and, two, to serve as a central reference source for advanced and timely topics in information security research and development. The scope of this series includes all aspects of computer and network security and related areas such as fault tolerance and software assurance.

ADVANCES IN INFORMATION SECURITY aims to publish thorough and cohesive overviews of specific topics in information security, as well as works that are larger in scope or that contain more detailed background information than can be accommodated in shorter survey articles. The series also serves as a forum for topics that may not have reached a level of maturity to warrant a comprehensive textbook treatment.

Researchers, as well as developers, are encouraged to contact Professor Sushil Jajodia with ideas for books under this series.

Additional titles in the series:

SECURE DATA MANAGEMENT IN DECENTRALIZED SYSTEMS edited by Ting Yu and Sushil Jajodia; ISBN: 978-0-387-27694-6
NETWORK SECURITY POLICIES AND PROCEDURES by Douglas W. Frye; ISBN: 0-387-30937-3
DATA WAREHOUSING AND DATA MINING TECHNIQUES FOR CYBER SECURITY by Anoop Singhal; ISBN: 978-0-387-26409-7
SECURE LOCALIZATION AND TIME SYNCHRONIZATION FOR WIRELESS SENSOR AND AD HOC NETWORKS edited by Radha Poovendran, Cliff Wang, and Sumit Roy; ISBN: 0-387-32721-5
PRESERVING PRIVACY IN ON-LINE ANALYTICAL PROCESSING (OLAP) by Lingyu Wang, Sushil Jajodia and Duminda Wijesekera; ISBN: 978-0-387-46273-8
SECURITY FOR WIRELESS SENSOR NETWORKS by Donggang Liu and Peng Ning; ISBN: 978-0-387-32723-5
MALWARE DETECTION edited by Somesh Jha, Cliff Wang, Mihai Christodorescu, Dawn Song, and Douglas Maughan; ISBN: 978-0-387-32720-4
ELECTRONIC POSTAGE SYSTEMS: Technology, Security, Economics by Gerrit Bleumer; ISBN: 978-0-387-29313-2
MULTIVARIATE PUBLIC KEY CRYPTOSYSTEMS by Jintai Ding, Jason E. Gower and Dieter Schmidt; ISBN-13: 978-0-378-32229-2
UNDERSTANDING INTRUSION DETECTION THROUGH VISUALIZATION by Stefan Axelsson; ISBN-10: 0-387-27634-3
QUALITY OF PROTECTION: Security Measurements and Metrics by Dieter Gollmann, Fabio Massacci and Artsiom Yautsiukhin; ISBN-10: 0-387-29016-8

Additional information about this series can be obtained from
http://www.springer.com

Synchronizing Internet Protocol Security (SIPSec)

by

Charles A. Shoniregun
University of East London
UK

Springer

Charles A. Shoniregun
Reader in Computing
KNURE/KSAC Distinguished Professor
School of Computing & Technology
University of East London
Docklands Campus, University Way
London E16 2RD
United Kingdom
Email: C.Shoniregun@uel.ac.uk

Synchronizing Internet Protocol Security (SIPSec) by Charles A. Shoniregun

ISBN-13: 978-1-4419-4099-5   e-ISBN-13: 978-0-387-68569-4

Printed on acid-free paper.

9 8 7 6 5 4 3 2 1

springer.com

DEDICATION

To my late mother Juliana O. Shoniregun (1934–2006)

TABLE OF CONTENTS

LIST OF FIGURES

LIST OF TABLES

LIST OF CONTRIBUTORS AND ORGANISATIONS

Alex Logvynovskiy	e-Centre for Infonomics, UK
Brendan Cotter	Kurt Geiger Ltd, UK
Sonny Nwankwo	University of East London, UK
Kasim Charhabagi	University of East London, UK
Harvey Freeman	Booze Allen Hamilton, USA
Charles Winer	Purdue University, Calumet, USA
Caterina Scoglio	Kansas State University, Kansas, USA
Victoria Repka	Kharkov National University of Radioelectronics, Ukraine
Maaruf Ali	Oxford Brooks University, UK
Vyacheslav Grebenyuk	Kharkov National University of Radioelectronics, Ukraine
Kia Makki	Florida International University, Miami, USA
Niki Passinou	Florida International University, Miami, USA
Siân Lambert	Manchester Metropolitan University, UK
Seamus Simpson	Manchester Metropolitan University, UK
Terry Cook	City University, USA.
Jen-Yao Chung	IBM Watson Research Centre, USA
Liang-Jie (LJ) Zhang	IBM Watson Research Centre, USA
Patrick Hung	University of Ontario, Institute of Technology, Canada
Dragana Martinovic	University of Windsor, Canada
Victor Ralevich	Sheridan Institute of Technology and Advance Learning, Canada
Pit Pichappan	Annamalai University, India

British Telecommunications Plc (BT), UK
CERT Coordination Centre, USA
Cisco, USA
Dell, UK
e-Centre for Infonomics, UK
Honeywell, UK
Internet Engineering Task Force (IETF)
InternetSecurity.org.uk, UK
Intrusion.com
Microsoft Corp, USA
National Security Agency, USA
Sun Microsystems, Inc., USA
TEISME.com, UK
University of Massachusetts, USA
VeriSign, Inc, USA

PREFACE

The open design of the Internet has not only opened many new opportunities for communications, but it has also opened many new avenues for attackers against organisations network and computing resources. This book is a critical investigation of the Internet Protocol Security (IPSec) based on combination of theoretical investigation and practical implementation, which provides an in-depth understanding of the IPSec framework. The benefits of IPSec were exploited while the delimiting factors cannot be ignored. Information security has become a major concern in recent times as more and more computers are being connected to the global Internet. With so much data transferring over public networks, the risk of sensitive information has increased exponentially and the increase of Internet hosts continuously requires additional security support. The IPSec may be used in three different security domains: Virtual private networks, Application-level security, and Routing security. It comprises of suite of protocols, which are developed to ensure that the integrity, confidentiality and authentication of data communications over an IP network. The IPSec is predominately used in virtual private networks (VPNs). But when used in application-level security or routing security, the IPSec is not a complete solution and must be coupled with other security measures to be effective. As with other security systems, poor maintenance can easily lead to a critical system failure. This research is concerned with an investigation of the vulnerabilities that impair the IPSec, and detailed the packet-by-packet analysis of the protocol transactions in IPSec. The IPSec uses a number of different algorithms and protocols to provide a cohesive security framework. But the Internet has also given intruders the opportunity to carry out diverse levels of attacks, which threatening the privacy of users and integrity of important data. In depth research has also led to more significant reasons why IPSec has failed in certain situation. The current standard for the Internet protocol (IP) is completely unprotected, allowing hosts to inspect or modify data in transit. However, the use of one technique to overcome one problem raised issues for another. A more general and flexible solution is require, which can be easily integrated with the current IPSec without changes to it specification. This book also identifies the security problems facing the Internet communication protocols; the risks associated with Internet connection, delimitations of the IPSec and finally proposed a 'Synchronisation of Internet Protocol Security (SIPSec)' model. I strongly believed that the readers of this book would gain an in-depth knowledge of the problematic nature of IPSec architecture/operations and why SIPSec is necessary.

ACKNOWLEDGEMENTS

My searching for knowledge enhancement in Internet security has triggered many questions relating to the conceptual operations and the limitations of the IPSec. Having authored many books, it became apparent that the amount of existing work in IPSec cannot be ignored and the work have contributed to what has led me to rethink what can be done to enhance the current IPSec security performance. However, it is difficult to acknowledge all the people that have directly or indirectly contributed to this book. But some names cannot be forgotten — many thanks to my editor Susan Lagerstrom-Fife, publishing director Jennifer Evans and Rudiger Gebauer for their support. Indeed, those kind reminders and useful comments from Sharon Palleschi are all appreciated.

A special thank you to a dear friend Dr Alex Logvynovskiy of e-Center for Infonomics, for his never-ending contribution.

I sincerely thank Prof Mike Thorne, Alan Ingle, Vice Chancellor's Group – University of East London and all my post graduate students for their support. Undoubtedly, my reflection to past experiences in industry and academia has help to bridge the gap in my understanding of the IPSec architechture and its limitations. I would also like to acknowledge my appreciation to the following organisations: Cisco, Dell, e-Center for Infonomics, IETF, HP, IBM, Microsoft Corp, AOL, BT, InternetSecurity.com, DTI, eBay, Lucent Technology, InternetSecurity.org.uk, TEISME.com and Sky Broadband.

Many thanks to all the organisations that voluntarily participated in the survey questionnaire and the security managers/analysts who gave their time to be interviewed and participated in the case study observations.

The time spent in research and writing this book has been particularly difficult on my family. My absence, irritability and frustration to carry on have often reached uncharted personal heights. Tangential thanks go to my beauty queen and my angels for all their support, of which even the most carefully chosen words cannot adequately represent.

Finally, to the memory of my late parents, their energetic approach towards education cannot be ignored in my contribution to knowledge—education is a lifetime learning experience. And also to the memory of my late grannies, their ideology has greatly impacted what I live to believed that twenty years is not forever and the experience gain within that period remains for ever and an additional value added bonus to individual knowledge.

Chapter 1

RESEARCH OVERVIEW AND CONCEPTUAL UNDERSTANDING OF INTERNET PROTOCOL SECURITY (IPSEC)

1.   INTRODUCTION

No technology symbolises our age better than the Internet and the activity on the Internet has seen an explosion in the past few years. The work of Shannon and Weaver (1949) laid the groundwork for a variety of further research(s) both in the communication theory and communication technology. The fact that you can use the internet search browsers to search and view or for receiving and transmitting of information — is possible because of the immense leaps in the technology of information transmission that Shannon and Weaver were interested in since the late 40's (Ettlie, 2000; Shannon and Weaver, 1949).

'The distance is nothing; it is only the first step that is difficult.'
—Madame Du Deffand (1697–1780)

The Internet Protocol (IP) is the standard protocol for the Internet that provides unique addressing to every host. Uniqueness is important to ensure data can be delivered correctly to every host in the Internet. The IP routes packets to their destination host even though it provides unreliable, and connectionless datagram delivery service. The reasons for the latter problems are based on the facts that there is no security associated with IP packets. These packets can be forged, source or destination addresses can be changed, contents can be modified, it can even be inspected and analysed during transit. Therefore, there is no assurance that the packets received are from the legitimate sender, who claimed to be the sender, contain the original data that was sent by the sender and have not yet been inspected and analysed during transit. So the authenticity of the legitimate sender is unreliable because there are no guarantees that the packet will successfully be delivered to the destination host. Whereas connectionless means packets are delivered independently. This sometimes can cause packets to arrive out of order. In other to ensure smooth communication between different types of computers, programmers write the programs in accordance with standard protocols. The TCP/IP is probably one of the all burst, and most widely used protocol for communications between computers/networks. The acronym TCP/IP derived from the two main protocols transmission control protocol (TCP), and IP.

2.   RESEARCH RATIONALE

The Internet is revolutionising the way organisations communicate and conduct business. By nature, the Internet is public, distributed, and very dynamic interconnection of several networks– with phenomenal growth in infrastructure, number of people online and number and types of applications running across it. This multi-dimensional growth is enabling tremendous business rewards, especially for those who stake their claims first. The infrastructure of the Internet is complicated and, today's security solutions are most effective when they are tailored to the unique elements of an installation but cannot always guarantee the data safety. As a result, many web hosting systems and networks inherited the generic problems of Internet architecture protocols. Any attack is a case in point that exploits the 'weakest link' syndrome of Internet architecture protocols. With the Internet growing at warp speed, it is not surprising to experience growing pains. Learning to build and maintain Web sites that are secure is simply one of the challenges. As gaps in security implementations are discovered, they are fixed; as gaps in security technology are discovered, new technologies and techniques are developed. When gaps are not completely fixable, techniques to minimise the risks associated with them are developed and adopted as best practices to avoid any vulnerable attacks, undoubted the Internet security issue is a night mere. Readily available tools and practices should be used to minimise the risks posed by security breaches, computer viruses, hackers, authenticity and the Internet frauds. Security approaches that take a holistic view of hardware, software, services and networks have the best chance of succeeding. A good place to begin is with three fundamental guidelines for managing Internet security:

* Understand global dependencies on Internet
* Maintain constant awareness of the status of those dependencies
* Be able to react in a pre-planned manner to changes in the environment

Although new security gaps will continue to emerge, enterprises can mitigate risk by exercising due diligence and by implementing processes for preventing and reacting to security incidents. More than ever, awareness and effective management of security risks is a distinguishing characteristic of successful online businesses. This gave a great interest to carry out a study and research on Internet attacks, implication and managements. Establishing secure channels between a pair of hosts is an attractive way of exchanging information that is directly. The IPSec provides security services for the traffic at the IP layer but it is difficult to use because there many parameters to set up for secure channels, and the configuration for the Internet Protocol Security (IPSec) is complicated. The IPSec is a framework of open standards for ensuring private, secure communications over the IP networks, through the use of cryptographic security services. IPSec supports network-level peer authentication, data origin authentication, data integrity, data confidentiality (encryption), and replay protection. The IPSec has been implemented by a large number of vendors, and interoperability between multi-vendor devices makes IPSec an ideal option for building Virtual Private Networks (Shoniregun, 2005b). The IPSec is designed to provide interoperable, high quality, cryptographically based security for IPv4 and IPv6 (Kent and Seo, 2005). It can be deployed to protect data going between two hosts, between a host and a router/firewall, or between two routers/firewalls. It also gives fine-grained control as to how the security is implemented - what services to use where, what combination, and what algorithms to use. In a nutshell, the IPSec is a standard that provide security at the network layer for securing the IP communications by encrypting and/or authenticating all IP packets. Many vendors support the IPSec and the policies can be assigned through Group Policy, which allows the IPSec settings to be configured either at the domain, site, or organisational unit level. Apart from the inherited problems of the Internet, the IPSec main problems lays in it ability to compression, multicast, Network Address Translation (NAT), Policy, Nested tunnel and poor standardisation that has prevented internetworking of existing Virtual Private Network (VPN) solution.

Furthermore, the unauthorised access to information is very easy, and it is hard to catch the intruders. The ability to view data sent over the network would allow data such as passwords to be viewed when connecting to some services like FTP, which does not encrypt passwords sent over the network. The computer connected to the Internet can be a weak link, allowing unauthorised access to the information in systems irrespective of the confidentiality. The intruders are always interested in security related information such as passwords, access control files and keys, personnel information, encryption algorithms, system configuration, access and authentication procedures that can enable unauthorised individuals to get access to important files and programs, thus compromising the security of the system. A security incident or an attack is refers to as "an assault on system security that derives from an intelligent threat, i.e., an intelligent act that is a deliberate attempt (especially in the sense of a methods or technique) to evade security services and violate the security policy of a system." This usually means that the activity violates an explicit or implicit security policy (Dekker, M 1997, Shirey, R 2000). A security incident or an intrusion may be a comparatively minor event involving a single site or a major event in which thousands of sites are affected. The intrusion can come from anywhere on the Internet in any shape and size, however some attacks must be launched from specific systems or networks. A typical attack pattern consists of gaining access to a user's account, gaining privileged access, and using the victim's system as a launch platform for attacks on other sites (Russell, D. 1992). Incidents can be come from anywhere from anyone. People commit online security breaches for the same reason they commit other illicit activities such as malicious sabotage, greed, to seek entertainment, intellectual challenge, a sense of power, political attention or recognition, ideology and for financial gain. Their targets can vary widely: theft or deletion of corporate data such as client, financial, or strategic documents; defacement of web site; and/ or denial of service (Dekker, M 1997). The Denial of Service (DoS) is well-known to the majority of system administrators. The most common types of DoS attacks is the Synchronising (SYN) flood attacks, because of the simplicity of program implementation and the lack of effective methods to secure the inspected intelligence system. The DoS is by far, the most prevalent security concern. The attacker requests the establishment of a new connection via SYN packet. The TCP protocol use SYN (SYNchronising segment) to synchronise the two ends of a connection, which opens the connection between the client and the server. The scientific and commercial interest in the impacts of SYN flood attacks has grows over the past few years with focus on detecting ill-intentioned activity in implementation of DoS attacks but also to block or mitigate attack stirs up. In critical cases, the Network/IT security managers should implement attack mitigation within a reasonable time frame.

The perpetrators of Internet attacks could be just above any one. It is difficult to characterise the people who cause the incidents. The short list of intruders includes an adolescent who is curious about what he or she can do on the Internet, a college student who has created a new software tool, an individual seeking personal gain, random hackers and a paid spy seeking information of a corporation or foreign country. The lack of adequate knowledge and understanding of software and security engineering leads to security vulnerabilities, such as inappropriate programming, getting even worse under deadline pressure and rush-to-market issues. Some solution may be effective today, but as technology changes, new risks and challenges appear. Moreover, different solutions must be combined to be effective against, different types of attacks, and the security of the system must be constantly monitored (Larochelle 2001; Shoniregun, 2006a).

3.   RESEARCH HYPOTHESIS

The documentation for the IPSec is complex and confusing, in majority of cases no overview or introduction is provided, and nowhere are the goals of IPSec identified. The user must assemble the pieces and try to make sense of the documentation that can be described as difficult to read at best but searching for knowledge enhancement in Internet security has triggered many questions relating to the conceptual operations and limitations of IPSec. As a result of the preliminary research, special consideration has been given to the null hypothesis, which relates to the statement clearly stated below, devoid of ambiguities and been tested. A null hypothesis may be rejected and alternatively it may not be rejected in our findings. In this situation we do not conclude that the null hypothesis is valid. To test the hypotheses a number of leading research questions have emerged:

i.   What precisely constitutes IPSec?
ii. Is classification and taxonomy of IPSec possible?
iii. What are the Impacts of IPSec on operating systems and Internet security?
iv. Can IPSec be 100 per cent secured?
v.   Is it possible to synchronised user's biometric profile with IPSec?

However, searching for knowledge can be very hypocritical at the beginning but always satisfactory when results are achieved. The following hypotheses have been formulated based on the literature review (which includes ongoing access to online resources and laboratory experiments).

It is too early to reject or accept the three stated hypotheses, but as the study progresses the facts will be noted either in support of 'Null' or 'Alternative' hypothetical statements:

Hypothesis 1:

*   Null hypothesis (H_0^1): The IPv4 is not complementary to v6.
*   Alternative (H_A^1): The IPv4 is complementary to v6.

Hypothesis 2:

- Null hypothesis (H_0^2): Absolute security is unattainable in the IPSec.
- Alternative (H_A^2): Absolute security is attainable in the IPSec.

Hypothesis 3:

- Null hypothesis (H_0^3): Synchronising the IPSec with the biometric user's profile is unattainable.
- Alternative (H_A^3): Synchronising the IPSec with the biometric user's profile is attainable.

Generally speaking, making the IPSec secured has been a hot debate for many years. The key issues in IPSec are contained in the generic architecture of IP. The traditional IPSec implementations have been in place for a long time but unlike today, the intermediate systems at the time had no requirement to access the information inside the encrypted headers. As the technology advanced much more sophisticated systems have been introduced. For example firewall, which can filter traffic intelligently and not just blocking traffic from and to a host and NAT devices, which are widely used to prolong the diminishing life of IPv4 and v6. These devices (intermediate systems) do an excellent job in enhancing network performance but at the same time they violate the end-to-end security model that IPSec was designed to enforce. Given the past record of information technology and its aversion to open discourse, we might expect many decades of failure, deceit, and dishonesty. The deployment of IPSec has raises some issues, which must be addressed. These issues are the rediscovery of end-to-end communication, the availability of IPSec stacks, the increase in the number and type of IP devices and the increase in the number of nomadic devices. The Request for Comments (RFCs) documented by Internet Engineering Task Force (IETF) defined the architecture and components of the IPSec. These components and their interrelationship comprises of the logical architecture of the IPSec. The IPSec protocols deployment and configuration is determined by the users/administrators. It is also the goal of the IPSec architecture to ensure that compliant implementations include the services and management interfaces needed to meet the security requirements of a broad user population.

4.   CONCEPTUAL RESEARCH CONTEXT

In the 80s, it was relatively straightforward to determine if an intruder had penetrated into systems, and discover what they did. The past decade has witness a stead growth in Internet technologies penetration into the society, intruders are able to totally hide their presence, by disabling commonly used services and reinstalling their own versions, then erasing their tracks in audit and log files. The intruders uses automated tools to enter commands on their personal computers to access interconnected systems on the Internet.

In the 80s and early 90s, DoS attacks were infrequent and not considered serious. But nowadays intruders sustain with new technology, to exploit vulnerabilities associated with the World Wide Web to gain unauthorised access to systems. The experienced intruders are getting smarter as demonstrated by the increased sophistication in the types of attacks, as it were the knowledge required on the part of novice intruders to copy and launch known methods of attack is decreasing. But instead of simply exploiting well-known vulnerabilities, intruders examine source code to discover weaknesses in certain programs, such as those used for electronic mail. Much source code is easy to obtain from programmers who make their work freely available on the Internet. Moreover, the targets of many computer intrusions are organisations that maintain copies of proprietary source code. Once intruders gain access, they can examine this code to discover weaknesses. The tools available to launch an attack have become more effective, easier to use, and more accessible to people without an in-depth knowledge of computer systems. A sophisticated intruder embeds an attack procedure in a program and widely distributes it to the intruder community. Thus, people who have the desire but not the technical skill are able to break into systems. Even, there have been instances of intruders breaking into a UNIX system using a relatively sophisticated attack and then attempting to run DOS commands. Tools are available to examine programs for vulnerabilities even in the absence of source code. Though these tools can help system administrators identify problems, they also help intruders find new ways to break into systems (Dekker, 1997). The Internet sites should be aware of the amount of trust they actually place in the infrastructure and the protocols, even though Internet users place unwarranted trust in the network. The Internet was originally designed for robustness from attacks or events that were external to the Internet infrastructure, that is, physical attacks against the hardware. However, the Internet was not designed to withstand internal attacks-attacks by people who are part of the network; and now that the Internet has grown to encompass so many sites, millions of users are effectively inside. The Internet is primarily based on protocols for sharing electronically stored information, and a break-in is not physical. Intruders are easy to get unauthorised access to the sites without knowing to the others, residing in programs, exploding at right time and collecting information. Internet attacks are easy in other ways. It is true that some attacks require technical knowledge, but technically unsophisticated intruders carry out many successful attacks (Allen, et al. 2000). The technically competent intruders will duplicate and share their programs and information at little cost, thus enabling inexperienced and immature intruders to do the same damage as the experts. As in the case of IP spoofing, attackers can lie about their identity and location on the network. Information on the Internet is transmitted in packets, which contains information about the origin and destination, but they can lie about it. Most of the Internet is designed merely to forward packets one step closer to their destination with no attempt to make a record of their source. There is not even a "postmark" to indicate generally where a packet originated. So it requires close cooperation among sites and up-to-date equipment to trace malicious packets during an attack. Moreover, the Internet is designed to allow packets to flow easily across geographical, administrative, and political boundaries. Consequently, cooperation in tracing a single attack may involve multiple organisations and jurisdictions, most of which are not directly affected by the attack and may have little incentive to invest time and resources in the effort. The attacks against the Internet typically do not require the attacker to be physically present at the site of the attack; the risk of being identified is reduced. In addition, it is not always clear when certain events should be cause for alarm and prevention. What appear to be probes and unsuccessful attacks may actually be the legitimate activity of network managers checking the security of their systems. Even in cases where organisations monitor their systems for illegitimate activity, which occurs in only a small minority of Internet-connected sites, real break-ins often go undetected because it is difficult to identify illegitimate activity. In the case of cross-site scripting, web users trigger malicious code without even knowing they have done so, and web sites can unknowingly pass the code along. Finally, because intruders cross multiple geographical and legal domains, an additional confusion is thrown over the legal issues involved in pursuing and prosecuting them (Cross, 2000). Security breaches can cause a loss of time and resources as personnel investigate the compromise, determine potential damage, and restore the systems. The systems may provide reduced service or be unavailable for a period of time. Sensitive information can be exposed or altered, and public confidence can be lost. After a successful computer system intrusion, it can be very difficult or impossible to determine precisely what subtle damage, if any, was left by the intruder. Loss of confidence can result even if an intruder leaves no damage because the site cannot prove none was left. Particularly serious for business are denial-of-service attacks and the exposure of sensitive information. Once an explicit denial-of-service attack has been resolved and the service returned, users generally regain trust in the service they receive. But exposure of sensitive information makes an organisation highly susceptible to lack confidentiality crisis.

Many attacks consist of large number of hosts, or computers, operating under the control of the attacker. These hosts may be referred to as zombies, agents, slaves, or bots. The huge number of hosts connected to the Internet gives attackers plenty of potential attack agents that are vulnerable to compromise. Root causes include the level of security at individual sites, the nature of attack tools, and vulnerabilities in software products (Householder, A., 2001). Other aspects of the new sophistication of intruders include the targeting of the network infrastructures such as network routers and firewalls and the ability to cloak their behaviour. Intruders use Trojan horses to hide their activity from network administrators; alter authentication and logging programs so that they can log in without the activity showing up in the system logs. Intruders also encrypt output from their activity, the information captured by packet sniffers. Even if the victim finds the sniffer logs, it is difficult or impossible to determine what information was compromised (Russell, D. 1992).

5. METHODS AND METHODOLOGY

The methods used in this research are questionnaires, case studies, and laboratory experiments. The deductive approach was adopted, which starts with theory, refined into a set of two hypothetical statements (null and alternative hypotheses), followed by observations, and with confirmation of the theory or otherwise. The research methods and methodology used within the framework of this study are based on the following combination:

i. Formal theory is the theoretical structure and relationships developed by inference from the set of axioms for proving the theorem or designing the SIPSec model.
ii. The questionnaire survey indicates the choice of sample and the size, design, target audience, analysis mechanism, hypothesis, methods of gathering data, and research strategy. The questionnaire survey was conducted among 21 large organisations. These large organisations consisted of 12 trans-national and 9 international. The business of the participated organisations includes banking, insurance, transport, retailing, electronics, IT consultants, automobile, aerospace, petroleum, services, food and drinks. The feedback of the questionnaire survey generated many open-ended questions that were adopted for the case studies observations.
iii. Case studies observations captured the nature of the Internet security problems encountered by 21 large organisations. These large organisations consisted of 9 international and 12 trans-national. The case histories were based on the reported facts from network and Internet security consultants, directors, managers, and network teams.
iv. Laboratory experiments was controlled and used for testing the reliability and validity of different IPSec installations (Windows 2003, Windows XP,

Linux, Solaris, and FreeBSD). The implementations of these IPSec are discussed in Chapter 4.

This study opts for all of the above options, hence it is propounded that research without methodology is like a ship without a captain. The questionnaire surveys, case studies, and laboratory experiments, are the primary method of data collection and information gathering for the purpose of satisfying the hypothesis and the secondary research was largely based on a review of literature on Internet security. The literature review exposed the ground knowledge of what have been done in this book and also opens up a number of questions and issues

6.   INTERNET ARCHITECTURE BOARD (IAB)?

The Internet Architecture Board (IAB) sets the technical direction and provides the focus for much of the research and development underlying the TCP/IP protocols because the TCP/IP Internet protocol suite did not arise from a specific vendor or from a professional society. The IAB was formed in 1983, but was placed under the ISOC (Internet Society) in June 1992. The IAB oversees the Internet Engineering Task Force (IETF) and Internet Research Task Force (IRTF), and the IAB has the responsibility for rectifying major changes as proposed by the IRTF and IETF. The IETF concentrates on short term or medium term engineering problems and was divided into over 20 working groups each focusing on a specific problem. No vendor owns the TCP/IP technology nor does any professional society or standards body. Therefore, the documentation of protocols, standards, and policies cannot be obtained from a vendor. Instead, the documentation is placed in online repositories and made available at no charge. Documentation of work on the Internet, proposals for new or revised protocols, and TCP/IP protocol standards all appear in a series of technical reports called Internet Request for Comments (RFCs) (Comer, 00).

6.1   The Internet Research Task Force (IRTF)

The Internet Research Task Force (IRTF) is responsible for examining the long-term research problems, and technical issues currently affected the Internet. Its main responsibility is to analyse issues that will become important in five to 10 years time e.g. how will the Internet handle the users (a landmark, which can not be fully estimated) and how the current user will be affected when homes are wired in to the Internet via computer television.

6.2 The Internet Engineering Task Force (IETF) industry standard

The IPSec working group at the Internet Engineering Task Force (IETF) has defined a number of Requests for Comments (RFC). This group was created in 1992 and the first version of the proposed mechanisms, was published in 1995. The RFCs define various aspects of IPSec architecture, and the mandatory transforms that can be use to implement the base protocols (see Table 1–1 for further detail discussion). The first version of the proposed mechanisms did not state anything about Key management. However, the Key management approach was later added to the IPSec architecture in the RFC document. The IETF coordinates the operations, management, and the revolution of the Internet. The primary responsibility of the IETF is in the developing and maintaining of the Internet communication protocol. The IETF is itself a large open community of network designers, operators, then does, and researchers concerned with the intranet and Internet protocols. The IETF is also responsible for the technical and operational problems, and thus propose solution to problems and provides a forum for the exchange of technical information within the Internet community. To establish trust between computers the IETF provides three standard based authentication methods provided by Internet Key Exchange (IKE) during implementation:

- The Windows 2000-based domain provides Kerberos v5.0 authentication infrastructure. This is used to deploy secure communications between computers and across trusted domains.
- Several certificate systems (Microsoft, Entrust, VeriSign, and Netscape) are use to provide Public/Private Key signatures.
- The pre-shared authentication keys are used strictly to establish trust not for application data packet protection.

The IPSec has been accepted in the industry for many years and its use is becoming very popular. The IPSec for Windows NT and 2000 is available from Microsoft. Other vendors have implemented IPSec for Win98, Win95 etc. The latest SUN Solaris release (Solaris 8) has IPSec built-in. IPSec can be added to Linux using a patch called 'freeswan'. The BSD operating systems (OpenBSD, FreeBSD, NetBSD) have IPSec built-in (see Chapter 4 for further discussion). All network companies that deliver routers, switches, and gateways, now have the IPSec built-in. The IPSec is clearly the emerging standard for IP security is specified in RFCs.

6.3   Multi-Protocol Label Switching (MPLS)

The Multi-Protocol Label Switching (MPLS) working group of the IETF is responsible for the standardisation of MPLS. The RFC 3031 document speci-fied the architecture for MPLS. With MPLS, the packets are forwarded through the MPLS VPN by switching on attached labels. The contents of the IP header are not looked at. The VPN endpoint adds a label to the packet, and 'subse-quent devices forward the data based on the incoming interface and the label'. The packet is then sent to the next device with a new label. The final device in the MPLS VPN removes the label and forwards the data to the ultimate desti-nation (Pepelnjak and Guichard, 2001). The devices that carry out the labelling are referred to as Label Switch Routers (LSR) and the path followed by the data is known as a Label Switch Path (LSP). The MPLS addresses a number of problems faced by present-day networks, most notably, speed, scalability and quality-of-service (QoS). MPLS traffic engineering can dedicate resources to an LSP and provide customers with guaranteed bandwidth. Although security is not the primary focus of MPLS, an Internet draft (Analysis of the Security of BGP/MPLS IP VPNs) published in July 2003 has shown that the security pro-vided by an MPLS VPN is in essence comparable to that offered by dedicated Frame Relay and Asynchronous Transfer Mode (ATM) virtual circuits (see Chapter 2 for further discussion). Although the likelihood of data being deliv-ered to the wrong destination is minimal (Harrison, 2003), it is still a sensible option to employ additional authentication and encryption mechanisms.

7.   IPSEC ROADMAP

The IPSec is a valuable option for protecting data in transit and perhaps one of the most complicated and confusing security standards ever put forward for universal implementation. What is the goal of IPSec? The goal of the IPSec was implicitly stated in the RFC 2401 to provide various security services for traffic at the IP layer, in both the IPv4 and IPv6 environments. The IPSec is actually a collection of techniques and protocols; therefore it is not defined in a single Internet standard. The architecture, services and specific protocols used in the IPSec is contain within collections of RFCs (see Table 1–1 for further details). The IPSec is an excellent set of protocols, developed out of significant work and collaboration from within the networking security community.

Table 1–1. IPSec related Requests for Comment (RFC) Documentation

RFC	Brief description
1256	Specification of router advertisement
1886	The AAAA and PTR records
1752	Recommendation for the IP next generation protocol
1828	IP Authentication using Keyed MD5
1829	The ESP DES-CBC Transform
RFC 2104	HMAC: Keyed-Hashing for Message Authentication: This RFC defines the authentication algorithm that uses a cryptographic hash along with a secret to verify the integrity and authenticity of a message. It is not written to be part of IPSec, but referenced in RFC 2403 and RFC 2404.
RFC 2401	Security Architecture for IPSec: This is the overview of the entire IPSec protocol suite from the point of view of the RFCs.
RFC 2402	Authentication Header (AH): This defines the format of the IPSec Authentication Header, in both Tunnel and Transport modes
RFC 2403	Use of HMAC-MD5-96 within ESP and AH
RFC 2404	Use of HMAC-SHA-1-96 within ESP and AH: These two RFCs define authentication algorithms used in AH and ESP. MD5 and SHA-1 are both cryptographic hashes, and they are part of a Hashed Message Authentication Code. AH always performs authentication, while ESP does so optionally.
RFC 2405	The ESP DES-CBC Cipher Algorithm With Explicit IV: This defines the use of DES (the Data Encryption Standard) as a confidentiality algorithm in the context of ESP.
RFC 2406	IP Encapsulating Security Payload (ESP): ESP is the encrypting companion of AH, and the maintained confidentiality of the contents in payload. ESP by itself does not define any particular encryption algorithms but provides a framework for them
RFC 2407	The Internet IP Security Domain of Interpretation for ISAKMP: This RFC describes the use of ISAKMP, which includes the Internet Security Association and Key Management Protocol within the context of IPSec. It has a framework for key exchange at the start of a conversation, and obviates the poor practice of using manual keys.
RFC 2408	Internet Security Association and Key Management Protocol (ISAKMP): Hand in hand with RFC 2407, this RFC detailed the ISAKMP protocol used to support key exchange (does not define the key exchange protocols).
RFC 2409	The Internet Key Exchange (IKE): The ISAKMP provides a framework for key-exchange. This RFC define the protocols within the IKE. The IKE includes initial authentication, as well as Oakley key exchange.
RFC 2410	The NULL Encryption Algorithm and Its Use With IPSec: The IPSec's ESP protocol performs encryption of payload using one of several available algorithms, but a NULL encryption algorithm is typically made available for testing. Of course, this provides no confidentiality for the "protected" data, but it may be useful for developers or those attempting to understand IPSec by sniffing the wire.
RFC 2411	IP Security Document Roadmap: This RFC provides an layout of the various IPSec-related RFCs, as well as provides a framework for new RFCs of particular types ("authentication algorithms", "encryption algorithms"). It's a good starting point.

RFC	Brief description
RFC 2412	The OAKLEY Key Determination Protocol: OAKLEY forms part of IKE (Internet Key Exchange), and it provides a service where two authenticated parties can agree on the secrets required for IPSec communications.
2460	The IPv6 Specification
2461	Specification of neighbour discovery
2474	Definition of the differentiated services field in the IPv4 and v6 headers
2675	Specification of jumbograms
3053	IPv6 tunnel broker
3056	Connection of IPv6 domains via v4 clouds
RFC 3884	Use of IPSec transport mode for Dynamic Routing: In contrast to the Schneier paper, it has been suggested that the transport mode is the only one that is strictly required to accomplish everything. The RFC3884 shows a way of providing tunnel mode. It has been suggested that the tunnel mode makes the implementation issues much easier.

The Table 1–1 presents the main references of the IPSec related documentation. The RFC are validated based on new contributions.

The IPSec is a suite of protocols for securing network connections, but the details and many variations quickly become overwhelming. This is particularly the case when trying to interoperate between disparate systems, causing more than one engineer to mindlessly turn the knobs when attempting to bring up a new connection (Friedl, 2005). The IPSec is an open industrial standard that helps to ensure interoperable with other operating systems. It is also completely transparent to the user as well as other applications. The IPSec works below the transport layer and is commonly used in Layer 2 Tunnelling Protocol (L2TP), using the tunnelling mode to establish and secure VPN connections. It can also be used to secure data transmission server-to-server, workstation-to-workstation, or server to workstation using transport mode (see Chapters 2 and 3 for further discussion on the tunnelling and transport modes). The IP and the cryptographically (security) approach are the two applications that make up the IPSec identity (see Figure 1–1 below for the diagrammatic illustration).

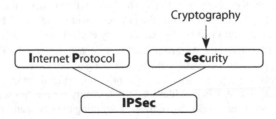

Figure 1–1. Conceptual ideology of IPSec identity

Although, the IPSec is meant to maintain a stand that is universally acceptable but the definition of the IPSec is not. There are so many definitions of

IPSec in existent, to agreed with one definition is more of injustice to others; the following are the most commonly used IPSec definition:

'IPSec is designed to provide interoperable, high quality, cryptographically based security for IPv4 and IPv6. The set of security services offered includes access control, connectionless integrity, data origin authentication, protection against replays (a form of partial sequence integrity), confidentiality (encryption), and limited traffic flow confidentiality. These services are provided at the IP layer, offering protection for IP and/or upper layer protocols.'

—RFC 2401(1998)

'Internet Protocol Security (IPSec) is a framework of open standards for ensuring private, secure communications over Internet Protocol (IP) networks, through the use of cryptographic security services. IPSec supports network-level peer authentication, data origin authentication, data integrity, data confidentiality (encryption), and replay protection.'

—Microsoft NetTech, (2002)

'IPSec is a framework of open standards developed by the Internet Engineering Task Force (IETF). IPSec provides security for transmission of sensitive information over unprotected networks such as the Internet. IPSec acts at the network layer, protecting and authenticating IP packets between participating IPSec devices ("peers"), such as Cisco routers.'

—Cisco, (2002)

In view of many definitions that has been reviewed in the process of defining 'what is IPSec?' it is most appropriate to propose a more simpler and less ambiguous definition:

'The IPSec is a combinations of open standard protocols developed by Internet Engineering Task Force (IETF) for maintaining secured communication over networks (including the internet) using cryptograph.'

—Shoniregun (2006a)

The IPSec combines several security technologies to achieve confidentiality, integrity, and authenticity, these security technologies are as follows:

• Diffie-Hellman key exchange is use for deriving the key material between peers on a public network.

- Public key cryptography is use for signing the Diffie-Hellman exchanges to guarantee the identity of the parties involve in the transaction (usually two users) to avoid man-in-the-middle attacks.
- Bulk encryption algorithms use Data Encryption Standard (DES) for encrypting data (see Chapter 2 for further discussion).
- Hash algorithms uses the Key-Hashing Message Authentication Codes (HMAC). The HMAC provides a framework to incorporate any cryptographic hash function for the MD5 and SHA1 (see Chapter 2 for further discussion).

The digital certificates signed by a certificate authority act as digital ID cards. The IPSec can be used either on a terminal host or a security gateway, thus allowing link-by-link and/or end-to-end security. The following are the three basic configurations that are possible (see Figures 1–2, 1–3 and 1–4 for diagrammatic illustration).

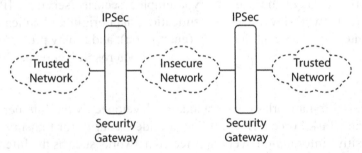

Figure 1–2. IPSec on two trusted private networks

The Figure 1–2 describes two trusted private networks that are connected over an unreliable network (Internet). The word unreliable is use to signify that the Internet cannot be 100 percent secured.

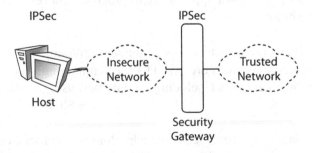

Figure 1–3. IPSec running on host machine

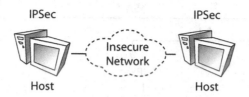

Figure 1–4. IPSec on host machines

The Figure 1–3 is based on mobile user, who is working away from the office. In this case the mobile user needs to be connected to trusted network over an unreliable network. The IPSec is running on the host machine to connect to the security gateway, which is also running the IPSec; this connection would enable access to the trusted network.

In Figure 1–4, two users need to be connected to each other over unreliable network in a secure manner. In this case both users runs the IPSec on their host machines and connect to each other. Many scenarios exist, that requires more complex configurations, involving security associations (SA) for different services. The latter services follow one another or can partially superimposed (see Figures 1–5 and 1–6 for diagrammatic illustration).

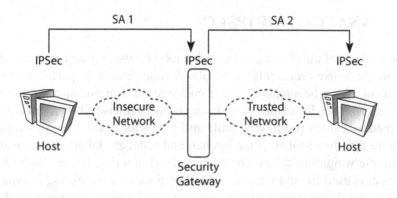

Figure 1–5. SA concepts of follow one another

In the Figure 1–5, the external security services (authentication and confidentiality) are satisfied by the first SA 1, while the internal security services (authentication) is satisfied by the SA2.

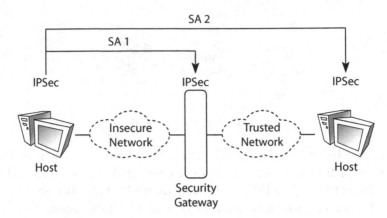

Figure 1–6. SA concept of partially superimposed

The security association in Figure 1–6, is based on the requirements of confidentiality and authentication, which reflect the use of ESP and AH. However, it is equally important to note that the IPSec can run in two modes (see Chapters 3 and 4 for further discussion).

8.   ANALOGY OF IPSEC

The analogy of the IPSec can be understood by using a house. Each of the rooms in the house represents protocols. A room can only perform specific requirement or can be adapted to be used for more than one specific function e.g. living room can be adapted as a dining room, likewise a bed room can also be adopted as a study room, with table and chairs for study. In reality a house have more than two rooms, if the kitchen and toilet are taken into consideration. But the weighting of each room been used in a day, is very high except if the room is used for storage purposes, then the usage weighting is expected to be low. The abstraction of IPSec packets from the above explanation shows that all the rooms used and their functions should be noted. (See Figure 1–7 for the diagrammatic illustration).

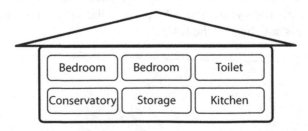

Figure 1–7. Analogy of IPSec as a House

The house cannot function without other entities such as electricity, water, telephone, and maintenance. The same ideology applies to the IPSec, it interacts with other software, hardware and requires maintenance (upgrade / configuration) as when it is necessary. The IPSec is software, but without the hardware, the software is redundant. The analogy of the IPSec as a house and conceptual understanding of Internet relationship with software and hardware was first presented by Shoniregun (2006b) (see Figures 1–7 and 1–8 for the diagrammatic illustration).

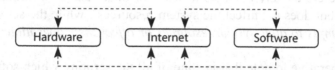

Figure 1–8. Internet relationship with software and hardware

Furthermore, the IPSec comprises of individual protocols built to work together to perform specific function. To show how this fit into the analogy of IPSec as house (see Figure 1–9 for diagrammatic illustration).

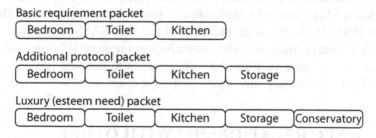

Figure 1–9. Analogy of IPSec Packets

There are obvious similarities in the three packets illustrated in Figure 1–9. The generic protocols (Bedrooms, Toilet, and Kitchen) shows that the IPSec has been evolving. What makes a difference is the functions that are performed by the additional protocol, which is added to the packet to enhance the performance. The

Internet provides uncontrollable opportunities, which are open to unlimited risks of information interception even with abundance of available security tools the Internet is and will always be vulnerable to security breaches (see section 10 for further discussion). The IPSec is said to gives the networks (including internet) users:

- The confidentiality of data being transmitted.
- Enabled secure branch connectivity.

- Provides some secure remote access
- Enabled secure extranet and intranet connectivity
- Enhanced e-Commerce security

Although the applicability of cryptographic authentication in the IPSec has proved to some extent to be useful in securing information that are transmitted. Other attacks, which have impacted the IPSec operations, are passive and active attacks on data/information. In the RFC 2828 documentation, passive attacks is refers to 'any attempts to learn or make use of information from the system but does not affect the system resources', while the active attacks is *'any attempts to alter system resources or affect their operations'* (see Table 1–2).

It is imperative to note that in spite of all the scrutiny which software undergo they are still vulnerable. Product vendors such as Cisco, Microsoft, Sun Microsystems, SAP and other software manufacturers/vendors have notoriety for patches and security issues; an example was the attack of the SASSER worm. The SASSER worm first appeared on 1 May 2004, by exploiting Microsoft Windows 2000 and Windows XP vulnerability, and spreading from machine to machine with no user intervention across the world. This worm scans random IP addresses for exploitable systems. It creates a remote shell on TCP port 9996. However, since the birth of the first SASSER version, many versions has been introduced, *'who knows how many more versions to come?'* It also scans so aggressively and infects networks to become congested with packets of data, eventually slow down system resources.

9.   IPSEC RELATIONSHIP WITH OTHER PROTOCOLS

The IPSec protects the IP datagrams by defining a method of specifying the traffic to protect, how the traffic can be protected and to whom the traffic can be sent. It can also protect packets between host, network security gateways (firewalls or routers) or hosts and security gateways. The IPSec datagram is an IP packet that nested other security services within the packet. These services can provide protection in the form of data origin authentication, connectionless data integrity, anti-reply protection, data content confidentiality and limited traffic flow confidentiality (Stallings, 2004). These features provide the IPSec, the ability to support several applications such as secure VPN and secure remote user access. The services mentioned are optional in IPv4 and mandatory for any implementation of IPv6. The operation of the IPSec in the IP layer is different from other security methods because it uses the Internet Key Exchange Protocol (IKE) to accomplish protocol and algorithm negotiation

Table 1–2. Classification of passive and active attacks

Types of attacks	Passive attacks	Active attacks
Passive wiretapping attack	• Able to interpret and extract information • Release of message contents	
Traffic analysis attack	• Observing the external flow of traffic	
Loss of Privacy		• It is difficult to detect because there is no change to content interpretation. • It is therefore better to prevent rather than detect
Loss of Data Integrity		• The modification of message portion of legitimate message is altered to produce an unauthorised effect • Replay passive capture of data transaction and active re-transmission causing an unauthorised effect. •
Identity Spoofing		• Masquerade (impersonation) • Replay sequence unauthorised access • Capture authentication sequence
Virus		• Code that copies itself into a larger program • It replicates to infect other programs by inserting its code in them • It infect memory, floppy disk, CD and other types of storage • Is not an independent program that execute by it self • It spread by passing copies of infected programs with or without intention on disk or via the networks (i.e. the internet)
Denial-of-service		• Preventing or inhibit normal usage
Worm		• An independent program • It copy itself from one system to the other and spread rapidly from one site to another • It attached to network resources • It can replicates via email, remote execution and login
Trojan horse		• It is use to disguise a virus or worm • It hides inside legitimate programs or files • It is used for penetrating into the defences of a system • Seizing the user's legitimate privileges again access to unauthorised data/ information

Types of attacks	Passive attacks	Active attacks
Trap doors		• Secret entry into a program • A back door mechanism that is built into the system by its designer • Gives the original designer a secret way to the software • It might not necessary be a loophole. Trap doors can be use to gain access to correct or debugged program errors.
Probe		• Unusual attempts to gain access to a system or to discover information about the system • Log in to an unused account
Scan		• A large number of probes done using an automated tool. • Direct attack on systems that the intruder has found to be vulnerable
Account compromise		• Expose the system to serious data loss • Unauthorised use of the system account
Root compromise		• Common with UNIX systems • Unlimited or super user privilege • Intruders who succeed in a root comprise has unlimited privilege
Packet sniffer		• It captures data. For example names, password, and proprietary information • Intruder can lunch widespread attacks on systems • The presence of a packet sniffer implies there has been a root compromise
Exploitation of trust		• Attackers can forge the trusted identity and gain unauthorised access to other systems
Malicious code		• If the program is executed, it would causes undesirable and undesired results • It can lead to serious data loss, downtime, and denial or service
Logic Bombs		• Logic bombs predate viruses and worms. • Integrated parts of the host program that are normally executed with it. • Set to explode (to destroy valuable systems resources) when a certain condition is met, it will trigger the logic bombs to explode. • The trigger could be a particular day of the week or date, or a particular user running the application.

Types of attacks	Passive attacks	Active attacks
Malware	• Others are installed from websites, pretending to be software needed to view the website.	• It can hijack browser, redirect search attempts, serve up nasty pop-up ads, track web sites visit • Can cause the computer to become unbearably slow and unstable • They reinstall themselves even after removed them, or hide themselves deep within Windows, and makes it difficult to clean. • It include programs such as viruses, worms, Trojans, and everything else generally detected by anti-virus software • It comes bundled with other programs (Kazaa, iMesh, and other file sharing programs seem to be the biggest bundlers) • It usually pop-up adverts, sending revenue from the ads to the program's authors. • CoolWebSearch variants, install themselves through holes in Internet Explorer
Bacteria	• It consume other system resources to cause a denial of service	• Does not always produce harmful effect • It replicate exponentially to fill disk space

and also for generating authentication and encryption keys. The IPSec uses one of the following protocols to protecting IP datagrams:

i. *Authentication Header (AH)* provides the origin authentication, data integrity and replay protection.
ii. *Encapsulating Security Payload (ESP)* provides data confidentiality, data origin authentication and integrity, and replay protection.
iii. *Internet Security Association and Key Management Protocol (ISAKMP)* is a mechanism for automatic set up of security associations and the management of keys.
iv. *Oakley determination protocol* is an automated key management protocol based on Diffie Hellman algorithm with additional security Tools. It uses cookies to thwart clogging attacks, which enables all the parties to form groups to exchange public parameters using nonce to repel replay.

The RFC 2401 documentation contains the blue print of IPSec implementations standards. The latter document also defines the security services, the usage, construction and processing of IP packets, and the interaction with the security policy enforced. The RFCs documentation on ESP, and AH describe the headers and payloads services that are provided. Certain packet processing rules are also defined within these documents but what is not defined is the transforms, which actually proved the services. The reason behind this is that has technology advances and other cryptographic algorithms are proving insecure, new transforms can be defined to replace the old transforms using the insecure algorithms. Transforms can be defined as the 'transformations applied to the data in other to secured the data'. The transformation take into account the algorithm and other security parameters.

The three main protocols use by IPSec to perform various services for secure network communications are 'Authentication Header' (AH), 'Encapsulating Security Payload' (ESP), and 'Internet Key Exchange' (IKE) or a combination known as ISAKMP. It is also important to understand how these protocols interact with each other and how they are tied together to implement the capabilities described by the IPSec architecture (Doraswamy and Harkins, 2003) (see Figure 1–10 diagrammatic illustration).

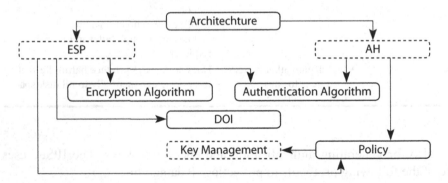

Figure 1–10. Protocols relationship within IPSec

The ESP and an AH Protocol documentation covers the packet format and general issues regarding the respective protocols. The documentation also contain default values if appropriate, such as the default padding contents, and mandatory to implement algorithms. The documents dictate some of the values in the Domain of Interpretation Document (DOI). The Encryption Algorithm (EA) document is describes 'how various encryption algorithms are used for ESP? These documents are intended to fit in this roadmap, and should avoid overlap with the ESP protocol document and with the Authentication Algorithm (AA) documents. When this or other encryption algorithms are used for ESP, the DOI document has to indicate certain values, such as an encryption algorithm identifier and provides input to the DOI. The AA documents describes 'how various authentication algorithms are used for both ESP and AH?' When this or other algorithms are used for either ESP or AH, the DOI document has to indicate certain values, such as algorithm type, so that the documents can provide input to the DOI. The DOI document contains values needed for the other documents to relate to each other. This includes encryption algorithms, authentication algorithms, and operational parameters such as key lifetimes. The Key Management Documents are described in the IETF standards-track key management schemes. The IKE has a very generic, payload format, and can be used to negotiate keys for any protocols apart from negotiating keys for IPSec. This is achieved by separating the parameters that the IKE negotiates from the protocol itself. The negotiator parameters as stored in a separate document referred to as the IPSec DOI, which contains values that would be required by other documents that related to each other such as list of approved encryption and authentication algorithms key lifetimes status. Other key components of the IPSec are security associations (SA's), and policy, which are built into the security policy database (SPD) (but not yet standard components). It is expected that the security policy within IPSec would enabled the:

- Sender to encrypt packets before transmitting them across a network.
- Receiver to authenticate packets sent by the IPSec sender to ensure that the data has not been altered during transmission.
- Receiver to authenticate the source of the IPSec packets sent. This service is dependent upon the data integrity service.
- Receiver to detect and reject replayed packets.

But when implementing the IPSec all of the above expectations are optional. The SPD contains information that defines the source, destination addresses, port numbers, and action to be taken (for instance, allow, permit, drop, or bypass). The SA is a logical connection between two devices transferring and provides data protection for unidirectional traffic using defined IPSec protocol keys, algorithms, and lifetime values SPD. The IKE generates keys used by the IPSec protocols. The SA's transmit and receive packets that are controlled by the security policy (rules that are built into the SPD) and also define the one-way protection of the message for specific IPSec mechanisms. There are usually two SA's used in protecting traffic between two hosts. The SA can control what to encrypt and what not to encrypt. It is a very important components as it differentiates whether two entities are allowed to communicate or not, and if allowed, which transforms to use.

9.1   IPSec Mode

The ESP and AH protocols can be used in two ways, either to protect entire IP payload or the upper layer protocols of the IP payload. These are referred to as IPSec modes. The modes are 'Transport' and 'Tunnel'. The transport mode only protects the upper layer protocols, while the tunnel mode protects the entire IP payload (see Figure 1–11 for the diagrammatic illustration).

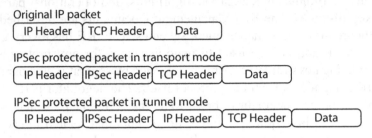

Figure 1–11. IPSec in different modes

The decision on whether to use transport mode or a tunnel mode depends on the types of network that the traffic has to pass through, and the network administrator (see Chapter 3 for detail discussion on IPSec mode).

10.   BUSINESS PERCEPTION

The businesses are utilising the Internet as a resource and a good medium for conducting their business activities. In essence there is a requirement to protect sensitive information that is potentially accessible via the Internet. The globalisation of Trade, Liberalisation, Economic reforms and Information economics, and the growth of global communication channels have redefined the role of network technologies in business operations. Examples of such applications include e-Commerce (eC), teleworking, multimedia communications, information access and entertainments. Unfortunately, the realisations of these applications are often hampered by insecurities typical of open networks: messages can be intercepted and manipulated, the validity of documents can be denied, and the personal data can be illicitly collected. The role of Internet as a result of networking technologies or Information and Communication Technologies (ICT) in business operations has rapidly risen during the past three decades. Almost all large organisations are automated and even the feedbacks from the market are analysed using the Internet to extracts information from various data-mining servers. This information is used for formulating new business strategies as well as for making better managerial decisions, which gives organisation a competitive edge in the global market place to compete without any additional cost 7/24 hours 365 days. The Internet also provides an organisation with front-end and back-end support for other business processes. Based on the advantages accrued from using the Internet, businesses are spending nearly half of their capital investments on IT infrastructure, while much of the workforce in the developed countries depending completely on the Information Systems (IS) and IT enabled Telecommunication Systems connected to Internet. Furthermore, with the convergence of transmission, the Internet technology compresses and stores digitised information so that it can travel through existing phone, wireless and wiring systems. This is advantageous to businesses as it results in accessing the Internet resources to create new, low-delivery channels (Shoniregun et al. 2005a) and helps to re-focus a product to global audiences. However, the issues relating to secure transactions cannot be ignored. But the fundamental security problems of the Internet, reside in the architecture, and one that is generic in nature. With all the countable advantages of businesses adaptation to the Internet, the Internet is not free from risk (Shoniregun, 2005b) and cyber criminalities. Indeed, the human race has not only brought its business to cyberspace, it has brought its exploration of the psyche there, too. In the digital world, just as everywhere else, humanity has encountered its dark side. Information age business, governments, and culture have led to information age crime, information age war, and even information age terror (Shoniregun et al. 2004). Many vendors have proposed different solutions, which have been applied but after a period time, such solution become absolute and a new solution has to be deployed based on the weaknesses of previous solutions. The IPSec is one of the solutions that have been deployed to provide a safe and secured communication transmission in both the application and transport layers.

The IPSec concept of Security association (SA) has many of its own inherited problems. The security of information on the Internet is by no means the greatest problems when transferring information from A to B. The 21st century businesses depended heavily upon the Internet to conduct their business transactions, which makes the entire business environment to be confronted with many technical and non-technical security challenges. However, the technical; challenges are far beyond the understanding of non-technical directors and their managers. The bottom line is that security of information transfer using the Internet has it root problem from the inherited limitations of the Internet technologies. The technological transition from centralised to distributed paradigm have created an open door for intruders to tap on the validity of information in transit.

11.   SUMMARY OF CHAPTER ONE

This chapter has set the scene for understanding the conceptual ideology behind IPSec. The direction to which this book is going has been made clear and the hypothesis have been postulated. The historical background of the Internet bodies has been established, to provide a springboard for a better

understanding of the IPSec. The IPSec provides the following security functions in the IP layer: authentication, data integrity, replay detection, data confidentiality, access control using security protocols covering various services and
joint management protocols for SA and key exchange. Despite all these security functions, the IPSec has limitations and is vulnerable to several kinds of
attacks (see Table 1–2 and Chapter 4 for further discussion). It was noted that
TCP/IP does not however, provided authentication and privacy functions, and
virtual anyone with the right tools will be able to spoof the IP addresses, and
intercept any data on the Internet. One of the advantages of TCP/IP is that it
is not restricted to one part only. This means that while message is in transmission, TCP/IP will choose from the least used path from the least of active
service. If for any reason, one of the routers is either non-operation or over
loaded with request, TCP/IP will then find an alternative route to the destination. However, the use of the IPSec renders the systems useless and degrades
overall network functionality. In most cases, the solutions implemented only
cover a part of the possible options; therefore the future of the IPSec depends
on synchronising the existing security policy with biometrics (see Chapter 5
for further discussion). The next chapter exploits the Internet communication
protocols.

REFERENCES

Allen, J., Alberts, C., Behrens, S., Laswell, B., and Wilson, W., 2000, Improving the Security of
    Networked Systems, Cross Talk, The Journal of Defence Software Engineering
Cisco, 2002, IPSec Network Security, Cisco Systems, Inc USA, http://www.cisco.com/univer-
    cd/cc/td/doc/product/software/ios113ed/113t/113t_3/ipsec.htm#xtocid0 (January 12, 2007)
Comer, D E., 2000, Internetworking with TCP/IP, 4th Edition, Prentice Hall, USA.
Cross S E, 2000, Cyber Security, 2000, Software Engineering Institute, Carnegie Mellon Uni-
    versity, USA.
Dekker, M., 1997, Security of the Internet, Froehlich and Kent Encyclopaedia of Telecommu-
    nications, Vol 15.
Doraswamy, N. and Harkins, D., 2003, IPSec: The New Security Standard for the Internet, In-
    tranets, and Virtual Private Networks, 2nd Edition, Prentice Hall USA.
Ettlie J. E., 2000, Managing Technology Innovation, John Wiley and Sons.
Friedl, S.J., 2005, An Illustrated Guide to IPSec, Unixwiz.net - Software Consulting Central,
    http://www.unixwiz.net/contact.html (January 18, 2007)
Harrison, J. 2003, VPN Technologies —A COMPARISON, http://vnu.bitpi pe.com/detail/
    RES/1046358922_393.html (December 27, 2006)
Householder, A., Manion, A., Pesante, L., and Weaver, G.M., 2001, Managing the Threat of
    Denial-of-Service Attacks, Research paper v10.0 presented at CERT Annual Conference,
    Carnegie Mellon University, USA
Kent, S. and Seo, K., 2005, Security Architecture for Internet Protocol, [see RFC 4301 docu-
    mentation for further details].
Larochelle, D., 2001, Statically Detecting Likely Buffer Overflow Vulnerabilities, in the Pro-
    ceedings of the 10th USENIX Security Symposium.

Microsoft NetTech, 2002, Internet Protocol Security, http://www.microsoft.com/technet/itsolutions/network/ipsec/default.mspx (January 11, 2006)

Pepelnjak, I., and Guichard, J., 2001, MPLS and VPN Architectures, Vol 1, Cisco Press.

Russell, D. and Gangemi Sr, G.T., 1992, Computer Security Basics, Published by O'Reilly & Associates, Inc.

Shannon C. E., and Weaver W., 1949, The mathematical theory of communication, University of Illinois Press, USA.

Shirey, R 2000, Internet Security Glossary, [see RFC 2828 documentation for further details].

Shoniregun C.A., Nwankwo S., Imafidon C., and Wynarczyk, P., 2005a, 'Information security challenges facing TEISME business operations in the UK', International Journal for Infonomics (IJI), vol. 1.

Shoniregun, C. A., 2005b, Impacts and Risk Assessment of Technology for Internet Security: Enable information Small-medium Enterprises (TEISMEs), Springer New York, USA.

Shoniregun, C.A., 2006a, Distinguished Lecture: Synchronising IPSec with Biomterics, Purdue University Calumet, Indiana, USA.

Shoniregun, C.A., 2006b, Distinguished Lecture: Phisihing for Information, Manchester Metropolitan University, Manchester, UK.

Shoniregun, C.A., Chochliouros, I.P., Laperche, B., Logvynovskiy, O., and Spiliopoulou-Chochliourou, A., 2004, Questioning The Boundary Issues of Internet Security, e-Centre for Infonomics, London.

Stalling, W., 2004, Network security essentials: applications and standards, Prentice Hall, USA.

Chapter 2

INTERNET COMMUNICATION PROTOCOLS

1.   INTRODUCTION

The Open Systems Interconnection (OSI) reference model incorporates SNA, DECNET, and TCP/IP. The ISO developed the OSI. Its purpose is to provide an easier way to describe the structure and functionality of data communication protocols, which encapsulates standards that must be met by two or more computers to communicate.

> 'Observe how system into system runs, what other planets circle other suns.'
> —Alexander Pope (1688–1744)

Although the TCP/IP protocols do not exactly match the OSI structure but it is an important protocol for the end-to-end computer communication and play a major role in the client to server data delivery. The two most important protocols in the Transport Layer are Transmission Control Protocol (TCP) and User Datagram Protocol (UDP). The UDP is a transport protocol too but it does not provide any quality control and assurance to deliver the data packet what so ever. It transports data unreliably between hosts. UDP is designed for applications where the sequences order of datagram is not important. This chapter provides an overview of the TCP/IP protocol, the OSI reference model (which is used in almost every discussion regarding computer networking), benefit and limitations of implementing security at the application, transport, network and data link, and the IPSec standards.

2.   TCP/IP PROTOCOL

The communication of data is vital part of today's society and a fundamental aspect of computing. There are literally hundreds of thousands of different networks present worldwide; these networks transmit data on a wide array of topics ranging from atmospheric conditions to genetics. The underlying principles and technologies are the same; network can nonetheless be described as independent entity. Each network is tailor made to meet the requirements of the organisation. The organisation will use technology that is best suited to meet their requirements. To obtain a fair appreciation of the technical side of the TCP/IP, it is necessary to understand the services provided by this protocol suite. The TCP/IP is the general name use for collection of over 100 protocols. Two of the protocols belonging to TCP/IP are TELNET and File transfer protocol (FTP). The TCP/IP protocol can be implemented independently of any machine platform, so it makes no difference to the type of systems the user is using, provided all the hosts are running the TCP/IP protocol. These have led to the enormous expansion in the networks hardware platform. Within the Internet, information is transmitted as a constant stream of data from host to host; more appropriately, the data is broken into small packages called packets. For example; when a long message is sent from one organisations network to another organisation, or between machines or even between VPN, the TCP/IP will divide the message in two packets, each packet is marked with a sequence number, the address of the recipient and inserts some error control information.

2.1   TCP/IP and OSI Layers

The TCP/IP is the most dominant protocol suite and the architecture can be categorised into five layers as opposed to the 7 layers in the OSI model (see Figure 2–1 for diagrammatic illustration). Each layer in the TCP/IP stack has a well-defined function that provides a communication interface for the layer directly above and below it. The layered architecture offers many benefits, including a simplified design and usage. Once the service required from a particular layer is identified, the layer can be designed independently, leading to vendor interoperability throughout the industry (Stevens, 2000). The TCP/IP communications architecture describes three facets, which are data exchange (intercommunications), data interpretation (inter operation), and system management.

There are many distinguished features that place TCP/IP as one of the most important protocol:

i. *Network technology independence:* The TCP/IP is independent of the hardware platform. Even though TCP/IP is based on conventional packet switching technology, it makes no difference as to each vendor's hardware. The Internet contains the first array of network technologies, ranging from network designed that operates within a single building to those that span across large geographical distances. The protocols within the TCP/IP suite

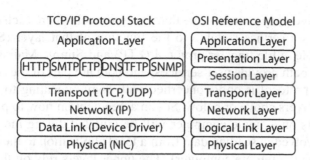

Figure 2–1. TCP/IP Protocol Stack and OSI Reference Model

also defined the unit of data transmission called datagram, and specify how to transmit the data.

ii. *Universal interconnection:* The use of TCP/IP within the Internet has facilitated communication between several computers. Every computer is assigned an address that is universally recognised throughout the entire Internet community. Each and every datagram carries the address of its origins and final destination. The destination addresses are used by the intermediate switching computers to make the routing decisions.

iii. *End to end acknowledgements:* The TCP/IP Internet protocols provide acknowledgements between the source and the final destination, rather than between successful machines, even when two machines do not connect to a common physical network.

iv. *Application protocol standards:* The TCP/IP protocols include standards for a large number of applications such as e-mail file transfer and remote login, as well as the basic transport levels service such as reliable stream connections.

It has now been the norm to reference or show the significant role of ISO in data communications subjects. The ISO encapsulated standards that must be met for at least two computers to communicate and incorporates other designs. The OSI Reference Model contains seven different layers, stacked on top of each other and each layer stack represents a function that performed specific requirement during data transferred (see Figure 2–1 diagrammatic illustration). The OSI order (top to bottom) exemplifies the path a data takes when sent. The reverse will be the order on the receivers end. Its operation is hierarchical with each layer performing a specific function and each layer is independent of the other. The layers can be grouped into two broad sections: the media layer (the physical and data link layers as they control the delivery of messages over the network); and the host layer (the application, presentation, session, and transport layers). These layers are blocks of protocols stack. A layer in the OSI model does not define a single protocol, but defines a data communications function that may be performed by any number of protocols.

Therefore, each layer may contain more than one protocol, where each of these protocols provides a service suitable to the function of that layer (Stevens, 1998). For example, a file transfer protocol (FTP) and Simple Mail Transfer Protocol (SMTP) both provide user services, and both are part of the Application Layer. Each protocol is only concerned with communicating to its peer and not with the layers above or below. So, an agreement on how to pass data between the layers on a single computer will be initiated during the process (every layer is involved in sending data from a local application to the equivalent application on the remote computer). The upper layers rely on the lower layers to transfer the data over the network. The data is passed down the stack from one layer to the next, until it is transmitted over the network (the physical cable) by the Physical Layer protocol, while at the remote end, the data is sent up the stack to the receiving application (see Figure 2–2 for diagrammatic illustration).

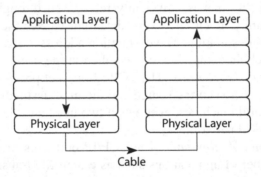

Figure 2–2. Data passing from one host to another

The upper and lower layers do not need to understand how the other parts function, but only need to know how the data between them are passed. The OSI model is a very useful protocol stack but the TCP/IP protocols do not exactly matches the structure.

3.   SECURITY PROBLEMS OF TCP/IP LAYERS

There are many security solutions available today that focus entirely on the TCP/IP suite, but no hard and fast rules to dictate, which layer of the TCP/IP stack we should or should not implement security. The decision really depends on the security requirements of the applications and users. However, implementing security at various layers of the TCP/IP stack is generic problem, which the IPSec has inherited. The Internet uses the TCP/IP protocol to function. It is a packet-based protocol that is composed of three different components: the IP, TCP, and sockets. The IP component is responsible for forwarding messages to the right IP address, which is made up of a four-byte destination number; this address is unique and has been assigned to different organisations that in turn assigned the IP address to their machines. The TCP/IP component ensures call rates delivery of packets to the clients. This is done by error detection and if a packet were corrupted in transit, the TCP would trigger the re-transmission of the packet. Furthermore, standardisation is an important aspect to ensure data can travel across network. The TCP/IP is a layered approach network and remains largely on changed for the past 20 years. The problems with TCP/IP security are briefly discussed below.

3.1   Data-link layer security

The data-link layer secured the 'Address Resolution Protocol' (ARP), which performs the task of translating hardware or Ethernet addresses on a local area network (LAN) or a wide area network (WAN), into IP addresses, but lack security. This protocol is vulnerable to manipulation. However not all systems will determine or check incoming ARPs for any possible outstanding requests. An example of such system is the UNIX system V, which is not commonly use nowadays. The most common or likely effect will be the denial of service (DoS), or an alternative form of attack possible is the "man- in-the- middle". This form of attack involves the manipulation of addresses so that traffic routed between two hosts is transmitted through a compromised system(s) that masquerades each host to the other.

3.2   Network-layer security

The IP implementation is seems to be very reliable, but it can however be manipulated. The routing of data packets is fairly open, which as a result lead to data not conforming to configured routing. Packets from the IP protocol can be injected directly onto the network as well. The Internet control message protocol (ICMP) has no authentication, which could permit manipulation of rooted message and also allows source of routing to specify the path a packet most take to its destination. An attacker can use source routing to force a device to pass a packet to an intended target. For this reason, source routing must be switch off in all firewall routers that are attached to the Internet. The ICMP is installed with every IP implementation, but by its nature it has inherited security problems. For instance, the ICMP redirect messages and instruct a host to send its packet to different router, falsifying such message can cause packets to follow the path to the attackers system. The purpose of including the first eight octets of the transport header in the message is to limit the scope of changes that may be dictated by ICMP. Upon arrival of the messages all connections between the same pair of hosts will be affected:

Example: If no destination unreachable, a message is received starting that some packet was unable to reach the target host, all connections to the host would be rejected.

It is equally important to say that if hackers can tamper with the knowledge of route to a destination, then they are probably capable of penetrating that host:

Example: A user with malicious intent will be able to subvert local routing tables, or ICMP could permit unsolicited mask reply packets. If incorrect routing table was broadcast to Internet backbone by the Internet Service Provider (ISP) it would result in a huge amount of traffic been routed to itself, denying large groups of users or the Internet communities of their service, as a result of the 'back hole created'.

The protocols managing the network routers are vulnerable enough to cause further compromise with the network attacks. Poor authentication is provided by SNMP, and unless routers are correctly configured, they remain open to malicious attackers who may reconfigure them with relative ease.

3.3   IP Security labels

The IP security option is one of the security features in the IP, mostly used by military sites, with commercial variants under research scrutiny, and further enhancements. The data packet is labelled with the level of sensitivity of the information and hierarchical component, which states the level of sensitivity. For example, secrets, top secrets—and also an option now categories as nuclear weapons, cryptography—within the networks the main portals of secret label is to constrain routing decisions. A packet marked "top security" may not be transmitted over an insecure link.

3.4   IP Origin forgery

The forgery of the origin of IP messages does not pose a serious security problem in itself, even though an IP message origin can be forged with relative ease. The seriousness of this problem however, comes to the forefront when taking into account the fact that most of the higher-level protocol uses the IP origin as a mode of identification. For example, the use of IP origin as an identification tool is the "r" commands (rlogin or rsh). These commands enabled access between UNIX systems without the use of authentication, as the IP source is used in the primary authentication method; this opens the doorway for the hackers who may use IP origin forgery.

3.5 Transport layer security

The mechanism for ensuring the consistent use of port number is weak within TCP. The UNIX systems assume that only privilege processes initiate connections from port numbers less than 1024, however, there is no reason to assume that such processes are trust worthy. Each IP packet must specify the kind of header that follows either the TCP or UDP, some applications use TCP. For example, fire transport protocol, and others deploy UDP. Once the type of packet is known, the attacker can look in the TCP or UDP header for the exact application to which this packet pertains. This is possible because many applications in the TCP/IP suite are assigned port numbers. The Internet assigned the first 1023 port numbers, which are available for viewing. For instance, Telnet requests users to enter a Telnet server on port 23, simple mail transfer protocol on port 25 and post office protocol (POP3), PC mail service is assigned port 110, therefore it is relatively easy to find out the source, destination, and contents of the packet.

The TCP/IP segments that follow the IP header also contain sequence numbers. The sequence numbers allow receiving TCP software to detect missing, duplicated, or out of order segments. It is possible for a "spoofer" to guess some of these sequence numbers pretty easily as they often follow a predictable sequence in some UNIX implementations. However, using a combination of predictable sequence and knowledge of the target IP address it is possible to prosecute an IP spoofing attack against a target. In addition the TCP check summing of IP packets is not very strong, which can lead to a potential for forgery, injection of data, and tailgating of packets. The randomness of TCP initial sequence numbers varies across the UNIX system, resulting in a potential to inject packets into a connection between two users.

3.6 Application security

Any network connected to the Internet is open to attack; the attacker will try to infiltrate an organisation's network by exploiting the numbers of higher-level protocols in the TCP/IP protocol suite. An attacker has the capability to obtain root privileges in a short space of time through Sendmail applications. The root privileges enabled the hacker to delete any audits of their actions, stop any further audits of their actions from being carried out, install malicious software, delete, read, or modify user applications, or data belonging to users. However, a large number of other software components/applications and protocols also contain similar bugs and vulnerabilities found in the

Sendmail system. The majority of the bugs found in the protocols are results of errors in the code, which may result from failures to check array bounds. As example of vulnerabilities in newer protocols, one may consider the World Wide Web (www) or web as the most notorious environment for propagating vulnerabilities. The Web servers provide information in response to requests from the web browsers:

Example: If a request exploits the bug in the Web server, the Web server's security mechanism may be bypassed. The information accessibility from the Web varies widely ranging from plain text to executable content. Others include PostScript, which can altar the behaviour of a printer, Java applets, and ActiveX,

The Java applets are pre-compiled, mini-applications, which are stored on a Web server. It can be downloaded to a network browser and executed locally. The Java program has been explicitly designed to address the security issues through various mechanisms that essentially restrict the behaviour of applets. Since Java programs are interpreted instead of being run in a native code, the Java Virtual Machine (JVM) can prevent program from running, if it violates the security policy. Although Java basic model is secured, the different levels in the model may introduce bug. Indeed the security policy in Java a applets and not correctly specified, but JVM assumes that the byte code verifier finds certain classes of errors, so bugs in the verifier may admit hostile programs. The interpreter may not detect every possible attack, and if Java applets are opened to ease access by Java programs to other parts of the operating system, then applications security may be bypass.

The Active X is a technology for distributing Internet software may allow access to computer resources that should be in assessable.

3.7   Security in the application layer

The application layer has several vulnerabilities that must be considered. These vulnerabilities generally occur above the application layer, which includes the following:

i.   *System access control and authorisation data structures:* The system password file is a common vulnerability in all system connected to the Internet, it allows the system password file to become compromised and leave the system open to hostile attacks of different kinds. The research on Windows

NT, dot NET and Microsoft IPSec have exposes many vulnerabilities that allows the hostile Web page to unobtrusively extract users details.

ii. *Malicious software:* The Trojan horse is a malicious piece of software that hides its true purpose. It will masquerade as a piece of software by providing useful service to the user, but in actual fact it will be exploiting user's right that is possessed by the initiator of the Trojan horse. The malicious software executed by connecting to the Internet is propagated within a very short time. In most cases they are used for sniffing password and mail copies of password file to the initiator. The malicious software can be a problem at many levels. A virus could be a set of macro commands; the macros would copy themselves into all documents, which are created using the word processing or visual basic program to write scripts. Alternatively the virus disguised as an object code, which will copy itself into other executable files when it is executed.

iii. *Hid in application features:* A considerable amount of information may be stored in a file by an application, which may not be visible when a file is open by the application. An example would be the very popular fast save option used in Microsoft word. Deleting the text in this application does not necessarily mean the information is removed. When deleting the text and saving the document a gain, the text is not deleted by Word, instead it is inserted in a note, instructing itself not to display the deleted information, however, it is possible to retrieve the deleted texts using a program, which disregards Word's instruction.

It is often more or less impossible to fully review the contents of a computer file, thus causing concern that sensitive information may inadvertently be exported from the system.

Example: It has been reported that most financial institution old computer systems that was sold at the auction or to private retailers have been found to contained customer confidential details. As mentioned above the files are still stored in the computer memory but not inactive state.

A frequently asked question is *'why do we requires both an IP layer security mechanism and a session layer security mechanism needed?'* The Table 2–1 below presents comparison features of IP layer security vs. session layer using IPSec and Secure Sockets Layer (SSL) (Freier and Karlton, 1996; Dierks and Allen, 1997).

The SSL was originally designed by Netscape to secure Hyper Text Transfer Protocol (HTTP) traffic passing through web browsers and is a session layer protocol. An alternative to IPSec is the SSL. The difference between SSL and IPSec is that IPSec works at the network layer, and secures entire networks, and SSL works at the application layer, and secures applications. Because the IPSec works at the network layer, it can be used to secure sub-net-to-subnet, network-to-network, or network-to-host communications. This means that IPSec traffic can be routed, while SSL traffic cannot. The IPSec and SSL are both used to provide confidentiality of data, and authentication, but they achieve these goals in different ways.

Unlike IPSec, SSL is based on a client/server model and is typically used for host-to-host secure transport. Although many people see SSL as a com-petitive technology to IPSec, this view is not entirely accurate. In most cases, IPSec and SSL are used to solve different types of problems. The Version 3 of the SSL was designed with public review and it was published as an Internet draft document. The SSL use the TCP/IP protocol in order to provide a reliable end-to-end secure service. The TCP/IP is responsible for the reliable transport and routing of data over the Internet, but it does not ensure security during the transmission of packets.

There are other protocols (HTTP, Lightweight Directory Access Protocol (LDAP), or Internet Messaging Access Protocol (IMAP)) that run on top of TCP/IP, meaning that they use TCP/IP to fulfil some applications. The latter is use for displaying web pages, running email servers, and enhancement of other applications.

The SSL provides confidentiality, server authentication, integrity and op-tional client authentication for a TCP/IP connection, but replay attack and man-in-the middle attacks still threaten its use. The SSL is placed on top of TCP/IP layer and below the application layer. It combines the public key and symmetric key encryption. The symmetric key encryption is much faster than public key encryption, but public key encryption provides better authentica-tion mechanisms. More specifically, the SSL secures the communications channel by providing end-to-end encryption that is sent between a Web client and a Web server. The SSL is a standalone solution because it is built into an application and it can support many other application protocols. Also, it does not need to be updated like other application protocols. Besides, it is quite flex-ible, and it also supported by all web browsers and servers making it reliable and proven protocol. While the IPSec based connections require a substantial amount of planning and implementation time, the SSL implementations are relatively quick to use, and sometimes require no planning at all, depending on what browser and how it is currently configured (Taylor, 2002). Providing security at different layers is a well-established fact, which has been in exist-ence for many years. However, the fact remains that the more levels of secu-rity available, the better, and difficult it will be for any intrusion; as different levels requires different password or authentication but with wider knowledge of programming back ground and abundant of free software it is possible to dismissed this conceptual believed.

Table 2–1. IP layer security vs Session layer security

Features	IPSec: IP Layer Security	SSL: Session Layer Security
Hardware-independence	Yes	Yes
Code	No modifications to applications. May need access to TCP/IP stack source code.	Modifications to applications. May need new DLL or access to application source code.
Protection	Entire IP packet. Includes protection for higher-layer protocols.	Only application layer.
Packet filtering	Based on authenticated headers, source or destination addresses, etc. Simpler and lower cost. Suitable for routers.	Based on content and higher-level semantics. More intelligent and more complex. But also desirable.
Performance	Less context-switching and data movement.	More context-switching and data movement. Larger data units may help speed up cryptographic operations and provide better compression.
Platform	Any systems, routers included.	Mainly end systems (clients/servers), also on firewalls.
Firewall/VPN	All traffic is protected.	Only application-level traffic is protected. ICMP, RSVP, QoS, etc., may not be protected.
Transparency	To users and applications.	To users only.
Current deployment	Emerging standard, supported by most firewall vendors.	Widely used by WWW browsers; also used by some products to provide session layer secure tunnel.

4. BENEFITS AND LIMITATIONS OF IMPLEMENTING SECURITY AT THE APPLICATION, TRANSPORT, NETWORK, AND DATA LINK LAYERS

One of the best ways to understand a network is to first understand the way in which traffic is passed across the network. The OSI can be use as a conceptual framework for understanding the benefits and limitations of implementing security at the application, transport, network, and data link layers. The OSI involves, navigation between applications running on different machines. It also paves way in understanding the TCP/IP protocol suit and Internet protocol address. Each layer within the OSI has a well-defined function. However, the benefits and limitations of implementing security at the application, transport, network, and data link layers are discussed below.

4.1   Application layer security (ALS)

The Application layer security is typically implemented at the end hosts. Implementing security at the application layer simplifies the provision of services such as non-repudiation by giving complete access to the data the user wants to protect. It is also possible to extend applications without being reliant on the operating system to provide basic security services. This is particularly useful, as 'applications normally have no control over what gets implemented in the operating system'. The end applications also tend to have a better understanding of the data and can therefore provide more appropriate security.

The major disadvantage of implementing security at the application layer is the need to independently design security mechanisms for end applications. This implies modification of existing applications to provide enhanced security. Since each application will inevitably have there own unique security requirements, it would not be feasible to individually modify the end applications (Kaeo, 1999). The custom-made security mechanisms should be defined when the application needs are specific. The Pretty Good Privacy (PGP), Kerberos, and Security shell, are some examples of application level product that provide key negotiation and other security services.

- *Benefits:* The ALS gives easy access to user credentials, and the application is execute in the context of the user. It simplifies the task of providing services like non-repudiation by giving a point access to the data that the user wants protected. An application can evolve independently since it does not need to depend on the operating system to provide these services.
- *Limitations:* The security mechanisms have to be designed independently for each application. This is tedious and lengthy task. Since each application has could find its once security mechanisms, it increases the probability of making errors and holds for attacks.

However, there are many examples of applications, which successfully provide integrated security to some extend, but at a lower level. One common example is email clients that make use of Pretty Good Privacy (PGP) to provide email security. In this particular case, the email client would be extended to provide the ability to look up user public keys in databases as well as provision of services such as encryption, authentication and non-repudiation of email messages. Although it would not be feasible to integrate security for all applications, there will always be some applications that will need to have application layer security services integrated into them due to their specific requirements. A common example of such a service cited by is non-repudiation. It is very difficult for lower layers to provide non-repudiation, as they do not have direct access to the user data.

4.2 Transport layer security (TLS)

The transport layer security (TLS) is rapidly becoming very popular for providing security over the worldwide web. Many organisations are now 'click and mortal' which means they have physical location and also transacts businesses online This online operations rely on TLS services like SSL for securing transaction made to and from their web servers.

- *Benefits:* The TLS provides security at the transport layer; the most definite advantage is that it does not require modification to applications. The TLS is total call specific and provide security services such as authentication, integrity, and confidentiality.
- *Limitations:* The TLS complicates the process of obtaining user contexts. In order to provide user specific services, TLS assumes that a single user uses the system, which might not always be true. It can only be implemented on end systems and need to maintain a contest for each connection. Currently, only the TCP implementations are available and none for UDP. The assumptions that applications do not require any changes, is not entirely accurate. Some modifications have to be made to enable applications, request security services from the transport layer.

Implementing security at the transport layer can provide transparent security services for end user and applications do not require modifications. The main problem with the TLS is that user-specific services cannot be provided. The TLS can only be implemented on an end system and it is only assumed that a single user is using the system. The TLS is protocol-specific, and provides security services such as authentication, integrity and confidentiality on top of TCP. For TLS to be properly implemented, it needs to maintain context for a connection. It is not possible to implement TLS for UDP because of lack of connection. Most web browsers nowadays provide security services through TLS. The major limitation of TLS is that the end applications will requires modification in order to request security services from the transport layer.

4.3 Network layer security (NLS)

The network layer security (NLS) is a widespread industrial standard. Implementing security at the network layer probably offers the greatest benefits. The general trend is that the lower down we move in the TCP/IP stack the less processing and overhead that will be encounter. This is certainly the case with network layer security as it significantly reduces the overhead involved in key negotiation. The Virtual Private Networks (VPNs) and intranets are typically based on IP subnets and the network layer supports the use of IP subnets, so it is relatively easy to implement VPNs and intranets. The IPSec is a common example of a protocol suite used to create VPNs at this layer.

*   *Benefits:* The most important advantage of implementing security at this layer is the ability to build VPNs. The NLS can be implemented at intermediate system is endorsed and gateways.
*   *Limitations:* It is difficult to handle issues such as non-repudiation of data. It is also more difficult to control security or on a per user bases in a multi-user machine.

The implementation of security at the network layers enables multiple applications and transport layer protocols to transparently share the common key management infrastructure that results in fewer changes in the end applications. One of the well-known services offered by the network layer is the ability to build VPNs and private intranets. Although the concept of VPNs has existed for almost a decade, it was only recently that there has been a rapid rise in the number and variety of VPN products and technologies. The old computer networks were implemented with two major technologies, dial-up lines for occasional connectivity and leased lines for permanent connectivity. The data communication industry and service providers attempted to develop a number of statistical multiplexing technologies to offer customers secure and cost effective alternatives. The first VPNs were based on X.25 and Frame Relay, and, later, Switched Multimegabit Data Service (SMDS) and ATM (Kaeo, 1999). However, since the service providers typically own the infrastructure, leased lines are still a costly option. Many customers also find the leased line option to be quite inflexible, since the customer may end up with a leased line with too little bandwidth or a *'much more expensive connection with more bandwidth than is needed, with nothing in-between'* (Perlman, 2000). In addition to this, customers often purchase Internet connectivity from providers and as a result end up paying an additional charge.

Nowadays, a common trend with many service providers is the migration from traditional Frame Relay and ATM backbones to pure IP or IP/MPLS networks. As a result of this the providers often increase the charges for traditional Frame Relay and ATM services since they have to manage these networks in addition to their IP/MPLS backbones. There have been significant developments in secure and cost effective VPN technologies. The modern VPN services span a variety of technologies and topologies. One way to deal with the increasing diversity of these technologies is to introduce some kind of VPN classification (Kaeo, 1999). One of the most common classifications is the OSI layer at which the VPN technology offers its services. As such, a large majority of VPN technologies available today can be categorised as being Layer 2 or Layer 3 solutions. For example, a VPN service could be a layer 2 solution

providing customers with Frame Relay or ATM leased-lines, or it could be a
Layer 3 solution providing customers with IPv4 connectivity between sites.
Layer 2 solutions tend to be more flexible as they can transparently carry almost any higher layer protocols. This allows layer 2 solutions to provide services for both IP and non-IP data. However, since the *'most common use of VPN*
is to route IP traffic' between sites, a layer 3 solution is suitable for most cases.
The Layer 3 solutions tend to be easier to manage since the networks have a
logical definition based on IP addresses. The main disadvantage with layer 2
solutions is that all the sites must use the same layer 2 protocol.

4.4   Data-link layer security (DLLS)

Implementing data-link layer security (DLLS) requires dedicated physical
connections between devices. If there were a need to encrypt data between
two hosts directly connected via a dedicated link, it would be possible to use
hardware encryption. Although such a solution would offer considerable speed
advantages, it would not be scalable since all devices in the network would
require dedicated physical connections between themselves. A good example
of DLLS implementation is the automatic Teller machines (ATMs).

- *Benefits:* Where speed is a concern DLLS is most suitable form of security.
  Can what on dedicated links and can be implemented in hardware like routers, which have to be physically connected. It provides end-to-end security,
  but not always guarantee.
- *Limitations:* The DLLS is not scalable and can only work well on dedicated
  links—it can be used to secure the link between two routers that are connected using a leased line.

However, security is given very low priority at the physical session, and
presentation layers. The set of rules, and proceedings governing transmission
between two points on a network or between two networks are commonly
known as Protocols. Each devise in a network must be able to interpret the
other device's protocol. The primary function of protocols in any network, re-
gardless is to identify each device in the communication path, and to secure the
oppression of the other devise. It also help to verify the correct receipt of the
transmitted information, and to determine whether the information requires
retransmission due to incompleteness or errors contained within it or it has
failed to reach the intended target destination. Examples of protocols used for
communications between computers in networks or between networks as in
the case of the Internet include the TCP/IP protocol suit.

5.   IPSEC STANDARDS

The IETF's IP Security (IPSec) working group is developing standards for IP-layer security mechanisms for both IPv4 (The version currently used on the Internet) and IPv6 (the next generation of TCP/IP). The IPSec architecture includes authentication (how to know if the site communicating to your site really who it claims to be) and encryption. These mechanisms can be used together or independently. The IPSec is a series of guidelines for the protection of Internet Protocol (IP) communications. The Network Working Group of the IETF defines the architecture of the IPSec compliant systems in RFC 2401 (Security Architecture for the Internet Protocol): IPSec as *'a framework that provides security services at the IP layer by enabling a system to select required security protocols, determine the algorithm(s) to use for the service(s), and put in place any cryptographic keys required to provide the requested services'*. Roland and Newcomb (2003) clarify this further by defining IPSec as: *'a collection of open standards that work together to establish data confidentiality, data integrity, and data authentication between peer devices'*. The IPSec works at the Network layer and can protect multiple data flows between peers, in both the IPv4 and IPv6 environments. IPSec uses the Internet Key Exchange (IKE) protocol to negotiate protocols between peers and generate encryption and authentication keys. IPSec can be implemented between, two hosts, two security gateways (e.g. routers or firewalls) or between a host and a gateway. The RFC 2401 defines 3 ways in which IPSec can be implemented:

- IPSec integrated into the native IP implementation of the host or security gateway.
- Introducing an IPSec layer between the IP layer and the network drivers, referred to as the "bump-in-the-stack" (BITS) implementation.
- Introducing an external device such as an outboard crypto processor. This option is referred to as the "bump-in-the-wire" (BITW) implementation.

The RFC 2411 (IP Security Document Roadmap) specification of the IPSec consists of numerous documents:

- RFC 2401 documentation presents the overview of a security architecture including general concepts, security requirements, definitions and mechanisms defining IPSec technology.
- RFC 2402 documentation describes the packet authentication extension to IPv4 and IPv6.
- RFC 2406: documentation describes the extension packet encryption in the IPv4 and v6.

- RFC 2408 documentation presents the specification of key management capabilities

The four RFCs discussed above have been published by the IP Security Protocol Network Working Group set up by the IETF. The IP Security architecture defines basic security mechanisms at the network level so that they can be available to all the layered applications. The IP security architecture consists of security variables, mechanisms, control, and management. The IPSec implementation operates in a host or a security gateway environment and attempts to solve two main VPN design issues:

- LAN-to-LAN IPSec – To provide seamless interconnection of two or more private networks.
- Remote-access IPSec – To extend a private network to allow remote-access users access to corporate resources.

In the most commonly used scenario, the IPSec allows an encrypted tunnel to be created between two private networks (Goncalves, 1999). It also allows for authenticating the two ends of the tunnel. It encapsulates and encrypts the IP data. The IPSec has been implemented by a large number of vendors, and interoperability between multi-vendor devices. The GNU/Linux FreeS/WAN project is an implementation of IPSec and IKE for GNU/Linux systems. Several companies are co-operating in the Secure Wide Area Network (S/WAN) project to ensure that products would be interoperated. There is also *a VPN Consortium fostering cooperation among companies in this area'. The primary objective is 'to promotes the widespread of IPSec by providing source code that is freely available and runs on a range of machines'* (Jayawickrama, 2003). The IPSec is defined in a number of RFC that defines the various security protocols, algorithms and mechanisms that comprise IPSec. The initial IPSec standards were defined in RFCs 1825-29 and have since been made obsolete by the current standards. The current RFCs addressing IP security issues include RFC 2401 – (Security Architecture for the Internet Protocol (IPSec)), RFC 2402 –(IP Authentication Header (AH)), RFC 2406 – (IP Encapsulating Payload (ESP)) and RFC 2409 – (Internet Key Exchange (IKE)).

The IPSec has evolved over time. The predecessor to IPSec was known as swIPe, an experimental protocol designed in 1993 (Kent and Atkinson, 1998). The IETF defined IPSec as a mandatory protocol for IP v6. The latest efforts by the IETF include looking into providing a more flexible and unified policy mechanism for IPSec. It is also hoped that support for common Application Program Interface (API) will be integrated, allowing end applications to request security services from IPSec. This will result in end user applications, such as email and instant messaging being able to take advantage of the IPSec.

Efforts are also underway to provide complete integration of the IPSec with the IP v6 stack. The two main operation modes in the IPSec are transport and tunnel modes. There are four possible combinations of these mode used has a protocols within the IPSec:

- AH in transport mode
- AH tunnel mode
- ESP in transport mode
- ESP tunnel mode

The ESP, and AH header do not change between transport and tunnel mode. The differences is that the ESP protects the whole IP packet, while the AH protects the IP payload.

5.1   IPSec transport mode

The operations of the transport mode start with the source and destination hosts, which directly perform all cryptographic operations using the cryptographic protocols. The transport mode can be compare to a house, the front door is the source and the destination is the back of the house (see Figure 2–3 for diagrammatic illustration). The house represents tunnelling protocol with different rooms, which contains encrypted data. Each user would require having keys that can open the doors. With this example it is assume that the front and back doors can be open. As this is the case in real life, system security cannot be 100 percent guarantee but many companies are striving to support IPSec software and hardware with many odds unfilled (see Table 2–3).

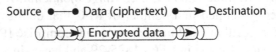

Source ●——● Data (ciphertext) ●——➤ Destination

Figure 2–3. IPSec transport mode

In a normal circumstance when no security is enabled, the TCP and UDP packets are active in the network layer (see Figure 2–4 for diagrammatic illustration). But when security is enabled, the transport layer packet becomes active. The latter adds either ESP or AH, or both headers to initiates the component of the network layer that adds the network layer header.

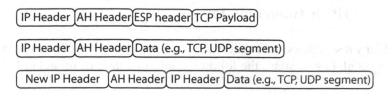

Figure 2–4. IP packet in IPSec transport mode

The transport mode provides security to the IP payloads. The functionality of transport mode is to intercept the IP packets flowing from the transport layer to the network layer and enforced the configured security. The transport mode of IPSec is used only when end-to-end security is required (see Figures 2–4 for diagrammatic illustration). For example, securing transmission within department A workstations and the database server in other to prevent data from being intercepted or altered. The IPSec can be implemented to encrypt the data, and protecting it from compromise but to do this, it is possible to use the built in default policies or to customise the policy. The policy is made up of one or more IP security rules. The rules must cover all the traffic that may be encountered, and can include a default rule to apply to traffic that do not need to be specified. The default policies include:

- Client (Respond Only) workstation using unsecured transmission, unless the server prompts it to use secure communications, then the workstation will comply.
- A Standard Server (Request Security) policy that the server will always request for secure transmissions, but will accept unsecured if the client does not support IPSec.
- Secure Server (Require Security) policy the server will require security and drop all communications with clients that do not support security.

Indeed, the users can always customise the policy requirements by creating filters and filter actions. The filters specify what the IP traffic is required to control. The parameters use by the filter traffic is the source and destination IP address or subnet, the protocol and port the traffic comes from, and the destination. The level of encryption is also specified in the filter action. As soon as the necessary filters are created with the filter actions, the new IPSec policy can be created. The IPSec policy is a set of rules that governs, when and how to use the IPSec protocol. The IPSec policy interacts directly with the IPSec driver. The policies determining which IP traffic that should be secured and the IP packets that should be left alone is accomplished through the use of an IP filter list (the IP filter list is a collection of individual filters that the filter action is applied to), individual IP filters, and filter actions. The IP filter recognised certain types of IP packets that requires immediate action.

5.2   IPSec tunnel mode

Many researchers and vendors use the word tunnel widely within the IPSec.
Cheng et al. (1998) states the following interpretation of tunnel in IPSec:

i.   Conceptually refers to a *secure passage* (or channel) between two systems
     across the insecure Internet. This passage is a realization of the *security
     policies* of two systems. In the context of IPSec, a security policy establish-
     es the specific requirements and *meta-characteristics* of a secure passage
     between two given systems. The meta-characteristics of a passage usually
     include the identities or addresses of its two endpoints, the encapsulation
     mode, the cryptographic algorithms to be used, parameters for the algo-
     rithms (such as key lifetime and key size(s)), etc. A security policy may
     also demand more than one secure passage between the two systems, each
     for a specific type of communication.

ii. Implementation-wise, the word tunnel refers to a set of items of informa-
     tion shared between the endpoints of a secure passage. This set enables the
     realization of a secure passage; it includes in particular the meta-character-
     istics and secret keys used by the cryptographic algorithms. In the IPSec
     terminology, such a set is called a *security association*. The next subsection
     elaborates on SAs in more detail. However, as the subsection subsequent
     to that explains, an SA is *not* a secure tunnel but an incarnation of a secure
     tunnel during a particular time interval. An SA is usually created and main-
     tained by a key management engine. The standard terminology of IPSec,
     tunnel refers to one of the two-encapsulation modes defined by the IPSec
     standard: tunnel mode and transport mode. Both modes can be used to
     construct a secure passage, although they provide slightly different protec-
     tion. The fourth section presents a more detailed discussion on the IPSec
     standard.

Moreover, the tunnel is used within this book to denote secure tunnel passage or an instance where it enhances the integrity of the data or information
transfer. On the other hand, when operating in tunnel mode, special gateways
perform cryptographic processing in addition to the source and destination
hosts. The network is usually assumed to be hostile, in that it may contain
intruders, who can read, modify, delete traffic, and control the network principals. The cryptographic protocol must be able to achieve its goals and face
hostile intruders. The protocols are often subject to non-intuitive attacks, which
are not easily apparent even to the careful inspector. Many of these attacks do
not depend upon any flaws or weaknesses in the underlying cryptography algorithm, and can be exploited by any attackers who are able to no more than
the basic operations.

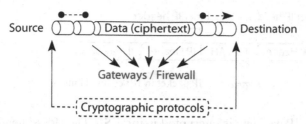

Figure 2–5. IPSec tunnel mod

The cryptographic protocols are protocols that use cryptography to distribute keys and authenticate principals and data over a network. An encrypted data is sent through a single tunnel that is created with L2TP (Layer 2 Tunneling Protocol). Data (ciphertext) is created by the source host and retrieved by the destination host. This mode of operation establishes end-to-end security. Many tunnels are created in a series of gateways, which enables gateway-to-gateway security. All the gateways should be provided with the ability to verify that a data packet is real and to authenticate the data packet at both ends. Any data packets that are suspected to be false or invalid must be dropped (see Figures 2–5 and 2–6 for diagrammatic illustration).

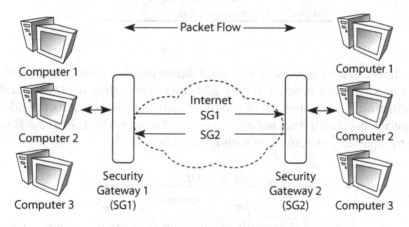

Figure 2–6. IPSec tunnel mode implementation

The IPSec tunnel mode is used when destination of the IP packets is beyond the security termination points. For example, when a security getaway (router or firewall) provides security on behalf of the host systems, in this case the getaway did not originate the packets. The getaway in this case only provides security services for the packets that it is forwarding (see Figure 2–6 for diagrammatic illustration).

The packet has two IP headers. The host that originated the packets creates the inner IP header and the outer IP header is generated by the security gateway (see Figure 2–7)

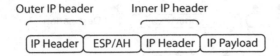

Figure 2–7. IP packet in IPSec tunnel mode

The entire IP packets, is encrypted using ESP. The IPSec header is created to encapsulate the entire IP packets (encrypted payload and ESP header) (see Table 2–2)

Table 2–2. Encapsulating Security Payload (ESP)

#octets	Field name
4	SPI
4	Sequence number
Variable	IV
Variable	Data (Original IP payload)
Variable	Padding
1	Padding length (in units of octets)
1	Next header/protocol type
Variable	Authentication data

The host can also provides end-to-end tunnel mode security, but in reality there is no significant benefits, it only adds more computing overhead. In the latter situation, the transport layer provides more beneficial results to end-to-end security, because it does not add an extra IP header. The ESP and AH can be use to separately or combined with IPSec tunnel mode.

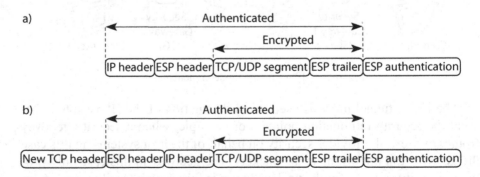

Figure 2–8. ESP Protocol (a and b)

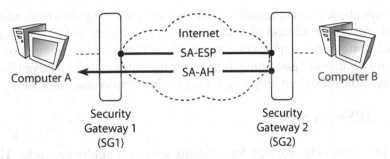

Figure 2–9. IP packet in IPSec nested tunnel implementation

The ESP puts the information before and after the protected data. For authentication, all fields are included (see Figure 2–8 a and b). The AH is responsible for the integrity while ESP does both encryption and integrity. Therefore, if just integrity, AH or ESP can be apply. The ESP always encrypts to protect the integrity, using null encryption algorithm. But if integrity and encryption, then both AH and ESP can be applied, or only ESP can be considered.

The IPSec tunnel also support nested tunnels, where tunnel lies within a tunnel. For example if host A wants to send a packet to host B, the policy defined, requires the packet to authenticate itself for the security gateway one (SG1) and encrypts the VPN connection between the security gateways one and two (SG1 and SG2). The Figure 2–9 shows how the packet will appears to the security gateways SG2. The operating systems, which natively support IPSec VPN connections, are:

* Windows XP Home and Professional
* Windows 2000
* Mac OS X 10.3 and later
* Solaris 8 and later version
* Various Linux distributions
* Free, Open, and NetBSD

For PDAs, Microsoft's Windows Mobile 2003 is currently the only operating system known to UITS to possess native IPSec support. The Pocket PC 2002 and Palm OS require third-party VPN clients.

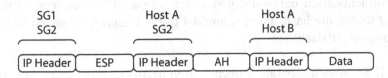

Figure 2–10. IP packet in IPSec nested tunnel mode

The outer header in the tunnelled ESP packet containing the source address SG1 and destination address of SG2 is presented in Figure 2–10. The original IP header contains the source address of host A and destination address of host B. In reality building nested tunnels are very demanding task and even harder to maintain, they are used only when it is absolutely necessary to do so.

5.3   IPSec services

The IPSec provides secured data transmission over public networks. These security functions in IP layer include confidentiality (encryption), authenticity (proof of sender), integrity (detection of data tampering), and replay protection (defence against unauthorised re-sending of data). The IPSec provides two mechanisms for providing authentication and confidentiality at the IP layer, which can be used separately or together. The IPSec also provides methodologies for key management. The IKE mechanism defines the exchanges of cryptography keys to protect the data. The IKE is a series of steps that establishes keys for encrypting and decrypting information, which uses AH and ESP.

6.   WHY AH

The AH provides data integrity to assured that the data was not changed in transit and authentication to claim the data received is the same as the data that was sent from actual sender but no confidentiality because it does not encrypt data. The address spoofing attacks can be prevented and protects against the replay attack. The AH contains the following fields:

- Next header (8 bit)
- Payload length (8 bit) for authentication header
- Reserved (16 bit): for future use
- Security Parameter Index (SPI)—a random value used in combination with the destination IP address to identify the Security Association for the datagram
- Sequence Number—counter value used to detect replayed IP datagrams in order to assure message sequence integrity
- Authentication data—integrity check value (ICV) obtained as the result of the secure hash function applied to the integrity protected fields of the original IP datagram

The IPSec uses a separate Authentication header (AH) to carry authentication information by containing an authentication value based on a symmetric-key hash algorithm such as a Message Authentication Code (MAC) function. IP Packet contains the following fields:

- The maximum size of IPv4 header is 60 bytes
- The Upper Layer Protocol Data Unit (PDU), usually consists of an upper layer protocol header and its payload (for example, an ICMP message, a UDP message, or a TCP segment).

The minimum IPv4 header's size is 20 bytes without options and padding. The total length of IPSec packet (combination of the headers and application data) size can be up to 65,535 bytes long. The AH provides services like data integrity, data origin authentication and anti-replay (optional). The AH does not encrypt any part of the protected IP datagram (see chapter 3 for further discussion on datagram and Figure 2–11 for diagrammatic illustration).

0	8	16	31
Next Header (NH): Identifies the header that immediately follows. The NH is 8-bits in length	**Payload Data (PD):** This field is 8-bits in length and shows the length of authentication header in 32-bits words.	**Reserved:** This field is 16-bits in length and has been reserved for future use as new specifications comes up.	
Sequence Number (SN): It is a monotonically increasing in value and is used to protect against anti reply attacks. It is also 32 bits in lengths			
Authentication Data: This field is variable in length but its length must be a multiple of 32-bits. This field contains the integrity check value (ICV).			

Figure 2–11. Contents of AH

The AH is similar to ESP operations, in that AH is inserted after the IP header; it flows after the extensions header. The AH is assigned a value 51 and protects the datagram. If an extension header is present then the next header field of the extension header just before the AH header will automatically be set to 51. The AH does not perform any encryption and there is no trailer, which eliminates the need for padding and pad length.

6.1 AH in transport mode

The AH in transport mode is used when end-to-end security is required. The originating host inserts the AH right after the IP header and before the upper layer protocol (see Figure 2–12 for diagrammatic illustration).

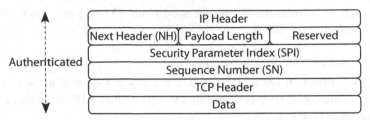

Figure 2–12. IP packet protected by AH in transport mode

The receiver finds the associated SA, by means of SPI in the AH. The sequence number is checked to protect against replay attacks. Then the Message Authentication Codes (MACs) is calculated again and compared to the integrity check value (ICV) present in the AH. If everything works out then the packet is accepted, otherwise it is silently discarded. The authentication algorithm used for the ICV is usually specified by the SAs.

6.2   AH in tunnel mode

The entire IP packet in AH tunnel mode is encrypted and AH is inserted before the IP header. The whole packet (AH and the original IP packet) is encapsulated in another IP header (see Figure 2–13 for diagrammatic illustration).

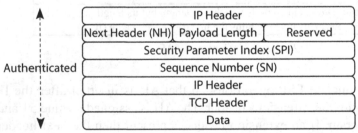

Figure 2–13. IP packet protected by AH in tunnel mode

The processing at the receiving end is exactly the same as for AH in transport mode. The transport mode can be use to protect against traffic analysis attacks as compared to AH transport mode, by concealing the actual destination of the packet.

7.   WHY ESP

The ESP is defined in the RFC 2406 as protocol header, which is inserted in the IP packet to provide confidentiality, data origin authentication, anti replay and data integrity. The ESP provides confidentiality (encryption) and authentication as AH. It is more complex than the AH. A value 50 in the protocol field of the datagram informs a receiver that the datagram carries the ESP. The IP ESP encrypts the data using symmetric key and encapsulates it with header information so that the receiving IPSec entity can decrypt it. The ESP packet contains following fields:

- Security Parameters Index (32 bits) identifies a security association
- Sequence Number increases counter value
- Payload Data (variable) is a transport-level segment (transport mode) or IP packet (tunnel mode) that is protected by encryption
- Padding (0-255 bytes) is required to fill the payload data field to the input size required by the encryption algorithm
- Pad Length (8 bit) is the number of pad bytes inserted by the encryption algorithm
- Next Header (8 bit) is the same as AH
- Authentication Data (variable) is Integrity Check Value (ICV) computed over the ESP packet minus the authentication data field

In the first release of RFC IPSec documentation, the ESP was used for encryption only and AH was used for authentication. As, RFCs allow using ESP without AH it was decided to add in the new RFC the capability to authenticates the ESP. So, it is possible to use AH to authenticate, and to use ESP also to authenticate and encrypt. The authentication algorithms uses in ESP are Data Encryption Standard (DES) (in CBC mode – the only mandatory one), 3DES, RC5, IDEA, 3 IDEA, CAST, and Blowfish. The most important three symmetric block ciphers are DES, 3DES, and Advances Encryption Standard (AES). The DES and 3DES algorithms were originally used for securing Internet traffic and first proposed in 1970. The cryptographic community considers DES insecure because 56-bit key can be discovered by a brute-force exhaustive attack in a relatively short period of time. Therefore, DES is not sufficient for many security applications. The DES was superseded by the 'Triple-DES' (3DES). The Triple-DES or 3DES has been used to replace DES. The 3DES encrypts each 64-bit block of a message three times. The operations may involve two or three different keys. The 3DES uses a key size of 112 bits in applications, as opposed to 56 bits for DES. The disadvantage of the 3DES is that the encryption and decryption time per block is three times that of the DES. However, the 3DES is more secure to 'brute force' attacks than DES. The DES is a rather old protocol that has proven to be more secured but a "brute force" attack could compromise the security of the data encrypted with the DES. Because of the DES lacks security, the National Institute of Standard and Technology (NIST) adopted the new Advance Encryption Standard (AES) and replace the DES encryption in their cryptographic devices. The AES offers three different key strengths: 128, 192, and 256 bit keys. The AES provides better security than DES and computationally more efficient than the 3DES.

The IPSec supports two modes of operation: transport and tunnel modes. In transport mode, the original IP header is followed by the AH or ESP header. Both the AH and ESP supports transport and tunnel mode. In the transport mode, only the IP payload, at the upper-layer (TCP, UDP, IGMP) that are encrypted and leaves the IP header unsecured. The real IP addresses are embedded in the new IPSec packet. The IP addresses of the hosts are used to route the packet. Commonly use for securing traffic on a LAN.

Within the tunnel mode, the entire packet including the encrypted payload is encapsulated in another packet before being sent off to the remote host. It means that the real IP addresses are embedded in the new IPSec packet. The host are not in charge of the IPSec. In the transport mode, AH header is inserted after the original IP header and before the IP payload and authenticates the entire packet, excluding mutable fields that are set to zero for MACs calculation. The authentication algorithms used by the IPSec is usually specified by the SAs. The two parties that share a secret key may use MACs to validate messages sent between them. Suitable authentication algorithms include HMAC, which is based on symmetric encryption algorithms and provides a framework to incorporate any cryptographic hash function for the MD5 and SHA1:

- The MD5 was developed and designed as an extension to MD4 (Rivest, 1991). It is slower than MD4 and more conservative thus providing more security. The MD5 does not require a large substitution table and is relatively fast on 32-bit processors. The MD5 algorithm takes an input message of any length and produces an output of 128-bit "message digest". The conjecture is that it is computationally impossible to produce the same message digest from two different messages.
- The SHA1 is a secret key authentication algorithm that superseded the SHA that was published in 1994. It corrects an unpublished flaw in SHA and similar MD4 design. The algorithm takes a message smaller than 264 bits in length and produces 160-bit authenticator value.

The cryptographic strength of the HMAC mechanism depends on the security provided by the underlying hash function [see RFC 2104 documentation for further details]. Even though the MD5 has been found to be vulnerable to some attacks such as the collision search attack (Dobbertin, 1996), the use of MD5 with HMAC is not compromised. The SHA1 is based on cryptographical function that produces larger message digest than MD5, but takes a longer computational time. The goal of HMAC is to use the available cryptographic hash functions without modifications and without degrading their performance. This allows for the ability to easily replace the functions in case they are not seen as secure at some point (Krawczyk, 1997). The two most widely used realisations of HMAC, when MD5 and SHA1 are used in IPSec, are denoted by HMAC-MD5-96 and HMAC-SHA1-96. The number "96" denotes the number of bits at which the output is truncated. After the message digest value is truncated to 96 bits, it is compared with the value in the authentication data field (Madson & Glenn, 1998)

In the tunnel mode, AH new IP header is included before the original IP header which means contrarily to transport mode, the entire original IP packet is authenticated and the AH header is inserted between the IP header and a new outer header. The inner IP header always carries the source and destination addresses, while the new IP header may carry different IP addresses such as firewall address or other security gateways' addresses (see Figure 2–15 for diagrammatic illustration).

The ESP header transport mode contains the original header. But only upper layer encrypted, the IP header is not encrypted which means this field is positioned in the clear text part of the IP datagram. Hence if the entire IP datagram including the protocol specific information also needs to be protected, tunnel mode should be used. While in tunnel mode, the original IP datagram including the original header is encrypted. However, unlike the AH authentication data field, the ESP authentication data field is optional and the authentication provided by only the ESP header, the ESP payload and the padding fields of the datagram. The IP header (the original one in transport mode or the new one in tunnel mode) is never protected by the ESP authentication service. Thus in cases where data integrity and confidentiality of the entire IP datagram are required, it is recommended to use IP ESP in combination with IP AH. As discussed above the ESP can be used in either tunnel and/or transport modes to encapsulate the entire IP packet. The confidentiality is provided using an encryption and authentication by an authenticator. Separate SAs are used for each encryption and authentication to determined the specific algorithms to be used and other crucial parameters (Kent and Atkinson, 1998) (see Figures 2–14 and 2–16 for diagrammatic illustration)

In an IP packet the ESP header always follows the IP header, but in the case of IPv6 the placement of the ESP header depends on the extension headers. In IPv6 the ESP header is always inserted after the extension headers. The extension headers contained route information in the form of hop-by-hop, routing and fragments headers. The protocol field in the IP header of an ESP protected packet will always be 50. If extension headers are present, then the next header field of the extension header just before the ESP header will automatically be set to 50. Immediately, after the ESP header, an upper layer protocol or another IP header is present, and end by the ESP trailer. The ESP header itself is not automatically encrypted but a part of the ESP trailer is encrypted.

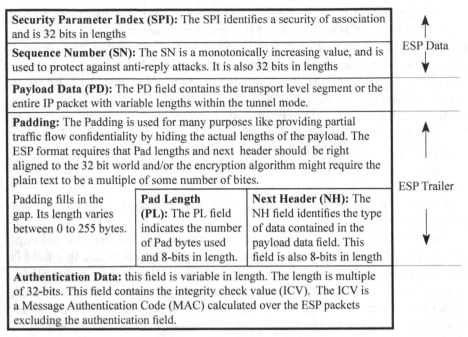

Figure 2–14. ESP header and Trailer

7.1   ESP in tunnel mode

The ESP in tunnel mode originating host encrypts the entire IP packet. The ESP header and trailer are inserted, everything after the ESP header are encrypted before adding it to the trailer. This action proves to be useful against traffic analysis attacks and intermediate routers trying to access IP header because the entire encrypted packet from the ESP header to the trailer is encapsulated in another IP header (see Figure 2–17 for diagrammatic illustration).

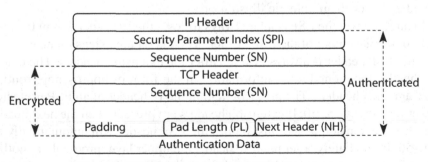

Figure 2–17. IP packet protected by ESP in tunnel mode

The receiving host or gateway examines the ESP header and the basis of SPI, decrypts the packet.

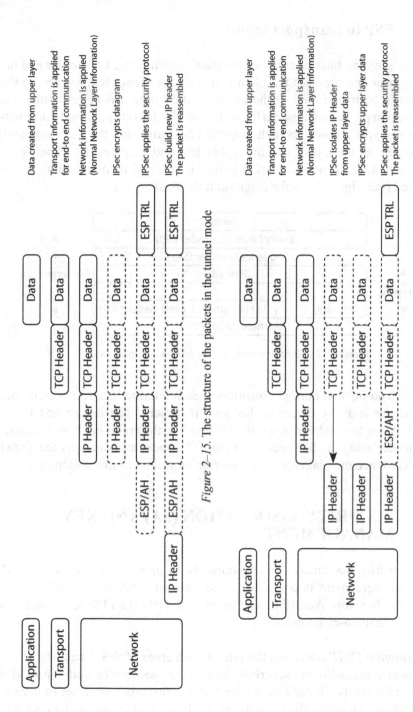

Figure 2–15. The structure of the packets in the tunnel mode

Figure 2–16. The structure of the packets in the transport mode

7.2 ESP in transport mode

The originating host encrypts all the data including the ESP trailer and the TCP fragment and replaces the plain text with the cipher text to prepare the IP packet to be transmitted. If the authentication option is selected then the authentication process will be performed. The ESP in transport mode originating host encrypts all the data including the ESP trailer and the TCP fragment, and replaces the plain text with the cipher text and prepares the IP packet to be transmitted. If the authentication option is selected then authentication is performed (see Figure 2–18 for diagrammatic illustration).

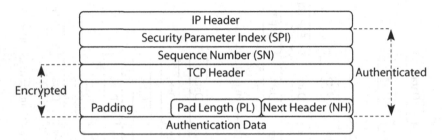

Figure 2–18. IP packet protected by ESP in transport mode

It worth noting that during transmission each intermediate router examines the IP header and any extension headers, if present. The cipher text is untouched. When the packet reaches the destination, the receiving host examines the IP header using the SPI present in the ESP header and decrypts the cipher text to reproduce the plain text and upper layer protocol information.

8. SECURITY ASSOCIATION (SA) AND KEY MANAGEMENT

The security association (SA) represents an agreement between two IP nodes. This agreement is provided in the form of a SA that establishes the security mechanisms. According to Cheng et al. (1998) an IPSec SA includes the following meta-characteristics:

- *Destination ID/IP* addresses the intended receiver of IPSec packets.
- *Security protocol* is the security—integrity or secrecy or both—provided by the SA on the IP packets. Under the security protocol, a set of cryptographic algorithms (called transforms in IPSec) and its parameters, such as key lifetime and key size, are specified.
- *Secret keys* are the keys to be used by the cryptographic transforms

- *Encapsulation mode* indicates which part(s) of the IP packet will be protected by the SA
- *Security Parameter Index (SPI)* is the identifier of the SA. On a given system, the SPI should be unique with respect to the destination address of the SA so that the pair (destination address, and SPI) uniquely identifies an SA. An IPSec packet constructed according to an SA carries the SPI of the SA so that the destination will know how to process the packet.

The SA is a protocol specific, meaning that if hosts use ESP or AH, the SA will be created for both ESP and AH and defines the rules for securing communication and their parameters. The two types of parameters within SA are detailed below:

i. Mandatory parameters
    - Authentication algorithm, mode and transform that are use with IPSec AH
    - Keys that are used with the authentication algorithm
    - Encryption algorithm, mode and transform that are use with IPSec ESP
    - Keys that are used with the encryption algorithm
    - Size of cryptographic synchronisation or initialisation of vector field for the encryption algorithm.
ii. None mandatory parameters
    - Authentication algorithm, mode and transform that are use with IPSec ESP
    - Authentication keys use in the authentication algorithm (part of the ESP transform)
    - Key life time or the time that it takes for the key exchange to occur
    - Source address of the SA, which can be a wild-card address
    - Sensitivity level of the protected data (secret or unclassified data)

The IPSec uses SA to specify the protocols to be used between these nodes. Before authenticated or encrypted IP datagrams are transmitted, both the sender and receiver must agree on the encryption algorithm, authentication algorithm, key or keys to use and their duration. The SA is one-way relationship; two SAs are required to secure communication between sender and receiver. For example, if hosts A and B needs to establish a secure communication. The host A will have two SAs IP packets: SAout for processing outbound and SAin for inbound with same configuration. The SAout of host A will share the same parameters with SAin of host B and SAin host A with SAout of host B. During IPSec implementation the SA database is created for maintaining the SAs that would use in securing IP packets. The IPSec architecture also contained the

Security Policy Database (SPD). The SDP works in conjunction with Security Association Database (SAD) to process packets and defines the security communication characteristics between two entities. The SAs can use either ESP or AH for security services. In cases when both ESP and AH services are to be applied to the same IP traffic stream, then two different SAs should be created (Egeland, 05). The SAs of a node are stored in the SADB, and a randomly chosen number called the security parameter index (SPI) and the destination IP address uniquely identifies each SAs. When a system sends a packet that requires IPSec protection, it looks up the SA in its database and applies the specified processing and security protocol, inserting the SPI from the SAs into the IPSec header. When the IPSec peer receives the packet, it looks up for the SAs in its database by inspecting the destination address, SPI and then processes the packet as required. Each SA entry in the SAD stores the following information:

i. List of negotiated values:
    • Selected IPSec operational mode (tunnel or transport)
    • List of selected AH or ESP services
    • Types of encryption and hashing algorithms
    • Value of specific parameters for security algorithms like the IV for encryption algorithms or the size of variable fields
ii. Keys for authentication and encryption
iii. Counter value for message sequence integrity.

The authentication and encryption algorithms used in ESP and AH require keys to work. As mentioned earlier, the SA contains all the necessary parameters for the IPSec operations and relies on the key exchange between communicating parties to provide this keys. The simplest way to distribute key is manual key exchange, where the keys are manually distributed to the communicating hosts. This method is the easiest, safest and still the most widely used. Although it works quite well for small environments however, it is not scalable.

9.   IKE: HYBRID PROTOCOL

The IKE is a hybrid protocol use for establishing a share security policy and authentication of keys for services that require keys and negotiate session key. The IKE initiates the following two candidates key:

- The Photuris used Diffie-Hellman key exchange (with signature). The Diffie-Hellman is based on "public-key" or "asymmetric" cryptographic keys.
- The Simple Key Management Protocol (SKIP) used long term Diffie-Hellman key exchange (i.e., ga mod p is publicly known)

If there were miss-configuration in shared security policy the candidate keys would not be able to select session key. The IKE is also defined as a hybrid of the ISAKMP framework, Oakley and SKEME protocols. The latter protocols are briefly describe below:

- Internet Security Association and Key Management Protocol (ISAKMP) provides a framework for authentication and key exchange, (not a protocol, suppose support different key exchange)
- OAKLEY describe a series of key exchanges and services (e.g. perfect forward secrecy, identity protection, and authentication)
- Secure Key Exchange MEchanism (SKEME) describes a versatile key exchange technique, which provides anonymity, repudiability, and quick key refreshment.

The IPSec provides the packet-level processing, while the Internet Key Management Protocol (IKMP) negotiates security associations. The IKE is an automated key exchange mechanism that is used to create SAs. The IKE creates an authenticated, secure tunnel between two entities and then negotiates the security association for the IPSec. The SA does not establish the keys itself, it uses generic framework, which allows the use of several key exchange protocols. The Internet Security Association and Key Management Protocol (ISAKMP) provides the standardised layout for negotiating SAs, the generation of cryptographic keys and the refreshing of the cryptographic keys [see RFC-2408 documentation for further details]. The IKE implements the OAKLEY, and SKEME key exchanges inside ISAKMP framework. The OAKLEY protocol supports perfect forward secrecy (PFS), compatibility with the ISAKMP protocol for managing security associations, user-defined abstract group structures with the Diffie-Hellman algorithm, key updates, and incorporation of keys distributed via out-of-band mechanisms [see RFC 2412 documentation for further details]. However, because OAKLEY is a generic key exchange protocol, and the keys that are generated might be used for encrypting data with a long privacy lifetime, 20 years or more. It is important that the algorithms underlying the protocol is able to ensure the security of the keys for that period of time, based on the best prediction capabilities available (Orman 1998). The OAKLEY is a key exchange protocol chosen by the IETF.

The ISAKMP defines the communication language for negotiation, payload format, the mechanics of implementing a key exchange and the negotiation of a security association. The ISAKMP does not define the key exchange algorithm but rather the message types in order to exchange keys. There are two SA negotiation phases within ISAKMP:

i.   *Phase 1 (Main Mode):* The Phase 1 is mutual authentication and establishes session keys (used in Phase 2) by key exchange, called IKE SA. This phase has two modes from which exchanges can occur: the 'main mode' and 'aggressive mode'. The authentication is pre-shared secret keys namely the public encryption and public signature.

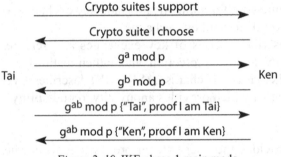

Figure 2–19. IKE phase 1 main mode

The established session key used Diffie-Hellman key exchange is protected by the keys. The Main Mode requires a six-message exchange between the initiator and responder, while the aggressive mode requires only a three-message exchange (see Figure 2–19 for diagrammatic illustration). The Main Mode is more secure and provides stronger authentication capabilities.

ii. *Phase 2 (Quick Mode):* The Phase 2 establishes multiple session keys (ESP SA, AH SA…) and uses quick mode as the method for message exchange. The quick mode is a three-message exchange that is used for the refreshing of key materials and for negotiation algorithms, data integrity hashes and features such as perfect forward secrecy (PFS).

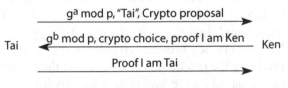

Figure 2–20. IKE phase 1—aggressive mode

The quick mode enabled any party to initiate a quick mode exchange to set up an ESP SA or AH SA in order to negotiates crypto parameters and what traffic will be sent on the SA. The Phase 2 can optionally do a Diffie-Hellman exchange, if perfect forward secrecy is required (see Figure 2–20 for diagrammatic illustration).

The Phase 1 establishes a protection suite with a master key from which all subsequent keys will be derived. Phase 1 also uses public key cryptography for the authentication of both parties that are involved in the negotiation and generation of the ISAKMP SA and the keys used to protect ISAKMP messages in Phase 2. The Phase 2 is used to establish the IPSec SA and generates the refresh keys (Spaulding, 02). The role of the networks is becoming greater and greater for nearly every aspect of our lives. But the Internet has also given intruders the opportunity to carry out diverse levels of attacks threatening the privacy of users and integrity of important data. Furthermore, the loss of security is always a major concern and subject to many threats such as loss of privacy, loss of data integrity, identity spoofing, and denial-of-service. The standard Internet protocol is completely unprotected, allowing hosts to inspect or modify data in transit. *The evolution of security will not come through technology, but through awareness* (Day, 03). The IPSec has been designed to prevent four different threats:

i. *Loss of data privacy:* Without end-to-end encryption, unauthorised parties can read messages sent across the network. For example intruders install packet sniffer to collect account names and passwords.
   A sniffer is a software program and/or device that monitors data travelling over a network. Sniffers can be used both for legitimate network management functions and for stealing information off a network. Sniffing is one of the most popular forms of attacks used by hackers. Sniffer as a product was originally created by Network General, which was acquired by Network Associates. Recently, Network Associates has decided to spin off the Sniffer product unit. The Sniffer unit has become a private company and has re-named itself as Network General.
   The trial version of password sniffer has been adopted for the laboratory experiment based on the reviews from 15 hackers websites (digital-hackers.com, ehap.org, elitechathacker.homestead.com, sascha-jung.de, hackerwar2002.cjb.net, thenewbiesarea.f2s.com, attrition.org, 2600.com, onething.com, attrition.org, mgmua.com, hacked.net, paybackproductions.com, turkeynews.net). The password sniffer has the following features:

• Displays the passwords as soon as it appears on network and supports various protocols.

- Fully supports application protocols of FTP, SMTP, POP3, and TEL-NET. That means user names and passwords used to send and receive e-mails, to log on a website, or to log on a server, can be fully captured and saved.
- Highlights syntax for application data in the format of HTML, HTTP and XML.
- Supports HTTP protocol, including proxy password, basic HTTP authenticate authorisation and most passwords submitted through HTML, no matter they are encoded by MIME or base64.
- Verifies whether the captured passwords are valid.
- It can tell whether the passwords captured are right. The replies from the server for the log-in are displayed, and it always keeps trying to get valid user name and password pairs.

Although there are over 100 sniffers available in the market today, the following are the most popular sniffers: ACE Password Sniffer, ICQ Sniffer, AIM Sniffer, EtherBoss MSN Monitor, Packet Sniffer, HTTP Sniffer, Password Sniffer, MSN Sniffer, RFC Viewer. The price of a sniffer, ranging from fifty pounds to tens of thousands of pounds, depends on who is the vendor. The trial versions of sniffer packets are available online for free download.

ii. *Loss of data Integrity:* Even if the data is not confidential we still do not want anyone to tamper with the data. We must make sure that data is not changed along the way.
iii. *Identity spoofing:* Many security systems rely on IP address to uniquely identify users. There are many tools that can fool this. Intruders may be able to impersonate your identity and have access to your data confidentiality.
iv. *Denial of Service:* When providing a service you always want yourself to be available. Intruders might send packets or overflow data to crash the system (see Chapter 4 for further discussion).

As long as we are on the Internet, we are vulnerable to all of the above issues. When security is addressed as a global network problem, the major issue is the management of security services. To achieve security in the Internet environment it is considered difficult because its involves understanding when and how the participating users, computers, services, and networks can trust one another, it also involves the understanding of the technical details of network hardware and protocols. A single computer can compromise the security of an entire network because every computer on the network is interconnected. Another factor to consider is that as the Internet compromises the wide array of political and organisational boundaries, participating individuals and organisations may not be agreeable on the level of trust required or policies for handling sensitive data. Security problems can arise because the Internet connects many organisations that do not have mutual trust. There are many techniques that help to ensures that information remains secured when been transmitted across the Internet. The client and server can use encryption to guarantee the identities; the clients need such authentication capabilities to determine whether a client has authorisation to assess the network or services.

10. POLICY

The IPSec is a layer-3 security protocol; it must be implemented in the kernel space. There are two auxiliary databases that IPSec consults with: SPD and SAD. The policy determines the security services allotted to an IP packet. All the IPSec implementations store policies in a database called SPD as mentioned earlier. The security policy is consisted of both inbound and outbound packet processing. A separate SPD can be maintained for inbound and outbound packets, in order to provide different security services to inbound and outbound packets. However, in practice a symmetric SPD is used. For example in the case of outbound, the SA uses the SAD pointer, provided that the SA is already established. The SA will be order to process the outbound packet as specified in the policy. At the receiving end, the inbound traffic is first processed with the relevant SA and the SPD is indexed to validate the policy on the packet. Furthermore, Cheswick and Bellovin (1994), and Cheng et al. (1998) explained the basic concept of how rules are applied within a policy, using a case of two sites or systems A and B that are connected to the Internet through two systems X and Y, respectively, where A and X, and B and Y may or may not be the same. As a first step toward having secure communication, A and B negotiate a (hypothetical) set of rules as the policy for communication between them:

Policy:
Rule 1—Packets of type 1 must go through a secure passage between X and Y, and the meta-characteristics of this passage are in set 1.
Rule 2—Packets of type 2 must go through a secure passage between X and Y, and the meta-characteristics of this passage are in set 2.

In the above policy, the type of packet is defined by the source and destination addresses of the packet. Another piece of information is needed, namely, the keys to be used with the cryptographic algorithms in sets 1 and 2 in order to enforce the policy. The references to sets 1 and 2 must be translated into references that will be use by SAs. To add, delete, and modify security policies' policy management is required (see Chapter 5 for further discussion). The SPD is stored in the Kernel and the IPSec implementation must define an interface that will be use to manipulate the SPD. These policies are not standard but the IPSec protocol standard defines the various capabilities of the policies. The IETF does not mandate any particular representation of policies and neither dictated specific implementation. On a serious note, all standard bodies refrain from dictating how policy should be implemented because different implementations require different security policies.

11.   SUMMARY OF CHAPTER TWO

The IPSec provides the following security functions in the IP layer: authentication, data integrity, replay detection, data confidentiality, access control using security protocols that cover various services and joint management protocols for security association and key exchange. Despite all these security functions, the IPSec has limitations and vulnerable to several kinds of attacks. The IPSec follows the end-to-end security model (i.e. information inside the IP packets are only available to end hosts). This approach does not allow for intelligence to be built into the networks, which might require access to encrypted information inside an IP protected packets. The intelligent system can be firewalls, NAT devices or sophisticated network monitoring tools. All of these require access to upper layer protocol information usually TCP in order to improve performance, reliability and reduce network management of overheads. It was noted that TCP/IP does not however, provided authentication and privacy functions, and virtual anyone with the right tools will be able to spoof the IP addresses, and intercept any data on the Internet. One of the advantages of TCP/IP is that it is not restricted to one part only —during message transmission, TCP/IP will choose from the least used path from the list of active service. If for any reason, one of the routers is either non-operation or over loaded with request, the TCP/IP will then find an alternative route to the destination. However, the IPSec can render the systems useless and degrades overall network functionality. In most cases, the solutions implemented only covers a part of the possible options, therefore the future of the IPSec will depend on synchronising existing policies with user's biometric profile. The next chapter presents an overview of IPv4 and v6.

Table 2–3. Companies Supporting IPSec software and hardware

Company	Features
ADTRAN	IPSec gateway, VPNC basic interoperability logo, IPSec client for Windows, IKE aggressive mode, IKE X.509 certificates, TripleDES encryption
Backbone Security. com	IPSec gateway, IPSec client for Windows, IPPCP compression, TripleDES encryption
Broadcom	IPSec gateway, IKE aggressive mode, TripleDES encryption, VPN toolkit
Caymas	IPSec gateway, VPNC basic interoperability logo, IPSec client for Windows, TripleDES encryption, Failover
Check Point Software	IPSec gateway, VPNC basic interoperability logo, VPNC AES interoperability logo, IPSec client for Windows, IPSec client for Macintosh, L2TP with IPSec, IKE aggressive mode, IKE X.509 certificates, IPPCP compression, TripleDES encryption, Certificate authority, Clustering, Failover
Cisco Systems	IPSec gateway, VPNC basic interoperability logo, VPNC AES interoperability logo, IPSec client for Windows, IPSec client for Macintosh, L2TP with IPSec, IKE aggressive mode, IKE X.509 certificates, IPPCP compression, TripleDES encryption, IPSec+Legacy, Clustering
Cryptek	IPSec gateway, IPSec client for Windows, TripleDES encryption, VPN toolkit
CyberGuard	IPSec gateway, VPNC basic interoperability logo, VPNC AES interoperability logo, L2TP with IPSec, IKE aggressive mode, IKE X.509 certificates, IPPCP compression, TripleDES encryption, VPN toolkit, Quality of service (QoS)
DigiSAFE	IPSec gateway, IPSec client for Windows, IKE aggressive mode, IKE X.509 certificates, TripleDES encryption, Certificate authority, Clustering, Failover
D-Link	IPSec gateway, IPSec client for Windows, IKE aggressive mode, TripleDES encryption, Quality of service (QoS), Fail over
Encore Networks	IPSec gateway, VPNC basic interoperability logo, VPNC AES interoperability logo, IKE aggressive mode, TripleDES encryption, IP VPN in layer 2, IP VPN in layer 3 , Frame Relay or ATM, Quality of service (QoS), IPSec+Legacy
eSoft	IPSec gateway, VPNC basic interoperability logo, VPNC AES interoperability logo, IPSec client for Windows, IKE aggressive mode, TripleDES encryption, Failover
F5	IPSec gateway, IKE X.509 certificates, TripleDES encryption, VPN toolkit, Certificate authority
Inkra	IPSec gateway, IPSec client for Windows, L2TP with IPSec, IKE aggressive mode, IKE X.509 certificates, TripleDES encryption, Quality of service (QoS), Failover
Internet Security Systems	IPSec gateway, VPNC basic interoperability logo, VPNC AES interoperability logo, L2TP with IPSec, IKE aggressive mode, IKE X.509 certificates, TripleDES encryption, Failover

Company	Features
Intoto	IPSec gateway, VPNC basic interoperability logo, VPNC AES interoperability logo, L2TP with IPSec, IKE aggressive mode, IKE X.509 certificates, TripleDES encryption, VPN toolkit, Quality of service (QoS), Clustering, Failover
Ixia	IPSec gateway, IKE aggressive mode, IKE X.509 certificates, TripleDES encryption, Certificate authority, IP VPN in layer 2, IP VPN in layer 3 , Quality of service (QoS), VPN test equipment
Jungo Software Technologies	IPSec gateway, VPNC basic interoperability logo, VPNC AES interoperability logo, L2TP with IPSec, IKE aggressive mode, IKE X.509 certificates, IPPCP compression, TripleDES encryption, VPN toolkit, Quality of service (QoS)
Juniper Networks	IPSec gateway, VPNC basic interoperability logo, VPNC AES interoperability logo, IPSec client for Windows, L2TP with IPSec, IKE aggressive mode, IKE X.509 certificates, TripleDES encryption, Quality of service (QoS), IPSec+Legacy, Clustering, Failover
Microsoft	IPSec gateway, VPNC basic interoperability logo, IPSec client for Windows, L2TP with IPSec, IKE X.509 certificates, TripleDES encryption, VPN toolkit, Certificate authority
NETGEAR	IPSec gateway, VPNC basic interoperability logo, VPNC AES interoperability logo, IPSec client for Windows, IKE aggressive mode, IKE X.509 certificates, TripleDES encryption
NetKlass	IPSec gateway, VPNC basic interoperability logo, IKE aggressive mode, TripleDES encryption, VPN toolkit
Nokia	IPSec gateway, IPSec client for Windows, IPSec client for Macintosh, L2TP with IPSec, IKE aggressive mode, IKE X.509 certificates, TripleDES encryption, Certificate authority, IP VPN in layer 3 , Quality of service (QoS), IPSec+Legacy, Clustering, Failover
Nortel	IPSec gateway, VPNC basic interoperability logo, VPNC AES interoperability logo, IPSec client for Windows, IPSec client for Macintosh, L2TP with IPSec, IKE aggressive mode, IKE X.509 certificates, TripleDES encryption, IPSec+Legacy, Clustering, Failover
Novell	IPSec gateway, IPSec client for Windows, IKE aggressive mode, IKE X.509 certificates, TripleDES encryption, IPSec+Legacy
Qno Technology	IPSec gateway, VPNC basic interoperability logo, IKE aggressive mode, TripleDES encryption, VPN toolkit
SafeNet	IPSec gateway, VPNC basic interoperability logo, VPNC AES interoperability logo, IPSec client for Windows, L2TP with IPSec, IKE aggressive mode, IKE X.509 certificates, IPPCP compression, TripleDES encryption, VPN toolkit, Certificate authority, Frame Relay or ATM, Failover
SonicWALL	IPSec gateway, VPNC basic interoperability logo, VPNC AES interoperability logo, IPSec client for Windows, L2TP with IPSec, IKE aggressive mode, IKE X.509 certificates, TripleDES encryption, Quality of service (QoS)

Company	Features
Stonesoft	IPSec gateway, VPNC basic interoperability logo, VPNC AES interoperability logo, IPSec client for Windows, IKE aggressive mode, IKE X.509 certificates, IPPCP compression, TripleDES encryption, Certificate authority, Clustering, Failover
Wind River	IPSec gateway, VPNC basic interoperability logo, VPNC AES interoperability logo, TripleDES encryption, VPN toolkit

Adopted from Virtual Private Network Consortium (VPNC)

REFERENCES

Cheng, P.C., Garay J.A., Herzberg, A., 1998, A security architecture for the Internet Protocol, IBM Systems Journal, Volume 37, Number 1, http://www.research.ibm.com/journal/sj/371/cheng.html (September 15, 2006).

Cheswick, W. R., and Bellovin, S. M., 1994, Firewalls and Internet Security, Repelling the Wily Hacker, Addison-Wesley Publishing Co., Reading, MA

Day, K., 2003, Inside the Security Mind: Making the tough decisions, Prentice Hall, PTR, USA

Dierks, T., and Allen, C., 1997, The TLS Protocol Version 1.0, [see draft-ietf-tls-protocol-02.txt documentation for further details] (December 5, 2006).

Dobbertin H., 1996, The Status of MD5 after Recent Attack, RSA Labs' Crypto Bytes, Vol. 2 No 2.

Egeland, G., 2005, Overview and Introduction to IPSec, Euroscom white paper.

Freier, A. O., Karlton, P., and Kocher, P. C., 1996, The SSL Protocol Version 3.0, , [see draft-ietf-tls-ssl-version3-00.txt documentation for further details] (January 20, 2006)

Goncalves, M., 1999, Checkpoint Firewall-1: An Administration Guide, McGraw-Hill.

Jayawickrama, W., 2003, Demystifying IPSec Protocol, Implementations and Limitations; www.bridgepoint.com.au/Documents/IPSecpaper.pdf, (January 15, 2007).

Kaeo, M., 1999, Designing Network Security, 1st Edition, Cisco Press.

Kent, S., and Atkinson, R., (1998), IP Encapsulation security payload (ESP), RFC 2406, http://www.cis.ohio-state.edu/cg-bin/rfc2402.html (December 7, 2006)

Krawczyk H, Bellare M, Canetti R., 1997, HMAC: Keyed-Hashing for Message Authentication, [see RFC 2104 documentation for further details] (January 13, 2007)

Madson C., and Glenn R., 1998, The Use of HMAC-SHA-1-96 within ESP and AH, [see RFC 2404 documentation for further details] (December 22, 2006)

Metz, C., and Phan, B., 2001, PF Key Management API Version 2, [see RFC 2367 documentation for further details] (January 17, 2006)

Orman, H., 1998, The OAKLEY Key Determination Protocol, [see RFC2412, documentation for further details] (January 3, 2007)

Pepelnjak, I., and Guichard, J., 2001, MPLS and VPN Architectures, Vol 1, Cisco Press.

Perlman, R., 2000, Interconnections: Bridges, Routers, Switches, and Internetworking Protocols, 2nd Edition, Addison-Wesley.

Rivest, R., 1992, The MD5 Message-Digest Algorithm, [see RFC 1321 documentation for further details], RSA Data Security, Inc. (January 14, 2007)

Roland, J.F., and Newcomb, M.J., 2003, CSVPN Certificate Guide, Cisco Press.

Spaulding, M., 2002, Using Public Key Infrastructure with Interoperable IPSec/IKE Virtual Private Networks, Business Brieging: Global info security.

Stevens, W.R., 1998, TCP/IP Illustrated: the protocols, Addison Wesley Longman, Inc.

Stevens, W.R., 2000, The Protocol: TCP/IP Illustrated, Vol 1, Addison Wesley.
Taylor L., 2002, Understanding IPSec, Intranet Journal.
Virtual Private Network Consortium (VPNC), Companies supporting IPSec software and hardware, http://www.vpnc.org/vpnc-IPSec-features-chart.html (January 19, 2007).

Chapter 3

INTERNET PROTOCOL VERSIONS 4 (IPV4) AND 6 (IPV6)

1. INTRODUCTION

The IP was designed in the early 1970s, when the Defence Advanced Research Projects Agency (DARPA) became interested in establishing a packet-switched network that would facilitate communication between different computer systems.

'Our watchword is Security...'

—William Pitt (1708–1778)

The IP version 4 (IPv4) was standardised in 1981 and is used in most IP-based networks including the Internet. Although the Dynamic Host Configuration Protocol (DHCP) and other features have been added to IPv4, and supported by most routers. The rise in popularity of the Internet and increasing number of Internet ready-devices as led to some of the limitations of IPv4. There are several opinions concerning the need for a new IPSec. The reasons why the IPv6 or IPng as been said to be appropriate for the next generation of the IPSec are as follows:

- it solves the Internet scaling problem
- it provides a flexible transition mechanism for the current Internet

The IPv6 is a new version of the IPSec and retains many of the features that contributed to the success of IPv4. This chapter presents an overview of IPv4 and v6.

2.   IPV4 STANDARD

The IP connects different kinds of hardware platforms using a unique addressing scheme. The current IPv4 (commonly known as TCP/IP) is defined in RFC 791 documentation. It provides the basic communication mechanism for the TCP/IP suite and the Internet. The evolution of IPv4 are as follows:

- 1974: IPv4 proposed
- 1981: IPv4 standardised
- 1992: The next generation IP became apparent, and proposals were requested. The main issue was a perceived shortage of address space, predicted the exhaustion of IPv4 addresses by 2005-2011, and routing table growth was also a concern.
- 1993: IPng Proposals solicitation [see RFC1550 documentation for further details]

The Internet protocol implements three basic functions: addressing, routing and fragmentation. The data is sent in blocks of characters called datagrams, or packets. The Internet modules use the addresses carried in the Internet header to transmit Internet datagrams toward their destinations. The selection of a path for transmission is called routing, and the node that performs this operation is called a router [see RFC-760 documentation for further details].

2.1.   Header

The Internet modules uses the fields in the Internet header to fragment and reassemble Internet datagrams when necessary for transmission through 'small packet networks'. This header identifies its sender and intended destination on each computer. A block of characters of data called the packet contents follows the header. After the packets reach their destination, they are often reassembled into a continuous stream of data; this fragmentation and re-assembly process is usually invisible to the user. As there are many different routes from one system to another, each packet may take a slightly different path from source to destination, because the Internet switches packets (packet switching network), instead of circuits. The Internet module resides in each host that engaged in the Internet communication and interconnects with different networks. These modules share common rules for interpreting address fields, fragmenting and assembling Internet datagrams. The Table 3–1 presents the fields that are contained within the IPv4. The IP treats each Internet datagram as an independent entity unrelated to any other Internet datagram. There are no connections or logical circuits (virtual or otherwise). The errors detected may be reported via the Internet Control Message Protocol (ICMP), which is implemented in the

Prec			D	T	R	Reserved	
0	1	2	3	4	5	6	7

0–2 Precedence
3 Normal delay low delay
4 Normal throughput/High throughput
5 Normal reliability/High reliability
6–7 Reserved

Figure 3–1. Content of precedence bit

Internet protocol module. The protocol between IP entities is best described with reference to the IP datagram format.

2.2 Addressing

The source and destination address fields in the IP header contain 32 bits each in the Internet address, which consisted of both network and host identifiers. The address is coded to allow a variable allocation of bits to specify network and host. The IPv4 current standard protocol for the Internet is a 32-bit address, which means that there are 4,294,967,296(2^{32}- over 4 billion) addresses available in theory (see Figures 3–1 to 3–3 for diagrammatic illustration). Each packet contains 64 bits of addressing information with 32 bits being reserved for the source address and 32 bits reserved for the destination address. The 32-bit address space is frequently represented as dotted quad notation. For example, the 32-bit IP address can be represented as 0xC0a8012A but looks much familiar when shows as 192.168.1.42. In order for packets to be routed effectively, the 32 bit address spaces are further divided into subnets, which split the address space into network and host sections [see RFC-997 documentation for further details].

The popular subnets are Class A, B and C with the number of bits reserved for the network portion being 8, 16 and 24, respectively. The remaining bits make up the host portion of the IP address. The class specifies how many bits

Table 3–2. Precedence field

P bits	Function
111	Network Control
110	Internetwork Control
101	CRITIC/ECP
100	Flash Override
011	Flash
010	Immediate
001	Priority
000	Routine

Table 3–1. IPv4 Header format

Version (4 bits) is the current version of the Internet header	**Internet Header Length** (IHL) (8 bits) includes options and padding and exclude payload. The length of the Internet header is 32 bit words. Options and padding are used for routing, security and time stamping. The minimum value is five, for a minimum header length of 20 octets.	**Type of Service** (16 bits) indicates the quality of service desired by specifying how an upper-layer protocol would like a current datagram to be handled and assigns datagrams various levels of importance. This field is used for the assignment of reliability (R), precedence (Prec), delay (D) and throughput (T) parameters	**Total Length** (32 bits) specifies the length, in bytes, of the entire IP packet, including the data and header. The maximum length could be specified by this field is 65,535 bytes. Typically, hosts are prepared to accept datagrams up to 576 bytes (Table 3–2).
Identification (16 bits) is a sequence number that is intended to identify a datagram uniquely. This number should be unique for the datagram's source address, destination address, and user protocol in the Internet.		**Flags** (3 bits) Only two of the bits are currently defined. The low-order bit specifies whether the packet can be fragmented. The middle bit specifies whether the packet is the last fragment in a series of fragmented packets. The third or high-order bit is not used.	**Fragment offset** (13 bits): This field indicates where in the datagram this fragment belongs. The fragment offset is measured in units of 8 octets (64 bits). The first fragment has offset zero and the second fragment shows data position (see Table 3–3).
Time to Live (8 bits): This field indicates the maximum time the datagram is allowed to remain in the Internet system. If this field contains the value zero, then the datagram must be destroyed. Every router that processes a datagram must decrease the TTL by at least one, so the TTL is somewhat similar to a hop count.		**Protocol** (8 bits): This field indicates the next level protocol used in the data portion of the Internet datagram. The TCP and UDP are transport protocols. The TCP is more reliable, connection-oriented protocol, and the ICMP is an error checking protocol.	**Header checksum** (16 bits): An error-detecting code applied to the header only. Since some header fields change (TTL value), which means the packet is examined at every router hop.
Source Address (32 bits) and is coded to allow variable allocation of bits to specify the network and the end system attached to the specified network			
Destination address (32 bits) contains the destination address.			
Options + padding: The options may appear in datagrams, but it must be implemented in all IP modules (host and gateways). What is optional is the transmission of any particular datagram, not their implementation. In some environments the security option may be required in all datagrams. The option field is variable in length; there may be zero or more options. There are two cases for the format of an option: The padding (variable) ensured that the datagram header is a multiple of 32 bits in length. The variable contains upper-layer information			

R	DF	MF
0	1	2

R: Reserved, must be zero
DF: 0 = May Fragment   1 = Don't Fragment.
MF: 0 = Last Fragment   1 = More Fragments.

Figure 3–2. Packet fragment

from the prefix (Network ID) and the suffix (Host ID). The first four bits of an IP address determines the class of the network. When interacting with humans, software uses dotted decimal notation, to differentiate one class from another by looking at the first four bits of IP address. The range and address format of each classes are presented in Figure 3–3 and Table 3–3.

2.3   Routing

The laboratory experiment has established that each IP datagram forwards a packet from its source to its destination by means of routers. All hosts and routers on the Internet contain IP protocol software and use a routing table to determine where to send a packet. The destination IP address in the IP header contains the ultimate destination of the IP datagram, but it might go through several other IP addresses (routers) before reaching that destination. The routing table entries are created when TCP/IP initialises. The entries can be updated manually by a network administrator or automatically by employing a routing protocol such as Routing Information Protocol (RIP). The routing table entries provide information to each local host regarding how to communicate with remote networks and hosts (Garfinkel and Sparfford, 1996).

Table 3–3. IPv4 classes

Class	High Order Bits	Number of bits of the network ID	Netmask	Number of bits of the host ID	Addresses
A	0	7	255.0.0.0	24	0.0.0.0– 127.255.255.255
B	10	14	255.255.0.0	16	128.0.0.0– 191.255.255.255
C	110	21	255.255.255.0	8	192.0.0.0– 223.255.255.255
D	1110	Multicast addresses on 28 bits			224.0.0.0– 239.255.255.255
E	1111	Reserved addresses for future use on 28 bits			240.0.0.0– 255.255.255.255

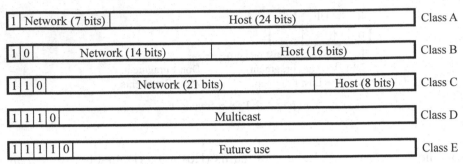

Figure 3–3. IPv4 Address formats

2.4   Fragmentation and Reassembly

The IPv4 reserves 16 bits for fragmentation and reassembly of information. If a router receives a packet that is too large for the underlying network, the IP will break the packet into manageable pieces before it is transmitted. When the pieces of the datagram arrive at their final destination, the IP assembles the pieces into the original packet. This process is called fragmentation. Three bits are provided as control flags. The remaining thirteen bits are used to sequentially label each fragment so that they may be reassembled in the correct order on the receiving end [see RFC-760 documentation for further details]. Any datagrams that cannot be reassembled successfully are simply discarded. The fragmentation often occurs in environments that have a mix of media (Ethernet and Token Ring). The fragmentation-offset field includes sequencing information, which the remote IP peer uses to reorder data fragments it receives from the network, and to detect missing packets. The identification field in the IP header of the receiving host can distinguish between fragments belonging to different datagrams and flag the header to indicate if data is fragmented.

3.   IPV4 LIMITATIONS AND POSSIBLE SOLUTION

The IPv4 has been in use for over 20 years and many of the related devices had already been connected to the Internet. But with the high demand of Internet usage, the IPv4 has encountered its dark side—limited IP address space, lack of security and quality of service issues, and various estimations have been made about exhaustion of the 32 bits space due to global Internet demand. The following are the major limitations currently facing IPv4:

3.1 Address Space and Network Address Translation (NAT)

According to IETF RFC 3194, there are 250 million usable addresses for hosts. However, the US Census Bureau estimating that the world's population will reach 9 billion people by the year 2050. But the current IPv4 addresses are only capable of around 4.3 billion network hosts (Lugani, 2002). Also the growth of new technologies such as PDAs, mobile phones, high-speed broadband access and integrated IP telephony services has driven the connection to the IP networks. The IP space is not allocated efficiently, the multiple large blocks are given to government agencies and large organisations. The Lucent technologies company in USA possesses 6,700,000 IP addresses and AOL (America online) posses 1,900,000. The allocated numbers are bigger than those allocated to china, the most populous country in the world, has the same number of official IP addresses as the Massachusetts Institute of Technology. The US holds approximately 75 percent of all IP addresses (Weiser, 2001).

The NAT inhibits host-to-host communications, which is one of the basic design principles of the Internet and the Classless Inter-domain Routing (CIDR). The NAT was developed and deployed to increase the number of network users on a network without the need for additional IPv4 addresses [see RFC-1518 documentation for further details]. Another solution is the use of Private addresses, which is defined in [see RFC1918 documentation for further details] 'the private enable network administrators to use these special addresses in their private networks without having to take permission from any authority. The Table 3—4 lists the range of these special addresses:

It worth noting that the private addresses are banned on the Internet to avoid ambiguity problems. In practice it is possible to use any kind of addresses (private or global) in private network as long as they do not leave the private network. If IP addresses are duplicated, it will have a serious consequences: It would be impossible to route IP datagrams to the right destination. To prevent the addresses flowing out of the private network, the IP headers of the outgoing packets from the private network should be changed as they pass onto the Internet and then changed back as responses are received and that is where NAT comes into play. However, the solutions described above regarding IP addresses are temporary, there are indeed many other serious limitations such as inability to scale and lower overall performance.

Table 3–4. Range of special addresses

Class Range	Private Address Range
A	10.0.0.0 – 10.255.255.255
B	172.16.0.0 – 172.31.255.255
C	192.168.0.0 – 192.168.255.255

3.2   IPv4 Security

The IPv4 lack security, not strong enough to provide reliable and efficient security mechanisms for authentication of connections or privacy of data transmitted over the Internet. The IPv4 header provides flags to indicate security, but the packet payload transmitted in clear text and can easily be intercepted and read using a network sniffer. Security of data on the Internet is an ongoing and increasing problem

3.3   Quality of Service (QoS)

Nowadays, multimedia applications need real-time and sensitive data transfer to the network but there is no structure that reflects IP address allocation, and huge routing tables are required to be maintained by routers. The QoS in IPv4 is using best effort delivery services, and for data to arrive at the destination as soon as possible. There is no guarantee that video or audio will have enough network bandwidth, although this is adequate for traditional applications such as Telnet and FTP. Therefore, an improved Quality of service needs to be implemented (Crouzard et al., 2003). Other issues which impacts the adaptation and effectiveness of IPv4 are discuss briefly below:

i.   The IPv4 have no auto configuration support. The nodes are not able to configure a public IP address by themselves. The only way to configure an IP address is by using a DHCP server or by manual configuration. However, a stateless Server mode will be a better solution and can save cost but does not guarantee 100 per cent security.

ii.   In the header format, the checksum decreases router performance. Since the Transport and Link layer already have their own checksum, so imposing another checksum at the IP Layer is redundant. The options and padding field is checked at every router hop and this uses up router processing time, which degrades router performance. These options are rarely used and not all hosts and routers support this option.

iii. Routing problems in the IPv4, the routing in IPv4 is a flat and hierarchical routing that had caused an explosion of backbone routing table. Header checksum in IP header is checked at every router hop and this take up router processing time. The fragmentation is also done by router, which causes degradation of routing performance.

iv.   Fragmentation problem, there will be no way of keeping track on how many fragments there is. If one of the fragments are lost or does not arrive on time all packets must be discarded. Fragmentation will take up router processing time, which will cause degradation in routing performance.

However, QoS is expressed as statistical statements based on transmission delay, jitter and bandwidth availability that the traffic experiences. Around the same time that NAT was being standardised as a solution for the IPv4 address space problem, work had begun on IPv6. The next section focuses on the IPv6 standard and stacks used in various operating platforms.

4   IPV6 STANDARD

The IPv6 standard was first documented in the RFC-1883. Previous to this document, the IPv6 was referred to as IP Next Generation IPng (Clauberg, 2001). The evolution of IPv6 are as follows:

* 1995: The first version of IPv6 was documented in RFC1883 as a proposed standard.
* 1996: The 6bone became operational and based on IPv6 over IPv4.
* 1998: The second version of IPv6 was documented in the RFC 2460 draft standard. A number of features were added beyond the bigger address space.
* 1999: The registries assigned to IPv6 prefixes and the IPv6 forum was formed.
* 2000: Major vendors bundle IPv6 in their mainstream product line.
* 2001: The RFC documentation containing the 6 to 4 was proposed.
* 2003: The RFC documentation containing the DHCPv6

The IPv6 features are detailed in RFC-1883 documentation and also define five broad categories of goals for the IPv6 design:

* Expanded Addressing Capabilities
* Header Format Simplification
* Improved Support for Extensions and Options
* Flow Labelling Capability
* Authentication and Privacy Capabilities

Most operating platforms and workstations support the IPv6. But there is little information concerning different distributions and implementations. The IPv6 addresses with prefix 3ffe::/16 known as 6bone address space. The prefix 2001::/16 is the productive address space and available through IPv6 enabled ISPs either via native links or tunnelling. The other prefix 2002::/16 is known as the 6to4 address space. The vendors and developers need to make their operating systems and network related applications IPv6 compliance. It is also part of the ongoing process that information regarding the Internet Exchange

Protocol (IXP) support for IPv6 should be readily available from the ISP. Bieringer (2005) gives an overview of the IPv6 status in Europe and vendors participation in the development process (see Tables 3–5 to 3–11).

Table 3–5. Support for IPv6 by IXPs

Country	IXP
Netherlands	AMX-IX, NDIX, XchangePoint, NL-SIX
Germany	BCIX, DE-CIX, INXS, NDIX, XchangePoint
UK	LINX, LIPEX, LoNAP, MaNAP, XchangePoint
Italy	MIX, NaMeX, TOPIX
France	PARIX, FNIX6
Spain	ESPANIX, mad-iX, CATNIX
Switzerland	CIXP, TIX
Others in Europe	…
Austria	VIX
Greece	AIX
Belgium	BNIX
Portugal	GIGAPIX
Ireland	INEX
Luxembourg	LIX
Russia	MSK-IX
Sweden	Netnod
Norway	NIX
Czech Republic	NIX.CZ

* All major IXPs in Europe are supporting IPv6.

Table 3–6. Support for IPv6 by ISPs

Country	IXP
	XS4ALL
Germany	Space.net, Versatel/Tesion, DFN-Beckbone (6WiN)
UK	British Telecommunication
Italy	Wind, Edisontel, Telecom Italia
France	PARIX, FNIX6
Spain	ESPANIX, mad-iX, CATNIX
Switzerland	CIXP, TIX

Table 3–7. Operating Systems IPv6 Status

Operating Systems	IPv6 Status
Microsoft	Windows 2000 (experimental) Windows XP (built-in) Windows 2003 (built-in)
Linux	Usable since 2.4 x Kernels
Mac OS X	Since version 10.2
FreeBSD	Since version 4.0
NetBSD	Since version 1.5
OpenBSD	Since version 2.7
BSD/OS	Since version 4.2
Sun	Since Solaris 8

* Basic IPv6 are already been implemented in most operating systems.

Table 3–8. IPv6 Status of Commercial Routers

Vendors	IPv6 Status
Cisco	Since May 2001 in IOS 12.2(2)T Since June 2003 in ISP Backbone IOS 12.2(2)S
Juniper	Since November 2001 in JunOS 5.1/5.2
Nokia IP	Since IPSO 3.6 (early 2002)
Hitachi	Since 1997

* Most commonly use routing protocols are already adopted the IPv6 for example, RIP (RFC 2080), BGP (RFC 2545) and OSPF (RFC2740). In addition to the latter non-hardware based routing applications are also IPv6 enabled e.g. MRTd, zebra, quagga, GateD NGC, GateD bird, uolsrd.

Table 3–9. IPv6 Status of Commercial Firewalls

Vendors	IPv6 Status
Nokia	IPSO since version 3.6 (packet filter)
Check Point	FW-1 since version R54 (NG AI) running on Sun Solaris, Nokia IPSO
Cisco (Routers)	IOS since version 12.2(2)T (packet filter)
Cisco (PIX)	Available but still not working properly
Fortinet	Since version 2.8
NetScreen	Since 2003

Table 3–10. Operating Systems IPv6 Status

Operating Systems	IPv6 Status
Linux	Working in current versions netfilter project supported by USAGI team
BSD	Working in current versions Ipfilter (FreeBSD, NetBSD, OpenBSD, Solaris) Pf (FreeBSD, NetBSD, OpenBSD) Ipfw (FreeBSD, Darwin, Mac OS X)

* The firewall is a requirement for IPv6 but the native end-to-end connectivity was a major problem. This problem has been inherited from the IPv4 NAT and PAT. Currently not all-

commercial firewall support IPv6. Some operating systems have built-in standard IPv6 fire-walling.

Table 3–11. Operating Systems IPv6 Status

Operating Systems	IPv6 Status
Linux	Working in progress
	Supported by USAGI team, based on BSD KAME project
BSD	Working in all version with KAME
Microsoft	Information

* The IPSec was defined as mandatory feature for IPv6 protocol stack, but unfortunately implementations in operating systems are not always fully available or complete.

4.1   IPv6 Addressing Capabilities

One of the most significant improvements of IPv6 is the size of its address space. Where the IPv4 used 32-bit addresses, the IPv6 uses 128-bit addresses. These additional ninety-six bits allow the IPv6 to address 3.40×10^{38} individual devices. It is important to note that IPv6 address being enlarged to 128-bit not only to provide bigger address space but also designed to be sub-divided into hierarchical routing domains that reflect the topology of the modern-day Internet. The use of 128 bits allows for multiple levels of hierarchy and flexibility in designing hierarchical addressing, which is currently lacking on the IPv4-based Internet. The IPv6 uses a standardised sub-netting scheme that splits the address into 64-bits for the network prefix and 64-bits for the host identifier. The IPv6 addresses are so large that a new notation needs to be used to represent them. The IPv6 uses hexadecimal numbers separated every four digits by colons. A sample of the IPv6 address could be expressed as A BC0:0123:0:0:0:4567:1040:A001 but when used the zero compression it was compress as ABC0:0123:4567:1040:A001 [see RFC-2373 documentation for further details].

4.2   Address type

The IPv6 addresses are identifiers for individual interfaces and for sets of interfaces that enabled addresses of all types to be assigned to the interfaces, not to the hosts or routers. A single interface may have multiple unique unicast addresses (Schnitzer, 2002; 3COM, 2004). In the IPv6, a node is any device that can implements the IPv6, which includes hosts and routers. The three types of addresses are unicast, anycast, and multicast:

4.2.1   Unicast address

Unicast is an identifier for a single interface. Unicast is a name for one-to-one address that identifies exactly one interface (see Figure 3–4 for diagrammatic illustration).

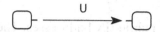

Figure 3–4. Underline principle of unicast

A packet sent to a unicast address will normally be delivered to that interface. The Aggregatable Global Unicast Addresses (AGUA) is specified in IPv6 addressing architecture. The addresses are characterised by FP (Format Prefix) = 001 (see Figure 3–5 diagrammatic for illustration).

3 bits	13 bits	8 bits	24 bits	16 bits	64 bits
FP	TLA	RES	NLA	SLA ID	Interface ID
Public topology				Site topology	Identifier

FP = Format Prefix (001)
TLA= Top Level Aggregation
NLA= Next-Level Aggregation
SLA= Site-Level Aggregation
RES= Reserved

Figure 3–5. Structure of AGUA

Range of AGUA structures:
- Topology is a collection of larger and smaller ISPs that provide access to the IPv6 Internet
- Site topology is a collection of subnets within an organization's site and interface
- The identifier identifies a specific interface on a subnet within an organization's site.

The AGUA is hierarchical structure that improves backbone routing; and sort networks traffic towards the Internet backbone. Without an address hierarchy, backbone routers have to store route table information on the reachability of every network in the world:

- TLA ID is assigned to an organisation providing public transit topology
- RES (8 bits) reserved for future use, either by TLA or NLA
- NLA ID (24 bits) is used by organisations assigned a TLA ID to create an addressing hierarchy and to identify sites (the ISP users)

- SLA ID (16 bits) identifies subnets within its site. With 16 bits of sub-netting flexibility, an aggregatable global unicast prefix assigned to an organization is equivalent to that organization being allocated an IPv4 Class A network
- Interface ID: Indicates the interface on a specific subnet. The size of this field is 64 bits.

The AGUA is equivalent to public IPv4 addresses. They are globally routable and reachable on IPv6 network. It is designed to be aggregated to produce an efficient routing infrastructure. Unlike the current IPv4-based Internet, which is a mixture of both flat and hierarchical routing, the IPv6-based Internet has been designed from its foundation to support efficient, hierarchical addressing and routing:

i. *Unspecified Address* (0:0:0:0:0:0:0:0 or::) is only used to indicate the absence of an address. It is equivalent to the IPv4 unspecified address of 0.0.0.0. The unspecified address is typically used as a source address for packets attempting to verify the uniqueness of a tentative address but never assigned to an interface or used as a destination address.

ii. *Loop back Address* (0:0:0:0:0:0:0:1 or ::1) is used to identify a loop back interface, enabling node to send packets to itself. It is equivalent to the IPv4 loop back address of 127.0.0.1. The packets addressed to the loop back address must never be sent on a link or forwarded by an IPv6 router.

iii. *Link Local Addresses* (LLA) (FP = 1111111010) is for use on a single link. The format is illustrated in Figure 3–6.

10 bits	54 bits	64 bits
1111111010	0	Node ID

Figure 3–6. Structure of Link Local Addresses

The LLA are used by nodes for communicating with neighbouring nodes on the same link. For example, on a single link IPv6 network with no router, link-local addresses are used to communicate between hosts on the link. A LLA is always automatically configured. An IPv6 router never forwards link-local traffic beyond the link [see RFC-2373 document for further details].

iv. *Site Local Addresses* (SLA) are used within an isolated intranet, independence of the changes to TLA/NLA. For example, private intranets that do not have a direct, routed connection to the IPv6 Internet can use site-local addresses without the need of aggregatable global unicast addresses (see Figure 3–7 for diagrammatic illustration).

10 bits	38 bits	16 bits	64 bits
1111111011	0	Subnet ID	Interface ID

Figure 3–7. Structure of Site Local Addresses

The site-local addresses are not reachable from other sites, and routers must not forward site-local traffic outside the site. Unlike link-local addresses, site-local addresses are not automatically configured and must be assigned either through stateless or state-full address configuration processes (Slvonen, 2003).

4.2.2   Anycast

The anycast is a one-to-nearest address that identifies a group of interfaces. A packet sent to an anycast address is delivered to one of the interfaces identified by that address (the nearest interface) and the routing protocols measure the distance (see Figure 3–8 for diagrammatic illustration).

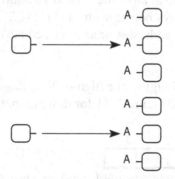

Figure 3–8. Underline principle of Anycast

The difference between multicast and anycast is in the transmission process. Instead of being delivered to all members of the group, packet sent to anycast address is normally delivered to only one interface, which is always the nearest member in the group.

4.2.3   Multicast

The Multicast is one-to-many address that identifies a group of interfaces. A packet sent to a multicast address will normally be delivered to all the members of the group. A packet sent to a multicast address is delivered to all interfaces identified by that address. The underline principle of Multicast is illustrated in Figure 3–9.

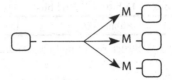

Figure 3–9. Underline Principle of Multicast

The IPv6 multicast address is an identifier for a group of nodes. The structure of Multicast addresses is illustrated in Figure 3–10.

8 bits	4 bits	4 bits	112 bits
11111111	Flags	Scope	Group ID

Figure 3–10. Structure of Multicast Addresses

In the IPv6, multicast traffic operates in the same way as it does in the IPv4. The IPv6 nodes listen for multicast traffic on an arbitrary IPv6 multicast address and the multiple multicast addresses at the same time. The nodes can join or leave a multicast group at any time. The IPv6 address is easy to classify as multicast because it always begins with "11111111". The multicast addresses cannot be used as source addresses or as intermediate destinations in a routing header:

- The Flags are set to 4 digits. The high-order 3 flags are reserved, and must be initialised to 0 (see Figure 3–11 for diagrammatic illustration).

0	1	2	3
0	0	0	T

T =0: Permanently assigned, well-known multicast
address, assigned by the global Internet numbering
authority
T =1: indicates a non-permanently-assigned, transient
multicast address

Figure 3–11. Structure of High–Order 3

- The scope indicates the operations of the IPv6 which the multicast traffic is intended to work with. The size of this field is 4 bits. In addition to information provided by multicast routing protocols, routers use the multicast scope to determine whether multicast traffic can be forwarded [see RFC-2373 documentation for further details]. The list of values for the scope filed is shown in Table 3–12.

Table 3–12. Values of scope filed

Value	Scope
0	Reserved
1	Node-local scope
2	Link-local scope
5	Site-local scope
8	Organization-local scope
E	Global scope
F	Reserved

- Group ID identifies the multicast group, either permanent or transient, within the given scope.

To allow host auto-configuration in the IPv4, there has to be a DHCP server. The host will send request to DHCP Server and DHCP will reply and assigned IP address to the host (see Figure 3–12). The IPv6 supports both stateful and stateless address configurations. IPv6 will work with or without a DHCP server (Jarvinen, 2002).

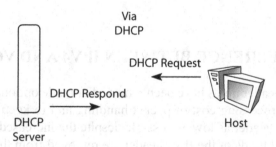

Figure 3–12. Stateful Server Mode

The IP configuration in IPv6 is carried out using two auto-configuration methods (Lucent, 2004):

- The IPv6 node creates a local IPv6 address for itself using 'stateless' address auto-configuration. The stateless auto-configuration makes it possible for the nodes to configure their own globally routable addresses in cooperation with a local IPv6 router. However, stateless auto-configuration cannot determine the DNS servers.
- Stateful mode method obtains interface address configurations and parameter information from a DHCPv6 server. The DHCPv6 allows more controlled configuration than stateless auto-configuration and offers same features as in the IPv4.

Another feature of the IPv6 addressing is auto-configuration capability. The IPv6 can be configured in three different ways as follow:

i. Manual configuration: This involves configuring the host with a static IPv6 address. This is similar to the IPv4 static IP method of configuration.
ii. Stateful auto-configuration method uses an IPv6 to create awareness of the DHCPPv6 server, in order to obtain the IPv6 address and any additional configuration held in the DHCPv6 server database (Koren, 05). This is similar to the IPv4 DHCP.
iii. Stateless auto-configuration method has no direct parallel in IPv4. With stateless auto-configuration IPv6 hosts can intelligently select their own IP address using their own Media Access Control (MAC) address and prefix information advertised by IPv6 aware routers on the local network segment. The stateless auto-configuration can work on segments without routers with the constraint that traffic will be isolated to the local segment [see RFC-2462 documentation for further details].

Moreover, the IPv6 have built-in support for mandatory security payload extension headers, but the differences between IPv4 and v6 cannot be ignored.

5.   DIFFERENCE BETWEEN IPV4 AND V6

Some IPv4 header fields have been removed or made optional to reduce the common case processing cost of packet handling and to keep the bandwidth cost of the IPv6 header as low as possible despite the increased size of the addresses. bIeveral fields of the IPv4 header are removed from the IPv6:

i. The Header Length in the basic IPv4 header is 20 bytes while the IPv6 header is 40 octets (see Figure 3–13 for diagrammatic illustration and Table 3–13). The IPv4 header length indicates the packet's total length, including the options field. The options field increases the length of the IPv4 header but in the IPv6 options field are not used, instead the IPv6 uses the Extension field. The Extension field is handled differently from how IPv4 handles the options field.
ii. Fragmentation field is handled differently in the IPv6. It is no longer done by intermediate routers but by the source node that originates the packet. Removing the fragmentation field, lower the cost of the CPU processing at the intermediate routers. The Path MTU discovery (PMTUD) mechanism is recommended for every IPv6 node to avoid fragmentation. If host tries to send larger packets they would be rejected by the network and this process

continues until the smallest MTU is found. The fragmentation and reassembly is a time-consuming operation; removing this functionality from the routers and placing it in the end systems, has considerably speeds up IP forwarding within the network. Besides, taking out fragmentation from IPv6 has saved the header from the segmentation control fields (identification, flags and fragmentation offset).

iii. Header Checksum are performs at the Internet layers using the transport layer (TCP and UDP) and data link (Ethernet) protocols. It reduced the cost of header processing for check and updating the checksum at each relay. The major risk in header checksum is that errors will not be detected by intermediate routers but only by the destined host.

iv. Options and Padding in the IPv4 header includes all options and each intermediate router must check for their existence and process them when present. This causes performance degradation in the forwarding of the IPv4 packets. In IPv6, these options are moved to extension headers, appended after the main header and not being processed at each intermediate. This increases the IPv6 header processing speed and improves forwarding process.

The RFC 2460 documentation defines the basic IPv6 header. This header contains fewer fields (8 fields) than IPv4 (12 fields). Thus, routers have less processing to do per header, which should speed up routing. The IPv6 protocol presents an upgrade of the IPv4 protocol (see Figure 3–13 for diagrammatic illustration), the Flow Label field and the extension headers with their variable length are new in IPv6.

The IPv6 extension headers are optional headers and several types of extension headers are defined in RFC 2460 documentation. The IPv6 packet includes zero, one, or multiple extension headers as shown in Figure 3–14. The only header that is required is referred to simply as IPv6 header. An IPv6 packet has the following general form:

40 octets		0 or more		
IPv6 header	Extension header	...	Extension header	Extension header

Figure 3–14. IPv6 Extension Header

The extension headers consists of the following:

- Hop-by-Hop Option header: defines special option that require hop-by-hop processing
- Routing header: provides extended routing, similar to IPv4 source routing
- Fragment header: contains fragmentation and reassembly information

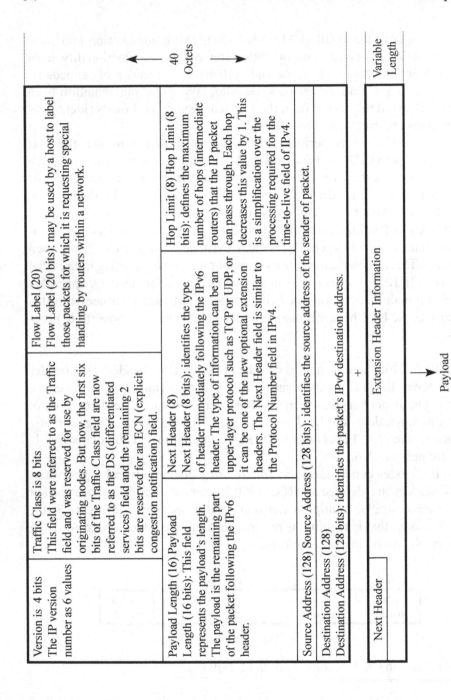

| Version is 4 bits The IP version number as 6 values | Traffic Class is 8 bits This field were referred to as the Traffic field and was reserved for use by originating nodes. But now, the first six bits of the Traffic Class field are now referred to as the DS (differentiated services) field and the remaining 2 bits are reserved for an ECN (explicit congestion notification) field. | Flow Label (20) Flow Label (20 bits): may be used by a host to label those packets for which it is requesting special handling by routers within a network. |
| Payload Length (16) Payload Length (16 bits): This field represents the payload's length. The payload is the remaining part of the packet following the IPv6 header. | Next Header (8) Next Header (8 bits): identifies the type of header immediately following the IPv6 header. The type of information can be an upper-layer protocol such as TCP or UDP, or it can be one of the new optional extension headers. The Next Header field is similar to the Protocol Number field in IPv4. | Hop Limit (8) Hop Limit (8 bits): defines the maximum number of hops (intermediate routers) that the IP packet can pass through. Each hop decreases this value by 1. This is a simplification over the processing required for the time-to-live field of IPv4. |

Source Address (128) Source Address (128 bits): identifies the source address of the sender of packet.

Destination Address (128)
Destination Address (128 bits): identifies the packet's IPv6 destination address.

40 Octets

Next Header | Extension Header Information | Variable Length

+

Payload

Figure 3–13. IPv6 Header format

- Authentication header: provides packet integrity and authentication
- Encapsulating Security Payload header: provides privacy (confidentiality)
- Destination Options header: contains optional information to be examined by the destination node

The IPv6 header and each extension header include a next header field, which contains the type of identifier of that header and the protocol identifier of the upper-layer protocol.

5.1 Flow Labelling Capability

The Flow Label field in the IPv6 header has been added to enable routers to identify and provide special handling. This means that Quality of Service (QoS) can be achieved even when the packet payload is encrypted. Since the demand for real-time processing capability keeps increasing, the IPv4 gives no guarantees, majority of organisations implementing real-time technologies turned to ATM because of quality of service capability.

The IPv6 flow labels and priority flags allow some packets to receive higher priority service than others. Typically routing information and real-time interactive traffic receives highest priority and bulk transfers, like email and Usenet news are relegated to the lowest ranks (see Table 3–13). In the IPv6, the use of IPSec is required for all packets [see RFC-1883 documentation for further details]. The IPv6 has the advantage of providing a standard network-layer encryption scheme for all packets with no special handling requirements for sensitive information. Requiring encryption on all packets also makes the potential system cracker's job much harder since he would not be able to differentiate between the packets that contain important information and the ones that contain spam email. The IPv6 includes the definition of extensions, which provide support for authentication, data integrity, and confidentiality. This is included as a basic element of IPv6 and will be included in all implementations. The Table 3–14, gives a detail comparison of both the IPv4 and v6. It also appears that the IPv6 design is more flexible and a modularised design, but security of data/information remains questionable. Migrating from the IPv4 to v6 technology is still a problem. If migrating to IPv6 were easy to do, it would have been done a long time ago. It is almost like saying that, starting tomorrow, everyone in the United Kingdom will have to start driving on the right hand side of road (Emigh, 2002).

Furthermore, there are some compelling reasons for businesses to move from IPv4 to v6 (see Chapter 1 for further discussion). Since the process is task consuming and fairly complex, it is not possible to throw away the existing IPv4 network and adopt the v6 immediately.

Table 3–13. Comparisons between the IPv4 and v6 Headers

IPv4 Field Header	IPv6 Field Header	Justification for both Headers
Version (4-bit)	Version (4-bit)	Same function but the IPv6 header contains a new value
Header length (4-bit)	—	Removed in IPv6. The basic IPv6 header always has 40 octets
Type of service (8-bit)	Traffic class (8-bit)	Same function for both headers
—	Flow label (20-bit)	New field added to tag a flow for IPv6 packets
Total length (16-bit)	Payload length (16-bit)	Same function for both headers
Identification (16-bit)	—	Removed in IPv6 because fragmentation is handled differently in IPv6
Flags (3-bit)	—	Removed in IPv6 because fragmentation is handled differently in IPv6
Fragment offset (13-bit)	—	Removed in IPv6 because fragmentation is handled differently in IPv6
Time to live (8-bit)	Hop limit (8-bit)	Same function for both headers
Protocol number (8-bit)	Next header (8-bit)	Same function for both headers
Header checksum (16-bit)	—	Removed in IPv6. Link-layer technologies and upper-layer protocols handle checksum and error control
Source address (32-bit)	Source address (128-bit)	Source address is expanded in IPv6
Destination address (32-bit)	Destination address (128-bit)	Destination address is expanded in IPv6
Options (variable)	—	Removed in IPv6. The way to handle this option is different in IPv4
Padding (variable)	—	Removed in IPv6. All optional data is moved to IPv6 extension
—	Extension headers	New way in IPv6 to handle Options fields, fragmentation, security, mobility, Loose Source Routing, Record Route, and so on. The following section presents IPv6's extension headers

However, user oriented transition plans will be required to ease the transition process but surely there is know one best solution for every network. It is foreseen that the transition will happen in stages with a few IPv6 nodes introduced into the IPv4 network until the entire network becomes IPv6 compliance. Therefore, it is really important to choose the most convenient mechanisms, defining where to be located and how to deploy them.

5.2   Multicasting

Many new functions are introduced in the IPv6 multicasting and handle all the functions that required broadcasts. In the IPv4 multicasting was extension of the basic specification, while specifications. The IPv6 limits the scope of a multicast address by using a fixed address field. The multicast tunnels were introduced to deployed multicasting in the IPv4 but in the IPv6, all routers have multicast-capabilities, which mean that multicast tunnels can be deployed by the IPv6 multicasting (Euroscom, 2000).

6.   TRANSITION

The Simple Internet Transition (SIT) is a set of protocol mechanisms implemented in hosts and routers, along with some operational guidelines for addressing and deployment, to make transitioning to the IPv6 work with as little disruption as possible. According to the IETF, translation is the key factor in successful deployment of IPv6 and also many experts agreed that IPv4 and v6 network would co-exist for many years to come because migration should not affect the traffic of current IPv4. The IETF has created the Net Generation Transition Working Group (NGT Working Group) to assist IPv6 transition and propose technical solutions to achieve it. Migrating from the IPv4 to v6 is not straightforward and mechanisms to enable coexistence of the transition between the two versions have to be standardised (Carmes, 2002). The transition should be a gradual implantation and easy to be integrated with the existing infrastructure without significant disruption of services (see Figure 3–15 for diagrammatic illustration).

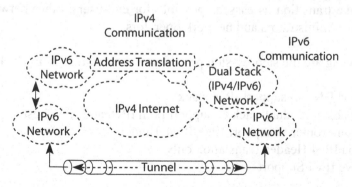

Figure 3–15. Different Transition technologies

The main aims of these transition mechanisms are to allow newly deployed IPv6 nodes to interoperate with existing IPv4 nodes and allow isolated IPv6

Table 3–14. Main differences between IPv4 and v6

Feature	IPv4	IPv6
Address bits	Source and Destination addresses are 32bits(4bytes) in length	Source and Destination addresses are 128bits(16bytes)
Header	See table 4.1	See table 4.1
Configuration	DHCP	Auto/DHCPv6
Security	IPSec is optional	IPSec is mandatory
Fragmentation	Done by both routers and the sending host	Not done by routers, only by the sending host
Multicast	IGMP is used to manage local subnet group membership. Broadcast addresses are used to send traffic to all nodes on a subnet.	IGMP is replaced with Multicast Listener Discovery (MLD) messages. There are no IPv6 broadcast addresses. Instead, a link-local scope all-nodes multicast address is used.

nodes to communicate with each other using the existing IPv4 infrastructure. The IPv6 transition plan is aimed at meeting the following requirements:

- Easy addressing of IPv4 devices to v6, the existing addressing will continue to be used (no need to assign new addresses)
- Low start-up costs and no preparation work is needed in order to upgrade the existing IPv4 to v6, or to deploy new IPv6 systems
- It allow IPv6 and IPv4 hosts to inter-operate
- It allow incremental deployment of hosts and routers
- Incremental upgrade of IPv4 devices to v6 at any time without any dependencies on any other devices
- Incremental deployment of new IPv6 devices can be installed at any time without any prerequisites (apart from upgrading DNS)
- To make transition as easy as possible for end-users, other network and system administrators and network operators

The following are the step-by-step procedure for migrating from IPv4 to v6:

- Upgrade DNS to support IPv6 stack
- Install host with dual stack to support both IPv6 and IPv4 host
- Configure router to support IPv6/IPv4 Tunnel
- Rely on IPv4 Header Translation only
- Remove IPv4 Support

The Transition from IPv4 to v6 has been discussed for years. There is no exclusive or correct mechanism but various organisations have defined and tested multiple methodologies. The three main categories of multiple methodologies are discussed below.

6.1   Dual IP Layer (Dual Stack)

The Dual IP layer (also known as Dual-stack) techniques allow IPv4 and v6 to co-exist in the same devices and networks. The dual IPv4 and v6 stack is a basic transition mechanism for providing complete support for both IPv4 and v6 in hosts and routers. It can be used as a first step in migration to IPv6 by deployment of systems that support IPv6. The diagrammatic illustration of Dual IP layer architecture in Figure 3–16 was adopted from Kwark (2002). This technique allows IPv4 and v6 applications to coexist in a dual IP layer routing.

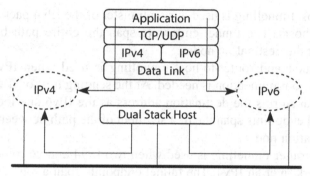

Figure 3–16. Dual IP layer architecture

One critical issue for the implementation of the dual stack mechanism is the dual-stack strategy relies heavily on the Domain Name Service (DNS). The Dual stack host has both IPv4 and v6 stack co-exists on the same machine. The DNS will check the record type either A type for IPv4 or AAAA or A6 for IPv6 stack, then it will decide on whether to use the IPv4 or v6 stack. The DNS support in dual stack mechanisms is a parameter that affects the network performance (Cho et al., 2004).

The Dual Stack Transition Mechanism (DSTM) is based on the DHCPv6 server, which temporarily assigns global IPv4 addresses to v6 hosts; in other to communicate with the IPv4 host (Tsirtsis, 2000). Assignment of the IPv4 addresses to IPv6 Hosts (AIIH). For example, the DHCPv6 and DNS handle the assignment and registration of the IPv4 address to dual stack nodes. The DSTM has advantage of removing the need for translation at the edge of the network but is limited by the availability of IPv4 addresses and the requirement to locally configure each node to use the DSTM service. Therefore, DSTM matches small and medium network size that already uses a DHCP server for sharing global IPv4 addresses but limited by the availability of the DHCPv6 server (Bouras et al., 2003).

6.2   Tunnelling Techniques

The tunnelling works by encapsulating and wrapping the IPv6 packet into the v4 packet and sends the packet through the IPv4 network. The tunnelling connects to the IPv6 network through the IPv4 Internet and can be used to deploy an IPv6 forwarding infrastructure when deploying the IPv4. The two endpoints of the tunnel need to be dual stack routers or hosts (Vieira, 2001). According to RFC 2893, there are different kinds of tunnelling scenarios to tunnel the IPv6 traffic between IPv6 and v4 nodes over an IPv4 infrastructure. The kind tunnelling configurations are defined as follows (Monga et al. 2003):

- Host-to-host tunnelling is used during transfer of the IPv4 packet, between two IPv6 hosts. The tunnel endpoints span the entire path between the source and the destination nodes.
- Host-to-router and router-to-host tunnelling is used when IPv4 to v6 or IPv6 to v4 communication is needed. At the sending host of IPv6 network, the host transforms the destination address as the IPv6 site local address. The tunnel endpoints span the first segment of the path between the source and destination nodes.
- Router-to-router tunnelling is used when two IPv4 and v6 routers connect to a network over an IPv4. The tunnel endpoints span a logical link in the path between the source and destination.

The two main categories of tunnelling mechanisms are 'Direct configuration on the endpoints of the tunnel' (configured tunnelling and tunnel broker mechanism) and 'Coding of the address of the endpoint into the IPv6 address' (automatic tunnelling mechanism, 6to4 transition mechanism, and 6over4 mechanism).

6.2.1   Configured Tunnelling

The configured tunnel mechanism is a connection between router to router or host to router. The router encapsulates the IPv6 packets into the IPv4 format and transmits it across the router. The router at the other end decapsulates the packets and send IPv6 packets to destination host –IPv6 nodes. Operationally, the tunnel consists of two routers that are configured to have a virtual point-to-point link over the IPv4 network. The implementation cost of the configured tunnelling mechanism is low because it allows the parallel development of the IPv6 infrastructure without usage of separate physical links but the tunnelling software needs to be installed on the gateway.

6.2.2 Broker Mechanism

The tunnel brokers is a mechanism designed for users who want to participate in the IPv6 network but are isolated from any native IPv6 network, or for users who wish an early IPv6 adoption [see RFC-3053 documentation for further details]. It is associated with a tunnel server, and is connected with DNS service. The tunnel broker provides quick and easy connectivity, even if the application use embedded IPv6 addresses in order to achieve the end-to-end service. The only exception is when NAT mechanisms are used; the configured tunnel would not achieved connection.

6.2.3 Automatic Tunnelling Mechanism

The automatic tunnelling mechanism that creates link with the IPv4 is compatible with the IPv6 addresses [see RFC-2893 documentation for further details]. The application of this mechanism requires only the installation of a software module to the hosts. It allows the IPv6 and v4 nodes to communicate over the IPv4 infrastructure without the need for tunnel destination pre-configuration. But the tunnel endpoints have to be manually configured and automatically derived from the IPv4 compatible v6 addresses. The problem with this method is that it does not solve the address exhaustion problem of IPv4 and routing table size. This mechanism can be combined with other mechanisms in order to achieve end-to-end communication [see RFC-3053 documentation for further details].

6.2.4 6to4 Transition Mechanism

The 6to4 mechanism enables the IPv6 sites to be connected to other v6 sites over the IPv4 network without explicit tunnel set up [see RFC-3056 documentation for further details]. The only requirement is that the IPv6 router has a routable IPv4 address. This mechanism used the IPv4 infrastructure for the interconnection of remote IPv6 network to communicate via 6to4 routers using encapsulation techniques The 6to4 mechanism is well-supported transitional tool that attracts large sites adaptation. It is typically implemented almost entirely in border routers. The 6to4 mechanism lack scalability for smaller sites; encapsulation adds an additional load to the network and the complexity of the IPv6 and v4 addresses in the routing tables are major issue.

6.2.5 6over4 Mechanism

The 6over4 mechanism allows isolated IPv6 hosts located on a physical link to act like fully functional IPv6 hosts even without direct contact with an

IPv6 router [see RFC-2529 documentation for further details]. This mechanism does not use IPv4 compatible v6 addresses or configured tunnels but requires dual stack support on hosts; specific configuration to work as 6over4 interface and the IPv4 domain has to support multicast operations. The 6over4 offers a very useful tool for sites that as yet have no IPv6 network but wish to deploy or test it. In this respect, it offers transitioning tool that is limited to when sites are in the process of moving to IPv6.

6.3   Translation Mechanism

The translation mechanism allows the communication between hosts that support different protocols. This is a simple NAT technique, which translates IPv6 to v4 and vice versa. The NAT is a device that translates IP addresses and converts non-unique IP addresses to globally unique IP addresses [see RFC-1631 documentation for further details]. The NAT can be inefficient and slow. The translation between the IPv4 and v6 can take place in one of the following three levels:

- The IP level translation is the simplest and fastest method and involves converting from one header to the other.
- In transport level the translator acts as a relay, working on TCP/UDP flows.
- Application level translation is the most complex form and generally operates in the form of an Application Level Gateway (ALG).

Translation tools may add extra functionality to basic translation, using caches for example, to improve performance and keep stateless information (Scholz et al., 2001). The most well-known translation mechanisms are discussed below:

6.3.1   Stateless IP and ICMP Translators (SIIT) and Network Address Translation- Protocol Translation (NAT-PT)

The Stateless IP/ICMP translator (SIIT) is one of the methods that translate the IPv6 and v4 payloads but the translation is limited to the packet header (needs to be done for every packet stateless mode), and only operates at the IP level. [see RFC-2765 documentation for further details]. The Network Address Translation- Protocol Translation (NAT-PT) is a well-established translation mechanism and is merely an extension of the existing NAT mechanism that provides an IPv4 and v6 translation tool based on SIIT translation mechanisms (see Figure 3–17 for diagrammatic illustration).

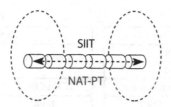

Figure 3–17. SIIT and NAT-PT

The NAT-PT operates at the application level because it is implemented in an Application Level Gateway (ALG) [see RFC-2766 documentation for further details]. The ALG is an application specific translation mechanism and enabled application on a host to be domain transparent. The SIIT is not a complete transition tool specification it is guide for translations. The NAT-PT offers better service by building on SIIT. The NAT-PT has the following characteristics:

- Supports both address and header translation.
- A stateful IPv4 and v6 translator.
- Serves multiple IPv6 nodes.
- Allocates a temporary IPv4 address to each.
- Act as a communication proxy with IPv4 peers.

The implementation of the NAT-PT mechanism is simple and does not require extra configuration to the hosts. It is stateful translator; each session must be routed via the same NAT-PT device. However, this mechanism does not support end-to-end security strategy and requires the usage of a large IPv4 space that inherited same problem as the existing NAT (Warfield, 2003).

6.3.2   The Bump in the stack (BITS) and Bump in the API (BIA)

The Bump in the stack (BITS) is a translator that allows IPv6 hosts to v4 only applications. This is achieved by adding segments to the IP stack to do the necessary translation. The BITS offers a very useful translator service, by making each host perform translation internally and improve the network performance [see RFC-2767 documentation for further details].

The translator translates outgoing IPv4 headers for the IPv6 headers and the incoming headers of the IPv6 into v4. It uses the header translation algorithm defined in SIIT. Like NAT-PT, there are associated problems in applications that embed IP addresses in their payloads.

The Bump in the API (BIA) is similar to BITS, but it does not translate between IPv4 and IPv6 headers. Instead it inserts an API translator between the API socket and the TCP/IP modules of the host stack (see Figure 3–18 for

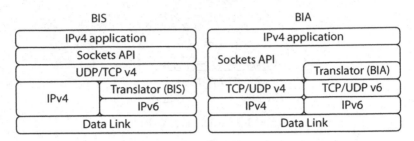

Figure 3–18. Bump in the stack (BITS) and Bump in the API (BIA)

diagrammatic illustration). In this way the translation can be done without the overhead of translating every packet headers. This mechanism will be needed in early migration stage (Feng et al., 2002).

6.3.3   Socks and Transport relay translator (TRT)

The socks are gateway mechanism implemented by a socks server that acts as a relay mechanism in TCP and UDP sessions, between two hosts support-ing different protocols (Toutain and Afifi, 2000). The socks are considered a unidirectional mechanism and may be used for connecting both the IPv4 and v6 networks. The Socks provides automatic translation for all applications but they must support Socks interfaces. The transport relay translator (TRT) is lo-cated in the transport layer and enables IPv6 only hosts to exchange TCP/UDP traffic with IPv4 [see RFC-3142 documentation for further details]. It uses proxy server to relay packet between the client and application server. The aim of a TRT relay system is to provide a way to gain access to the IPv4 network resources outside and IPv6 only network (see Figure 3–19 for diagrammatic illustration).

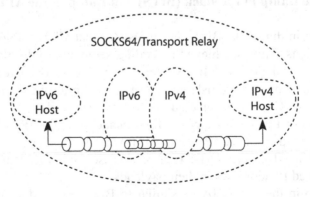

Figure 3–19. Socks and TRT

The TRT translates the IPv4 and v6 of the TCP and UDP sessions, which is similar to the NAT mechanism. The TRT can be useful as a temporary measure to allow IPv4 and v6 to interoperate. Both the TRT and Socks64 are examples of relay translators that provide a convenient method of implementation for transport level translator. The routing information is configured to route the prefix towards the dual-stack TRT router, which terminates the IPv6 session and initiates IPv4 communication to the final destination (Savola, 2003).

7.   SUMMARY OF CHAPTER THREE

The IPv4 packet is composed of header and data. The data portion is classed as the upper layer packet such as TCP or UDP packet. The IPv4 addresses, which are 32 bits length, are represented in a dotted decimal notation, and are divided into parts, network ID and host ID. It has different bits numbers according to which class the IP address belongs. Some of the limitation of IPv4 and v6 has been highlighted in this chapter. Surely, the IPv6 has many advantages over the IPv4 as a result of the extended IP address space, simple header format, auto-configuration, QoS, and security –but not 100 per cent safe free. However, problems may arise for new applications that require the IPv6. It is not cost effective to throw away the existing IPv4 network and adopt IPv6 immediately, what has been foreseen is that the transition will happen in stages with a few IPv6 nodes introducing into the IPv4 network until the entire network becomes IPv6 full compliance! With all the limitations and the ambiguity of IPv4 and v6, the question to ask is *'how can biometrics be integrated with IPSec'* —this will be the topic of discussion in chapter 5. The next chapter focuses on the implementations and the limitations of IPSec.

REFERENCES

3COM, 2004, IPV6 Technology Brief, 3COM Technical Paper.
Bieringer, P., 2005, Status of IPv6 (Information and Workshop), in the Proceeding of IEEE 2005 Symposium on Applications and the Internet, Trento, Italy
Bouras, C., Ganos, P., and Karaliotas, A., 2003, The deployment of IPv6 in an IPv4 world and transition strategies, Internet Research: Electronic Networking Applications and Policy, Volume 13, No2.
Carmes, E., 2002, The Transition to IPv6, Internet Society ISOC Member briefing.
Childress, B., Cathey, B., and Dixon, S.D., 2003, The adoption of IPv6, Journal of Computing Sciences in Colleges, Volume 18 Issue 4.
Cho, K., Luckie, M., and Huffaker, B., 2004, Identifying IPv6 network problems in the dual-stack world, in the Proceedings of the ACM SIGCOMM workshop on Network troubleshooting.
Clauberg, A., 2001, IPv6 Deployment, Manager, SP Consultant, Cisco Systems Inc.

Crouzard, L., Gawinowski, G., Robert, O, and Smith, P., 2003, IPv6 and Internet technology for the aeronautical telecommunication network —A new networking approach, Eurocontrol Experimental Centre.

Emigh, J., 2002, What you need to know?, Enterprise networking planet pressed, June.

Euroscom, 2003, IP Multicast", Project P911-PF, Deliverable 1, State-of-the-Art

Feng, M., Chown, T., and Saywell, M., 2002, Review of IPv6 Transition Scenarios for European Academic Networks, IPv6 Conference in Paris.

Garfinkel, S., and Spafford, G., 1996, Practical UNIX & Internet Security, 2nd Edition, O'reilly, April, 1996

Jarvinen, A., 2002, Comparing IPv4 and IPv6 mobility and auto configuration for residential networks, Helsinki University of Technology Department of Computer Science and Engineering, Seminar on Internetworking; http://www.tml.hut.fi/Studies/T-110.551/2002/papers/May/antti.jarvinen.pdf (January 20, 2007).

Koren, D., 2005, Are we ready for IPv6? Is IPv6 ready for us?, International Journal of Network Management, Volume 15 Issue 1.

Kwark, G.H., 2002, IPv4/IPv6 Coexistence with Application Perspective, i2soft; http://www.ipv6.or.kr/ipv6summit/Download/4th-day/Session-VII/s-7-4.ppt#1 (January 31, 2007).

Lucent Technology lab, 2004, The Challenges of Next Generation IP Address Management;http://www.larta.org/LAVox/ArticleLinks/2003/030609_ipv6.asp (January 23, 2007).

Lugani, S., 2002, Introduction to Internet Protocol – version 6, WIPRO Infortech white paper, 2002

Monga, P., Ahmed, I., and Gupta, I., 2003, Ipv6-Coexistence and Integration with Next Generation Networks, Faculty of Computer Science, Dalhousie University; http://www.cu.ipv6tf.org/pdf/IPv6-Coexistence.pdf (January 18, 2007).

Networks CSC/FUNET; http://staff.csc.fi/~psavola/residential.html (January 3, 2007).

Savola, P., 2003, Migration and Co-existence of IPv4 and IPv6 in Residential

Schnitzer, D., 2002, Applied IPv6 Security, http://www.schnitzer.at/dominik/uni/ipv6sec.pdf (January 23, 2007).

Scholz, G., Evans, C., Flores, J., and Rahman, M., 2001, Internet protocol version 6, Journal of Computing Sciences in Colleges, Volume 16 Issue 3.

Slvonen, P., 2003, Migration and Co-existence of IPv4 and IPv6 in Residential Networks, CSC/FUNET; http://staff.csc.fi/~psavola/residential.html (January 13, 2007).

Tatipamula, M., and Grossetete, P., 2004, IPv6 Integration and Coexistence Strategies for Next-Generation Networks, IEEE Communications Magazine.

Technologies, Products, and Services Volume 1 of 3, http://www.eurescom.de/~pub-deliverables/P900-series/P911/D1/Vol1/p911d1vol1.pdf (January 28, 2007).

Toutain, L., and Afifi, H., 2003, Dynamic tunnueling a new method for the IPv4-IPv6 transition, IETF documentation: draft-ietf-ngtrans-6to4-dstm-00.txt.

Tsirtsis, G., 2000, Dual stack deployment using DSTM and 6 to 4, IETF documentation: draft-ietf-ngrans-6to4-dstm-00.txt.

Vieira, J., 2001, Description of IPv4/IPv6 available transition strategies, Long laboratories.

Warfield, M. H., 2003, Security Implications of IPv6, Internet Security Systems, white paper.

Weiser, M., 2001, Whatever happened to the next generation Internet, Communication of the ACM, Vol. 44, No. 9.

Chapter 4

IMPLEMENTATIONS AND LIMITATIONS OF THE IPSEC

1. INTRODUCTION

The IETF created the Net Generation Transition Working Group (NGT Working Group) to assist IPv6 transition and propose technical solutions to achieve it purpose. The IPv4 to v6 is not straightforward and the mechanisms to enable co-existence of the two versions have to be standardised.

> 'I'll put a girdle round about the Earth in 40 minutes.'
> —William Shakespeare (1564–1616)

However, the IPSec does not include mechanisms for specifying more granular security policy issues, but the hosts are authorised for sessions with certain other entities or whether hosts are authorised to exchange specified kinds of traffic. There is few information concerning different distributions and implementations. This chapter presents the classification and taxonomy of the IPSec, and evaluates various IPSec implementations and their limitations. The laboratory experiment was conducted to show the implementation problems of most popular IPSec products.

2. CLASSIFICATION AND TAXONOMY OF THE IPSEC

The Internet security have made great progress since the IETF standardised the IPSec, as a result of this standardisation the IPSec have evolved, taking advantage of new technologies. The classification and taxonomy of the IPSec operations is based on existing networks paradigm (see Table 4–1). Over the past few years, we have seen evidence of an increasing number of the IPSec implementation requirements within different types of networks.

Table 4–1. Classification and Taxonomy of the IPSec operations

Type of Networks	IPSec Configuration		
	Open IPSec	Inter-Lock IPSec	Close-in IPSec
Local Area Network (LAN)	✗	✓	✓
Wide Area Network (WAN)	✓	✓	✗
Metropolitan Area Network (MAN)	✗	✓	✓
Intranet	✗	✓	✓
Extranet	✓	✓	✓
Value Added Network (VAN)	✗	✓	✓
Internet	✓	✓	✗

- ✓ (Applicable)
- ✗ (Not Applicable)

i.   *Open IPSec* is an inter-connected and un-trusted network. It is open to interaction within and outside its geographical area; Examples of Open IPSec networks are WAN, Extranet, and Internet.

ii. *Inter-lock IPSec* is enable niche access to those who are given permission. The Inter-lock IPSec provides partially secured operation. Examples of Inter-lock IPSec networks are MAN, Intranet, Extranet, VAN, and Internet.

iii. *Close-in IPSec* is a restricted inter networks and can be trusted to some extent but not totally secured. Access to the network is granted to approve users only. Examples of Close-in IPSec networks are LAN, MAN, Intranet, Extranet, and VAN.

It is evident from the survey conducted that a staggering number of organisations agreed that absolute security is unattainable using the IPSec. Similarly, the IPSec is complementary to, but not in direct competition with anti-virus or any other security software.

3.   COMBINING THE IPSEC PROTOCOLS TO CREATE A VIRTUAL PRIVATE NETWORK (VPN)

The IKE is the protocol that brings all the previously discussed protocols together. The IKE operates in two separate phases when establishing the IPSec for VPNs. In Phase 1, the IKE authenticates the IPSec peers, negotiates an IKE security association between peers, and initiates a secure tunnel for the IPSec. While in the Phase 2, the IPSec peers use the authenticated, secure tunnel from Phase 1 to negotiate the set of security parameters for the IPSec tunnel. Once the peers have agreed on a set of security parameters, the IPSec tunnel is created and stays in existence until the SAs are terminated or until the SA lifetimes expire. The IPSec can be configured on routers by first identifying the five parameters that the IKE uses in Phase 1 to authenticate peers and establish the secure tunnel:

- Encryption algorithm—56-bit DES (default) or the stronger 168-bit 3DES.
- Hash algorithm—MD5 (default) or the stronger SHA-1.
- Authentication method—Pre-shared keys, RSA encrypted nonces, or the most secure and the digital signatures.
- Key exchange method—768-bit Diffie-Hellman Group 1 (default) or the stronger 1024-bit Diffie-Hellman Group 2.
- IKE SA lifetime is 86,400 seconds (1 day). Whatever parameters are chosen for the IKE Phase 1, they must be identical on both peers otherwise the connection would not be established.

Once Phase 1 is configured, the IKE Phase 2 values need to be supplied:

- IPSec protocol—AH or ESP.
- Hash algorithm—MD5 or SHA-1 (These are always HMAC derivatives for IKE Phase 2).
- Encryption algorithm (if using ESP)—DES or 3DES.

The AH and ESP are fully discussed in chapters 1 and 2. The SHA-HMAC and MD5-HMAC are now available to provide additional packet integrity for ESP. In order to facilitate the configuration process for devices that need to support a variety of the IPSec in VPNs. The IPSec parameters are grouped into predefined configurations called transforms (see chapter 3 for further discussion). The transforms identify the IPSec protocol, hash algorithm, and when needed, the encryption algorithm.

3.1   IPSec in VPN Pre-Configuration

The IPSec was designed to use a robust set of protocols and processes, although it is possible to establish VPNs without knowing too much about these protocols, the end results are likely to be haphazard. It is highly recommended to follow a sequence of pre-configuration steps before the actual configuration of devices. The policy must be identical on both ends of a VPN. The elements of an IKE policy include:

- *Key distribution method* (Manual or Certificate Authority).

- *Authentication method* - Manual distribution uses pre-shared keys. Certificate Authority distribution uses RSA encrypted nonce or RSA digital signatures.
- *IP address* and host names of peers—The IPSec configuration requires the IP address or hostname of the peers.
- *IKE policy parameters* - Used by ISAKMP to establish the secure tunnel of IKE Phase 1. The IKE policies consist of the following five parameters:
- *Encryption algorithm* (DES/3DES).
- *Hash algorithm* (MD5/SHA-1).
- *Authentication method* (Pre-shared, RSA encryption, RSA signatures).
- *Key exchange* (D-H Group 1/D-H Group 2).
- *IKE SA lifetime* (86,400 seconds by default).

When choosing to implement the IPSec VPN, both ends of the VPN must implement identical IPSec policies. The following information is needed for the IPSec policy:

- AH or ESP.
- Authentication—MD5 or SHA-1.
- Encryption—DES or 3DES.
- Transform Set—ah-sha-hmac esp-3des esp-md5-hmac or one of the other allowable combinations.
- Traffic to be protected—Protocol, source, destination, and port.
- SA establishment—Manual or IKE (IKE is always used).

If there is any existing IPSec configuration on the device to be configured, this must be checked to avoid conflicts. It is important to ensure that there is network connectivity before any IPSec configuration is in place (pinging the peer devices. When configuring access control lists (ACLs) with IPSec, the specific IPSec protocol must be given permission to:

- UDP port 500—For ISAKMP traffic.
- Protocol 50—For ESP traffic.
- Protocol 51—For AH traffic.

The protocols 50 and 51 are actual protocols within the TCP/IP stack. They are not used in port 23 for telnet traffic.

3.2   Establishing the IPSec in VPNs

It is possible to have absolute control over the traffic that gets processed by the IPSec. It may be desired that only certain traffic between peers be authenticated. For example, we may want to encrypt only email or client/server traffic or just encrypt everything going between two peers. The security policy of the organisation is ultimately mirrored in what is called crypto ACL. Two VPN peers must mirror the ACLs. It simply extended the IP ACL, but the permit and deny features have a different function to normal IP ACLs (Matkovich, 2003; Jayawickrama, 2003):

i. Permit at the source peer passes the traffic to the IPSec for authentication, encryption, or both. The IPSec modifies the packet by inserting an AH or ESP header and possibly encrypting some of or all of the original packet and then sends it to the destination peer.
ii. Deny at the source peer bypasses the IPSec and sends the clear-text packet to the destination peer.
iii. Permit at the destination peer passes the traffic to the IPSec for authentication, decryption, or both. The ACL at the destination peer uses the information in the header to make its decision.
iv. Deny at the destination peer bypasses the IPSec and assumes that the traffic has been sent in the clear.

A certain level of planning is required when dealing with crypto ACLs. When the permit and deny keywords are used in the proper combinations, data is successfully protected and transferred (Roland and Newcomb, 2003). However, when the permit and deny are not used in the proper combinations, data is simply discarded. It is now clear why it is so important for crypto ACLs to match on both ends of the IPSec in VPN. All crypto ACLs must be extended IP ACLs, giving permission to identify source, destination, and protocol.

The IKE Phase 1 uses either main mode or Aggressive mode to authenticate the IPSec peers and establish an IKE SA between the peers. The main mode is the default mode used on Cisco routers. With Main mode, the IKE performs three bi-directional (6 in total) exchanges between peers:

• Algorithms and hashes are agreed upon.
• Diffie-Hellman exchange is made to produce matching shared secret keys.
• Verified other peer's identity.

However, with Aggressive mode only three messages are exchanged and since more information is packed into the messages, it means that more key information is available for eavesdroppers. Whichever modes are used (Main or/and Aggressive), the end result of the IKE Phase 1 is a secure tunnel between the peers that protects the ISAKMP exchanges of the IKE Phase 2 as the IPSec SA is negotiated. But the Cisco Systems Inc. and Juniper Networks

Inc. have confirmed that some implementations of ISAKMP in some products could put users at risk.

The only mode of operation in the IKE Phase 2 is the Quick mode. This begins immediately after the secured tunnel is established in IKE Phase 1. The following is done during IKE Phase 2:

- The IPSec SA parameters are negotiated and agreed on by both peers (within the secure IKE SA established in Phase 1).
- The IPSec SAs are established.
- The IPSec SAs are renegotiated periodically as needed

Once the IPSec SAs have been established, secured traffic can be exchanged over the VPN. The IP packets across the IPSec VPN are authenticated and/or encrypted, depending on the transform set used. In some cases, the IPSec VPNs are terminated when one of the peers chooses to leave the connection. This is commonly found in remote access VPNs when the mobile user disconnects from the corporate resources (Sandsmark, 2004). However, it is more common for the IPSec VPNs to be terminated based on the negotiated SA lifetimes in the IKE SA and the IPSec SA. When the SAs are timed out, the associated keys are discarded. If the IPSec SA times out and there is still IPSec traffic to be sent, the peers immediately go into IKE Phase 2 negotiations to establish the IPSec SA using new keys. However, if the IKE SA times out, the peers must start with IKE Phase 1 negotiations to re-establish new IKE SAs and then re-negotiate the IPSec SAs. The sole purpose of the IKE is to establish SAs for the IPSec. Before IKE can do this it must negotiate an SA (ISAKMP SA) relationship with the peer. Because the IKE negotiates its own policy, it is possible to configure multiple policy statements with different configurations, and then let the two peers come to an agreement (Matkovich, 2003). The ISAKMP policy is defined using IOS commands. The syntax are expressed in Commands 4.1, 4.2, and 4.3:

Router(config)#crypto isakmp policy *priority*   (4.1)

Router(config)#crypto isakmp policy 1   (4.2)

Router(config-isakmp)#   (4.3)

The above example changes the router prompt to the (config-isakmp) mode. The priority is a unique number between 1 to 10,000 that is used to identify the priority for the ISAKMP policy —the lower the number, the higher the priority. The Figure 4–1 presents the IKE/ISAKMP configuration policy programme.

```
Router(config-isakmp)#?
ISAKMP commands:
authentication {rsa-sig | rsa-encr | pre-share}
default
encryption {des | 3des}
exit
group
hash {md5 | sha}
lifetime seconds
no
```

Figure 4–1. IKE/ISAKMP configuration policy

The authentication command is used to manually tell IKE what key to use. Two other options are rsa-encr and rsa-sig. The rsa-encr option uses RSA encrypted nonce and the rsa-sig option uses RSA Signatures. The syntax is expressed in Command 4.4:

```
Router(config-isakmp)#authentication pre-share                    (4.4)
```

The encryption command is used to define the algorithm used for encrypting the IKE negotiations. The syntax is expressed in Command 4.5:

```
Router(config-isakmp)#encryption 3des                             (4.5)
```

The group command is used to declare what size modulus to use for Diffie-Hellman calculations. The group 1 is 768 bits long, and group 2 is 1024 bits long. The group 2 is significantly CPU intensive and more secure than group 1. The hash command is used to set the hashing algorithm. The two options are MD5 and SHA. The SHA is more secure than the MD5. The syntax are expressed in Commands 4.6 and 4.7:

```
Router(config-isakmp)#group 2                                     (4.6)
```

```
Router(config-isakmp)#hash sha                                    (4.7)
```

The lifetime command is used to set the lifetime for the IKE SA and the default value is 86400 seconds (one day). Once the lifetime time expires the SA is renegotiated. The syntax is expressed in Command 4.8:

Router(config-isakmp)#lifetime 500   (4.8)

Since, pre-shared keys are chosen as the authentication mechanism, the key must be defined manually. There are two ways to specify the pre-shared keystring. The first method uses the peer router's IP address and the second method uses the peer router's hostname. The syntax are expressed in Commands 4.9 and 4.10:

Router(config)#crypto isakmp key *keystring* address *peer-address*   (4.9)

Router(config)#crypto isakmp key *keystring* hostname *peer-hostname*
(4.10)

In order to specify which method the peer should use for IKE identity (i.e. address-based or hostname-based), the following command is used. The syntax is expressed in Command 4.11:

Router(config)#crypto isakmp identity *{address | hostname}*   (4.11)

Using the IP address-based identity method is more secure. It is recommended to use the same identity method on peers. The command below sets the key to MyKey. The address 172.16.172.20 is the IP address of the other side peer. The syntax is expressed in Command 4.12:

Router(config)#crypto isakmp key MyKey address 172.16.172.20   (4.12)

When using pre-shared authentication, the other peer must have the same key configured. Although pre-shared keys are easy to configure, they are not scalable for large deployments.

3.3   Configure Transform Sets

The transform set represents a combination of security protocols and algorithms. During the IPSec SA negotiation process, it is necessary for the peers to agree on a particular transform set for protecting the data flow. The multiple transform sets can be specified and one or more of these transform sets can be a crypto map entry. The transform set that is defined in the crypto map entry would be the one used in the IPSec SA negotiation to protect the data flow. During the IPSec SA negotiations using IKE, the peers search for a transform set that is the same at both peers. When a matching transform set is found, it is selected and applied to the traffic. The command is expressed in 4.13:

Transform set = AH transform + ESP transform + Mode   (4.13)

The transform set specifies one or two of the IPSec protocols (AH or ESP or both) and the algorithms to use with each selected protocol. In order to define a transform set, it is necessary to specify one to three transforms. Each transform has the IPSec protocol (ESP or AH) plus the algorithms to use with it. The transform sets are limited to one AH and one or two ESP. The default IPSec mode is tunnel. The syntax are expressed in Commands 4.14 to 4.23:

Router(config)#crypto ipsec transform-set transform-set-name
transform1 [transform2 [transform3]] modetransport | tunnel   (4.14)

Router(config)#crypto ipsec transform-set MySet?   (4.15)

ah-md5-hmac AH-HMAC-MD5 transform   (4.16)

ah-rfc1828 AH-MD5 transform   (4.17)

ah-sha-hmac AH-HMAC-SHA transform   (4.18)

esp-des ESP transform using DES cipher (56 bits)   (4.19)

esp-md5-hmac ESP transform using HMAC-MD5 auth   (4.20) esp-null ESP transform w/o cipher   (4.21)

esp-rfc1829 ESP-DES-CBC transform   (4.22)

esp-sha-hmac ESP transform using HMAC-SHA auth   (4.23)

When a particular transform set is used during the negotiations for the IPSec SAs, the entire transform, (i.e. the combination of protocols, algorithms and mode) must match a transform set at the remote peer. The syntax is expressed in Command 4.24:

RouterA(config)#crypto ipsec transform-set
MySet1 ah-md5-hmac esp-3des   (4.24)

This transform uses AH authentication with MD5 hash, ESP with 3DES encryption and the IPSec tunnel mode (default). The syntax is expressed in Command 4.25:

RouterB(config)#crypto ipsec transform-set
MySet2 esp-md5-hmac esp-des   (4.25)

This transform uses ESP authentication with MD5 hash, ESP encryption with 56-bit DES and the IPSec tunnel mode (default). The syntax is expressed in Command 4.26:

RouterC(config)#crypto ipsec transform-set
MySet3 ah-sha-hmac   (4.26)

The above transform uses the AH authentication with SHA and no encryption.

3.4   Configure Crypto Access Lists

The crypto access lists are used to define which IP traffic needs protection. The extended IP access-lists used have exactly the same syntax as normal IP extended access lists. However, crypto access lists are used with crypto map entries referencing specific access lists that define whether the IPSec processing is applied to the traffic that matches the access list. The IP-extended access lists are used to specify which packets must be encrypted as they exit the interface. The TCP traffic from the subnet is attached to initiator router that would be encrypted as it exits the router interface. The permit keyword causes all the TCP traffic that matches the specified conditions to be protected. The access list criteria are applied in the forward direction to traffic exiting the router and in the reverse direction to traffic entering the router. When a router receives encrypted packets back, it uses the same ACL to determine, which inbound packets to decrypt by looking at the source and destination addresses in the access list in reverse order (Roland and Newcomb, 2003). It is therefore important that peer routers have access lists that mirror each other. It is also discouraged to use any keyword in a permit statement, since this will cause all traffic to be protected and will consequently require protection for all inbound traffic. It is therefore, required to create explicit access lists to allow IKE, AH and ESP protocols.

3.5   Configure Crypto Maps

The crypto map maps the entries that are used to pull together the various parts used to set up the IPSec and also maps the entries group of the IPSec policies into a crypto map set. The map set is then applied to an interface and the all traffic passing through that interface is checked against the applied crypto map set. The syntax is expressed in Commands 4.27:

```
Router(config)#crypto map <name> <seq> <method>
[dynamic dynamic-map-name]                                      (4.27)
```

The above command ties together the configuration for the IPSec policy and SAs. The method keyword defines the key management method in ipsec-manual, and ipsec-isakmp. The ipsec-isakmp is the most commonly used method. The [dynamic dynamic-map-name] option is used to associate a dynamic crypto map to a static crypto map set. The latter is typically used in connection with remote access clients.

The crypto map entries with the same crypto map name (but different map sequence numbers) are grouped into a crypto map set. These crypto map sets are then applied to interfaces. The policy described in the crypto map entries is used during the negotiation of SAs. If the local router initiates the negotiation, it will use the policy specified in the static crypto map entries to create an offer to be sent to the remote IPSec peer. Every time the remote IPSec peer initiates the negotiation; the local router will have to check the policy from the static crypto map entries whether it is valid to accept the peer's offer or not. The success of negotiation between two IPSec peers depends on the peers' crypto map entries compatible configuration statements. If two peers try to establish a security association, they must both have at least one crypto map entry that is compatible with one of the other peer's crypto map entries. The two crypto map entries must be compatible and least meet the following criteria:

- The crypto map entries must contain compatible crypto access lists (mirror image access lists).
- The crypto map entries must be able to identify the peer.
- Both crypto map entries must have one transform set in common.

The crypto map entries with different map-numbers but the same map-name are considered to be part of a single map set. It is possible to apply only one crypto map set to a single interface. When creating more than one crypto map entry for a given interface, the sequence -number of each map entry is used to rank the map entries: the lower the sequence number, the higher the priority. The crypto map programme is presented in Figure 4–2 using the ipsec-isakmp as the key management method:

```
Router(config)#crypto map VPN 10 ipsec-isakmp!
Router(config-crypto-map)#?
match address [access-list-id | name]
peer [hostname | ip-address]
transform-set [set_name(s)]
security-association [inbound|outbound]
set
no
exit
```

Figure 4–2. Crypto Map Configuration

The available subcommands are as follows:

- Match address: Specifies the crypto access list number.
- Set peer: Specifies the IPSec peer IP address.
- Set transform-set: Selects the transform set(s) to use.
- Set security-association: Sets manual AH and ESP keys.
- No: Deletes the entries

Applying the crypto map set to an interface enabled the router to check all the interface's traffic against the crypto map set and to use the specified policy during connection or SA negotiation. SAs are initialised when the crypto maps are applied. The syntax is expressed in Commands 4.28 and 4.29:

```
RouterA(config)#interface ethernet1/0
```
                                                                                    (4.28)

RouterA(config-if)#crypto map VPN   (4.29)

The global lifetime values are used when negotiating new IPSec SAs. These lifetimes only apply to SAs established via IKE (used the ipsec-isakmp keyword). The manually established SAs (used the ipsec-manual keyword) never expire. There are two lifetimes: a timed and traffic-volume. An SA expires after the first of these lifetimes is reached. The default lifetimes are 864000 seconds (1 day) and 4,608,000 kilobytes (10 Mbytes per second for one hour). The SA and the corresponding keys expires according to whichever comes sooner, either after the number of seconds has passed or after the amount of traffic in kilobytes has passed.

4.   IPSEC IN WINDOWS

There has been many work put into the development of IPv6 compatibility by Microsoft. Efforts are still being made to improvise on the IPv4 and number of Internet drafts on the IPv6 is overwhelming. The key steps taken by Microsoft to deliver the IPv6 are detail below:

- The transition to IPv6 began in 1998 with the availability of an IPv6 implementation from Microsoft research.
- In March 2000, a technology preview was released for Windows 2000.
- In October 2001, Window XP was released with a developer preview IPv6 stack and key components of the system enabled for IPv6, so that developers can begin the task of IPv6-enabling their applications.
- In July 2003, the advanced network pack for Windows XP was released. This pack includes the IPv6 Internet connection firewall, a teredo client, and support for Windows peer-to-peer networking.

The Microsoft IPSec comprised of five main components, which are Active Directory, Policy Agent, IKE module, the IPSec driver, and TCP/IP Driver. These five components work with each other to provide seamless IPSec functionality in Windows 2000, XP and 2003 (see Table 4–2). It is best to distribute the IPSec policies by using Group Policy to configure Active Directory domains, sites, and organisational units before assigning the IPSec policies to Group Policy objects. This means that applying the IPSec policies to domains, organisational units, or individual machines and users, depend on the organisational requirements and how the Group Policy is used (Weber, 2002). Although, it is possible to assign the local IPSec policies to the computers that are not members of a trusted domain, but distributing the IPSec policies, managing the IPSec policy configuration and trust relationships is much more time-con-

Table 4–2. Microsoft IPSec Components

Component	Description
Active Directory	The Windows Active Directory stores domain-wide IPSec policies for computers that are members of the domain. Active Directory-based IPSec policies are polled and retrieved by the Policy Agent.
Policy Agent	The Policy Agent retrieves IPSec policy from an Active Directory domain, a configured set of local policies, or a local cache. The Policy Agent then distributes authentication and security settings to the IKE component and the IP filters to the IPSec driver.
Internet Key Exchange (IKE)	IKE receives authentication and security settings from the Policy Agent and waits for requests to negotiate IPSec Security Associations (SAs). When requested by the IPSec driver, IKE negotiates both kinds of SAs (main mode and quick mode) with the appropriate endpoint requested by the IPSec driver based on the policy settings obtained from the Policy Agent. After negotiating an IPSec SA, IKE sends the SA settings to the IPSec driver.
IPsec Driver	The IPSec driver monitors and secures outbound unicast IP traffic and monitors, decrypts, and validates inbound unicast IP traffic. After the IPSec driver receives the filters from the Policy Agent, it determines which packets are permitted, which are blocked, or which are secured. For secure traffic, the IPSec driver either uses active SA settings to secure the traffic or requests that new SAs be created. The IPSec driver is bound to the TCP/IP driver to provide IPSec processing for IP packets that pass through the TCP/IP driver.
TCP/IP Driver	The TCP/IP driver is the Windows Server 2003 implementation of the TCP/IP protocol. It is a kernel-mode component that is loaded from the tcpip.sys file during start-up.

suming for computers that are not members of a trusted domain. However, the IPSec policy design and management must take into account the delays that result from the replication of Group Policy data from domain controllers to domain members. Normally, the first step in troubleshooting a problem with the IPSec connectivity is to determine whether the computer in question has the most current Group Policy assignment. To do this, the client must be a member of the local administrators group on the computer for which troubleshooting is being performed. The Policy Agent retrieves the IPSec policy information, which handles the internal interpretation and processing of the policy, and sends it to the other IPSec components that require the information to perform security services (Microsoft, 2003). The Policy Agent has two main functions - to acquire and distribute the IPSec policies that the administrator has defined. It first acquires the IPSec policy from the appropriate policy store, which will either be the Active Directory, a set of local configuration policies, or a local cache of policies. The appropriate policy components are then distributed to either the IKE module where the authentication and security settings go or to the IPSec Driver where the IP filters go.

The IKE generates keys for the IPSec protocols. It is also used to negotiate keys for other protocols that need keys. The IKE performs mutual authentication between two parties and establishes an IKE SA that includes shared secret information that can be used to efficiently establish SAs for ESP, AH and a set of cryptographic algorithms to be used by the SAs for protecting the traffic they carry [see RFC 4306 documentation for further details]. The IKE probably has the most complex job of the IPSec architecture. The SA contains set of policies and keys that are used to protect information. The ISAKMP SA is the shared policy and key(s) used by the negotiating peers, for protecting the communication [see RFC 2409 documentation for further details]. The function of the IKE is to negotiate SA for both the ISAKMP and the IPSec. It does this based on the authentication and security settings received from the Policy Agent. The IKE component is controlled (started, stopped and restarted) by the Policy Agent service.

The IPSec driver is instrumental to the enforcement of the policy and stores the SA information in the internal SA database before initiating the go-between among the TCP/IP driver, application and IPSec policy. It is a kernel-mode component that monitors and secures IP packets. In addition to the Policy Agent and IKE, the IPSec driver uses the following components: the SAD, the SPD, the TCP/IP driver, TCP/IP applications, and the network interface. The IPSec driver must matches IP packet information with the IP filters that are configured in the active SPD. If traffic must be secured, the IPSec driver used the appropriate SA to determine how to provide packet security or requests the IKE module negotiates the IPSec to be used to provide packet security. After the IPSec driver determines which SA to use, it creates and validates encrypting, decrypting, and hashing to create or interpret the AH and ESP headers on the IPSec -protected packet (Bragg, 2001; Microsoft, 2003).

The Microsoft's support for IPv6 is quite thorough and develops its own IPv6 stack. But this stack is only included in windows XP and above. The Windows 2000 (with service pack 1 or above) requires the installation of the Microsoft IPv6 Technology Preview for Windows 2000. When installed it provides the basic IPv6 functionality for testing purposes. It was never planned to have the production quality of IPv6 for Windows 2000 or earlier versions. The package is difficult to install, it would not install if the service pack 2 or above is installed. The procedure may need to be manually installed after a service pack upgrade. Microsoft considers the patch a technology preview and do not recommend running it in a production environment. For these reasons, Windows XP or Windows 2003 are a better choice for running IPv6 on a Windows platform, which includes the following command line utilities used to configure and monitor the IPv6 functionality of the host. The syntax is expressed in Commands 4.30 and 4.31, while Figure 4–3 presents the screen shot:

C:\net start tcpipv6 (4.30)

C:\net stop tcpipv6 (4.31)

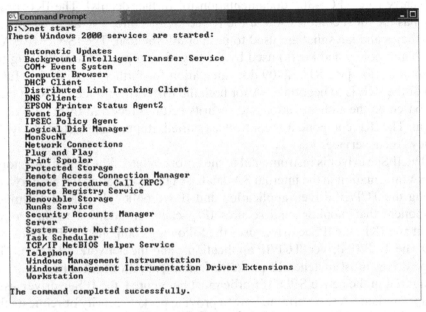

Figure 4–3. Screen shot: net.exe

Other executable basic utility are as follows:

- Ipv6.exe: basic utility that configures network interfaces and updates the routing table. It also retrieve and displays information about the IPv6 protocol
- 6to4cfg.exe: utility that sets up and configures 6to4
- ping6.exe: tracert6.exe: the IPv6 versions of the utilities
- ttcp.exe: utility that sends TCP or UDP data between two network nodes. It is useful to test speed and throughput both for IPv4 and IPv6
- ipsec.exe: utility that configures policies and security associations for the IPv6 IPSec traffic.

4.1 Windows XP

The Windows XP comes with IPv6 support by default, although it needs to be enabled manually, the service pack 1 and update q817778 are both in the command shell. Without updating the q817778 in a command prompt, the command ipv6 would not be installed. The syntax is expressed in Commands 4–32 and 4–33; while Figure 4–4 presents the screen shot:

C:\ netsh interface ipv6 install (4.32)

C:\ netsh interface ipv6 set privacy disabled persistent (4.33)

```
C:\>ipv6 install
Installing...
Succeeded.

C:\>
```

Figure 4–4. Screen shot: IPv6 install

Windows XP Service Pack 1 also supports the IPv6 via the Network Connections control panel (see Figure 4–5 for the screen shot).

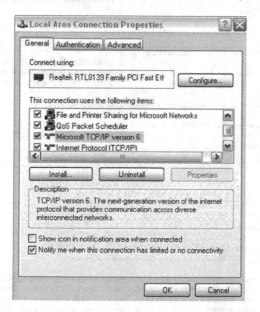

Figure 4–5. Screen shot: IPv6 via network connections control panel

The stack shipped with Service Pack 1 is of production quality, and the earlier versions are developer previews. Despite this, the stack shipped with Service Pack 1 identifies itself as a developer's edition. This is slightly confusing but not actually harmful. Service Pack 2 extends this support even further, including an IPv6 firewall by default and Toredo, which allows IPv6 through

NAT. Most of the configuration in the stack shipped can be done with the IPv6 command, with finer control over the stack available using netsh. The basic testing of IPv6 and IPv4 connectivity can be accomplished with ipconfig, ping6 and tracert6 (see Figures 4–6 to 4–12 for the screen shots).

```
Command Prompt                                                    _ □

Windows IP Configuration

Ethernet adapter Local Area Connection:

        Media State . . . . . . . . . . . : Media disconnected

PPP adapter Speedtouch Connection:

        Connection-specific DNS Suffix  . :
        IP Address. . . . . . . . . . . . : 80.42.195.41
        Subnet Mask . . . . . . . . . . . : 255.255.255.255
        Default Gateway . . . . . . . . . : 80.42.195.41

Tunnel adapter Teredo Tunneling Pseudo-Interface:

        Connection-specific DNS Suffix  . :
        IP Address. . . . . . . . . . . . : fe80::5445:5245:444f%4
        Default Gateway . . . . . . . . . :

Tunnel adapter 6to4 Tunneling Pseudo-Interface:

        Connection-specific DNS Suffix  . :
        IP Address. . . . . . . . . . . . : 2002:502a:c329::502a:c329
        Default Gateway . . . . . . . . . : 2002:c058:6301::c058:6301
                                            2002:836b:213c:1:e0:8f08:f020:8

Tunnel adapter Automatic Tunneling Pseudo-Interface:

        Connection-specific DNS Suffix  . :
        IP Address. . . . . . . . . . . . : fe80::5efe:80.42.195.41%2
        Default Gateway . . . . . . . . . :

C:\>
```

Figure 4–6. Screen shot: ipconfig command

```
C:\>ping6 www.kame.net

Pinging www.kame.net [2001:200:0:8002:203:47ff:fea5:3085]
from 2002:502a:c329::502a:c329 with 32 bytes of data:

Reply from 2001:200:0:8002:203:47ff:fea5:3085: bytes=32 time=326ms
Reply from 2001:200:0:8002:203:47ff:fea5:3085: bytes=32 time=328ms
Reply from 2001:200:0:8002:203:47ff:fea5:3085: bytes=32 time=328ms
Reply from 2001:200:0:8002:203:47ff:fea5:3085: bytes=32 time=328ms

Ping statistics for 2001:200:0:8002:203:47ff:fea5:3085:
    Packets: Sent = 4, Received = 4, Lost = 0 (0% loss),
Approximate round trip times in milli-seconds:
    Minimum = 326ms, Maximum = 328ms, Average = 327ms

C:\>
```

Figure 4–7. Screen shot: ping6 command

```
C:\>tracert6 www.kame.net

Tracing route to www.kame.net [2001:200:0:8002:203:47ff:fea5:3085]
from 2002:502a:c329::502a:c329 over a maximum of 30 hops:

  1      39 ms     62 ms     46 ms   2001:620:0:c000::9
  2      46 ms     62 ms     62 ms   swiZH2-10GE-1-3.switch.ch [2001:620:0:c015::2
]
  3      46 ms     46 ms     46 ms   swiCE3-10GE-1-1.switch.ch [2001:620:0:c027::1
]
  4      46 ms     78 ms     46 ms   swiCE2-10GE-1-4.switch.ch [2001:620:0:c03d::1
]
  5      46 ms     46 ms     46 ms   2001:798:2012:10aa::1
  6      62 ms     78 ms    140 ms   ch.fr1.fr.geant.net [2001:798:20cc:1201:1601:
:2]
  7      62 ms     78 ms     62 ms   fr.uk1.uk.geant.net [2001:798:20cc:1601:2801:
:2]
  8     155 ms    140 ms    140 ms   uk.ny1.ny.geant.net [2001:798:20cc:1c01:2801:
:1]
  9     136 ms    140 ms    140 ms   nycmng-geant.abilene.ucaid.edu [2001:468:ff:1
5c3::1]
 10     156 ms    156 ms    140 ms   chinng-nycmng.abilene.ucaid.edu [2001:468:ff:
f15::1]
 11     187 ms    140 ms    140 ms   iplsng-chinng.abilene.ucaid.edu [2001:468:ff:
f12::2]
 12     156 ms    156 ms    155 ms   kscyng-iplsng.abilene.ucaid.edu [2001:468:ff:
1213::2]
 13     171 ms    171 ms    156 ms   dnvrng-kscyng.abilene.ucaid.edu [2001:468:ff:
1013::1]
 14     203 ms    187 ms    218 ms   snvang-dnvrng.abilene.ucaid.edu [2001:468:ff:
1017::2]
 15     327 ms    328 ms    328 ms   3ffe:80a::b2
 16       *         *       311 ms   2001:200:0:8002:203:47ff:fea5:3085

Trace complete.

C:\>
```

Figure 4–8. Screen shot: tracert6 command

```
C:\>ipv6 rc
2001:200:0:8002:203:47ff:fea5:3085 via 3/2002:c058:6301::c058:6301
     src 3/2002:502a:c329::502a:c329
     PMTU 1280
     252 seconds since ICMP error
2002:c058:6301::c058:6301 via 3/2002:c058:6301::c058:6301
     src 3/2002:502a:c329::502a:c329
     PMTU 1280
     395 seconds since ICMP error
2002:836b:213c::836b:213c via 3/2002:836b:213c::836b:213c
     src 3/2002:502a:c329::502a:c329
     PMTU 1280
     396 seconds since ICMP error
C:\>
```

Figure 4–9. Screen shot: ipv6 rc (view the route cache)

```
C:\>ipv6 nc
5: fe80::220:edff:fe35:36ab                              incomplete
4: fe80::5445:5245:444f 0.0.0.0:0              permanent
3: 2002:c058:6301::c058:6301 192.88.99.1           permanent
3: 2002:836b:213c::836b:213c 131.107.33.60         permanent
3: 2002:502a:c329::502a:c329 127.0.0.1             permanent
3: 2002:836b:213c:1:e0:8f08:f020:8 131.107.33.60        permanent
2: fe80::5efe:80.42.195.41 127.0.0.1              permanent
1:            fe80::1                    permanent
1:              ::1                      permanent

C:\>
```

Figure 4–10. Screen shot: ipv6 nc (view the neighbour cache)

```
▨ Command Prompt                                                    _ 5
C:\>ipv6 if
Interface 5: Ethernet: Local Area Connection
  Guid <9F9E9130-F387-4BE4-A8F1-B01FB19054D3>
  cable unplugged
  uses Neighbor Discovery
  uses Router Discovery
  link-layer address: 00-20-ed-35-36-ab
    tentative link-local fe80::220:edff:fe35:36ab, life infinite
    multicast interface-local ff01::1, 1 refs, not reportable
    multicast link-local ff02::1, 1 refs, not reportable
    multicast link-local ff02::1:ff35:36ab, 1 refs, last reporter
  link MTU 1500 (true link MTU 1500)
  current hop limit 128
  reachable time 43500ms (base 30000ms)
  retransmission interval 1000ms
  DAD transmits 1
  default site prefix length 48
Interface 4: Teredo Tunneling Pseudo-Interface
  Guid <528BE5F9-A887-4D27-9E95-25C3670436AB>
  zones: link 4 site 2
  cable unplugged
  uses Neighbor Discovery
  uses Router Discovery
  routing preference 2
  link-layer address: 0.0.0.0:0
    preferred link-local fe80::5445:5245:444f, life infinite
    multicast interface-local ff01::1, 1 refs, not reportable
    multicast link-local ff02::1, 1 refs, not reportable
  link MTU 1280 (true link MTU 1280)
  current hop limit 128
  reachable time 31500ms (base 30000ms)
  retransmission interval 1000ms
  DAD transmits 0
  default site prefix length 48
Interface 3: 6to4 Tunneling Pseudo-Interface
  Guid <A995346E-9F3E-2EDB-47D1-9CC7BA01CD73>
  does not use Neighbor Discovery
  does not use Router Discovery
  routing preference 1
    preferred global 2002:502a:c329::502a:c329, life infinite
  link MTU 1280 (true link MTU 65515)
  current hop limit 128
  reachable time 30000ms (base 30000ms)
  retransmission interval 1000ms
  DAD transmits 0
  default site prefix length 48
Interface 2: Automatic Tunneling Pseudo-Interface
  Guid <48FCE3FC-EC30-E50E-F1A7-71172AEEE3AE>
  does not use Neighbor Discovery
  does not use Router Discovery
```

Figure 4–11. Screen shot: ipv6 if (view interface information)

```
C:W>ipv6 ifc
usage: ipv6 [-p] [-v] if [ifindex]
       ipv6 [-p] ifcr v6v4 v4src v4dst [nd] [pmld]
       ipv6 [-p] ifcr 6over4 v4src
       ipv6 [-p] ifc ifindex [forwards] [-forwards] [advertises] [-advertises]
mtu #bytes] [site site-identifier] [preference P]
       ipv6 rlu ifindex v4dst
       ipv6 [-p] ifd ifindex
       ipv6 [-p] adu ifindex/address [life validlifetime[/preflifetime]] [anyca:
t] [unicast]
       ipv6 nc [ifindex [address]]
       ipv6 ncf [ifindex [address]]
       ipv6 rc [ifindex address]
       ipv6 rcf [ifindex [address]]
       ipv6 bc
       ipv6 [-p] [-v] rt
       ipv6 [-p] rtu prefix ifindex[/address] [life valid[/pref]] [preference P
[publish] [age] [spl SitePrefixLength]
       ipv6 spt
       ipv6 spu prefix ifindex [life L]
       ipv6 [-p] gp
       ipv6 [-p] gpu [parameter value] ... <try -?>
       ipv6 renew [ifindex]
       ipv6 [-p] ppt
       ipv6 [-p] ppu prefix precedence P srclabel SL [dstlabel DL]
       ipv6 [-p] ppd prefix
       ipv6 [-p] reset
       ipv6 install
       ipv6 uninstall
Some subcommands require local Administrator privileges.

C:W>_
```

Figure 4–12. Screen shot: ipv6 ifc (configure interface attribute)

4.2   Windows 2003

The Windows Server 2003 has the IPv6 support, but does not switched on by default. This version of Windows also includes the option to install the IPv6 protocol through the graphical user interface. The IPv6 command have been deprecated in Server 2003, and the equivalent netsh commands are now preferred. The graphical user interface works very well, so there is no need to experiment with the command line just for installing the IPv6. The IPv6 can be enabled via the command line by running netsh interface IPv6 install, or from the Network Connections control panel and right click on a LAN interface to edit its Properties -> Install -> Protocol -> Add -> Microsoft TCP/IP version 6 (see Figure 4–13 for the screen shot).

The support for the IPv6 ping and traceroute are also available in the traditional ping and tracert commands without the "6" suffix.

5.   LINUX

The first IPv6 related network code was added to the Linux kernel 2.1.8, in November 1996 by Pedro Roque. It was based on the BSD API but due to

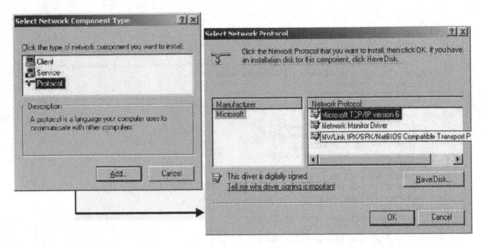

Figure 4–13. Screen shot: Windows 2003 IPv6 via network connections

lack of manpower, the IPv6 implementation in the kernel was unable to follow the discussed drafts or newly released RFCs. In October 2000, a project was initiated in Japan, called USAGI (Universal play Ground for IPv6) project, which aim at implementing all missing, or outdated IPv6 support in Linux. It tracks the current IPv6 implementation in FreeBSD made by the KAME project. Unfortunately, the USAGI patch is so big, that current Linux networking maintainers are unable to include it in the production source of the Linux kernel 2.4.x series. The 2.4.x series is missing some extensions and does not confirmed to all current drafts and available RFCs documentation. The latter can cause some interoperability problems with other operating systems. Another problem is a lack of user support. Linux distributor should provide the documents or user guide for the IPv6 to work with the Linux system (Murphy and Malone, 2005).

6.   SOLARIS

The SUN Microsystems's IPv6 implementations began with an early prototype for Solaris 7, which could be additionally installed. Solaris 8 and 9 are fully IPv6-capable. The IPv6 is enabled when the Solaris software is install. To manually enabling the IPv6, it is necessary to login as a super user because the super user access enabled the IPv6 on the node and create file /etct/hostname6.interface by using the command touch/ etct/hostname6.interface at the command line. When the system is rebooted, it requires the ifconfig at the command line, which displays both the IP and MAC addresses, and the IPv6 address is added to the appropriate name service (NIS, NIS+ or DNS). For the

NIS+ a table named ipnodes.org_dir is added, which contains both IPv4 and IPv6 addresses of the host. The existing host.org_dir table that contains the IPv4 addresses within the host remains the same in other to facilitate existing applications. To enable the IPv6 addresses, appropriate DNS zone file should be edited by adding AAAA records to the host. The full detail explanation of AAAA and PTR records are available in the RFC 1886 documentation. The following commands are used for monitoring IPv6 in Solaris OS:

i.   ifconfig displays the systems IP and MAC address. It enabled the Ethernet interface to be marked up and down, and the IPv6 and tunnelling module to be plumbed.
ii. netstart displays network status information. The network interface shows how many packets are passing through and the errors that are occurring. This command is used in identifying overloaded networks where the packet collision rate would be much higher than what is expected. It is also possible to choose which protocol information to display by setting the default_IP value in the /etc/defaul/inet_type and –f command line option. The ARP table for IPv4 and the neighbour cache for IPv6 are display by –p option.
iii. snoop captured and inspects the packet. The captured packets can be displayed as they are received or saved into a file and analysed later. This command produced large amounts of data and also displays IPv6 headers, extension headers, ICMPv6 headers and the neighbour discovery protocol data. If the ip or ip6 protocol keywords are specified, the snoop command displays both the IPv4 and IPv6 packets.
iv. ping (packet Internet groper) send the ICMP packet to another host to test the network status, which allows continuous packet or specified number of packets to be sent. The ping uses both IPv4 and IPv6 protocols to probe the target hosts.
v.   traceroute probe all multi-homed host addresses and for tracing both IPv4 and IPv6 routes to specific host.

In our laboratory experiment, the Unix systems were used to demonstrate Solaris implementation. The telnet command was use to login to the systems, the primary Ethernet interface was 'hme0' but the ls command were used instead of 'hme0' in this experiment (see Figure 4–14 for the screen shot).

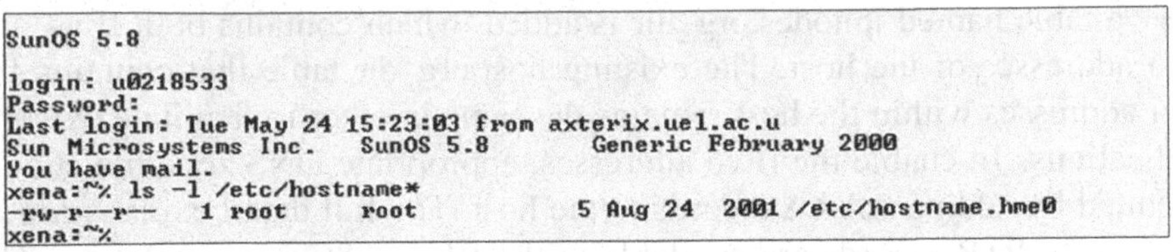

```
SunOS 5.8

login: u0218533
Password:
Last login: Tue May 24 15:23:03 from axterix.uel.ac.u
Sun Microsystems Inc.    SunOS 5.8      Generic February 2000
You have mail.
xena:~% ls -l /etc/hostname*
-rw-r--r--   1 root      root            5 Aug 24  2001 /etc/hostname.hme0
xena:~%
```

Figure 4–14. Screen shot: find out hostname. * files

To enable the IPSec security policies, /etc/inet/ipsecinit.conf file should be created to initialise configuration file with specific IPSec entries (see Figure 4–15 for the screen shot).

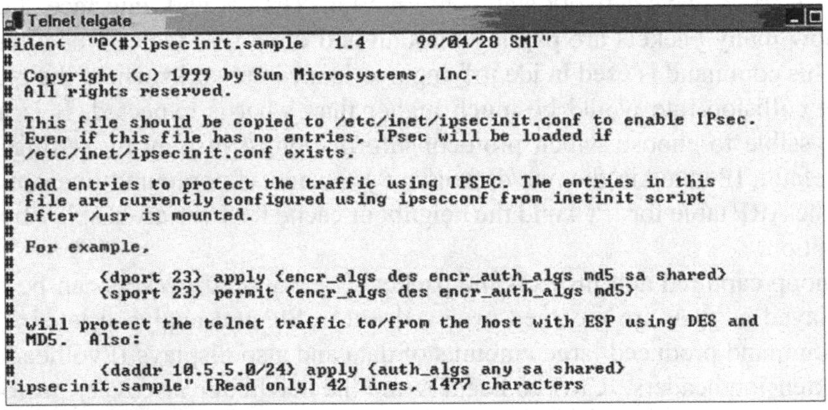

```
Telnet telgate                                                          _ ▢
#ident  "@(#)ipsecinit.sample   1.4     99/04/28 SMI"
#
# Copyright (c) 1999 by Sun Microsystems, Inc.
# All rights reserved.
#
# This file should be copied to /etc/inet/ipsecinit.conf to enable IPsec.
# Even if this file has no entries, IPsec will be loaded if
# /etc/inet/ipsecinit.conf exists.
#
# Add entries to protect the traffic using IPSEC. The entries in this
# file are currently configured using ipsecconf from inetinit script
# after /usr is mounted.
#
# For example,
#
#        {dport 23} apply {encr_algs des encr_auth_algs md5 sa shared}
#        {sport 23} permit {encr_algs des encr_auth_algs md5}
#
# will protect the telnet traffic to/from the host with ESP using DES and
# MD5.   Also:
#
#        {daddr 10.5.5.0/24} apply {auth_algs any sa shared}
"ipsecinit.sample" [Read only] 42 lines, 1477 characters
```

Figure 4–15. Screen short: Sample of ipsecinit.conf file

Solaris software include sample of ipsecinit.conf file, which is use as a template to create ipsecinit. An empty file /etc/hostname6.hme0 for IPv6 can be created using the vi editor: # touch /etc/hostname6.hme0. The vi editor was used to create the hostname.* files and execute the following command for every interface to initialise the IPv6 stack (inet6). The syntax is expressed in Commands 4.34:

ifconfig hme0 inet6 plumb up   (4.34)

The netstat command displays the IPv6 network status (see Figure 4–16 for the screen shot).

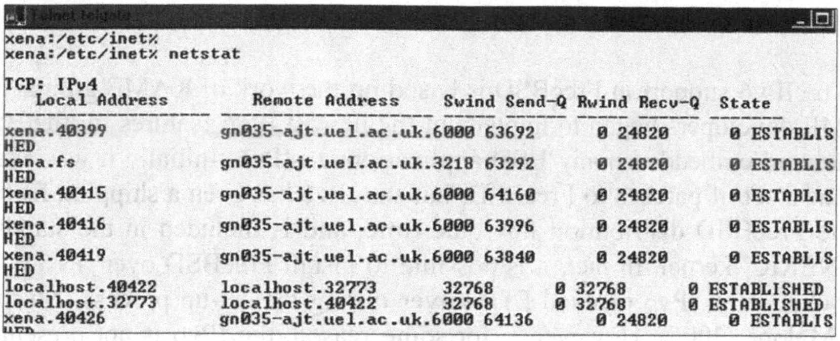

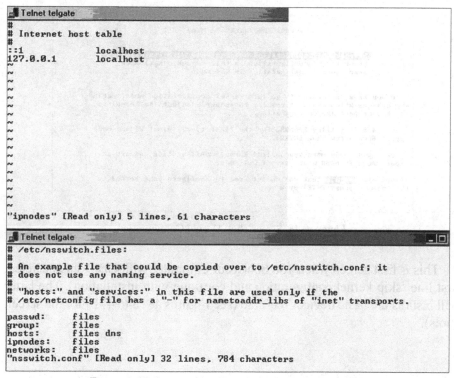

Figure 4–16. Screen shot: netstat command

The traditional /etc/hosts database is a symbolic link to /etc/inet/hosts that is only used for IPv4 addresses in Solaris.

Figure 4–17. Screen shot: IP nodes and nsswitch.conf file

The /etc/inet/ipnodes, can be used by both the IPv4 and v6 name lookups that controlled the settings in /etc/nsswitch (see Figure 4–17 for the screen shot).

7.   FREEBSD

The IPv6 support in FreeBSD is based on the work of KAME group. The KAME developers began to implement the newest IPv6 features for the BSD kernel and embedded many BSD applications to IPv6. Initially it was available as a set of patches to FreeBSD, but the IPv6 has been a shipping feature of the FreeBSD distribution for some time, and is included in the standard 'GENERIC' kernel. In fact, it is possible to install FreeBSD over IPv6 if the user choose an IPv6 enabled FTP server during the set-up process (Murphy and Malone, 2005). However, if for some reason, the IPv6 is not present in the system kernel, the user will need to recompile it after adding the options INET6 line to the kernel configuration (see Figure 4–18 for screenshot). It is possible to install from FTP, http, nfs, or CD Rom. The CDRom installation was used in the laboratory experiments.

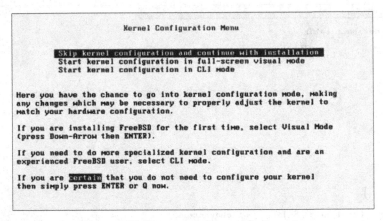

Figure 4–18. Screen shot: Kernel Configuration

This is first screen when you boot your computer with CD Rom and select first line 'skip kernel configuration and continue with installation'. The latter will installs the basic devices required (see Figures 4–18 to 4–19 for the screen shots).

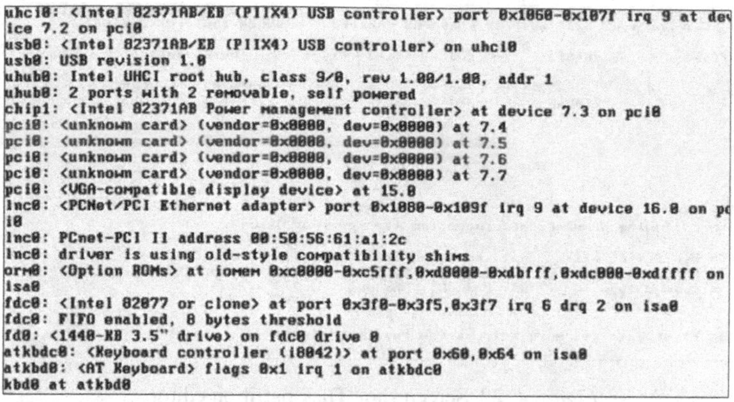

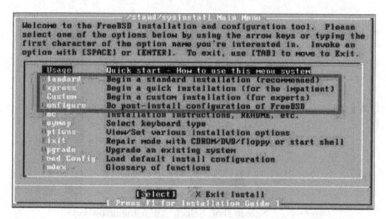

Figure 4–19. Screen shot: Kernel automatically recognises devices

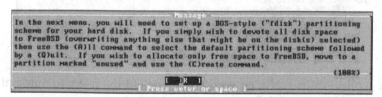

Figure 4–20. Screen shot: Installation main menu

The installation main menu has a unique inner triangle, which captured the standard/express/custom menu. The user can choose the option of how to proceed. Ideally, it is recommended to chose standard and press enter (see Figures 4–20 to 4–29 for the screen shots).

Figure 4–21. Screen shot: Disk partition

This message is for the disk partition and format. It is the same as windows installation.

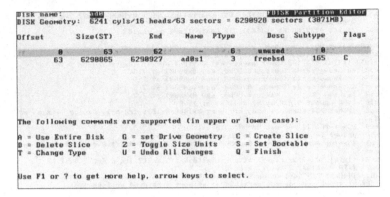

Figure 4–22. Screen shot: Disk partition editor

The user will be required to proceed by pressing 'Q'.

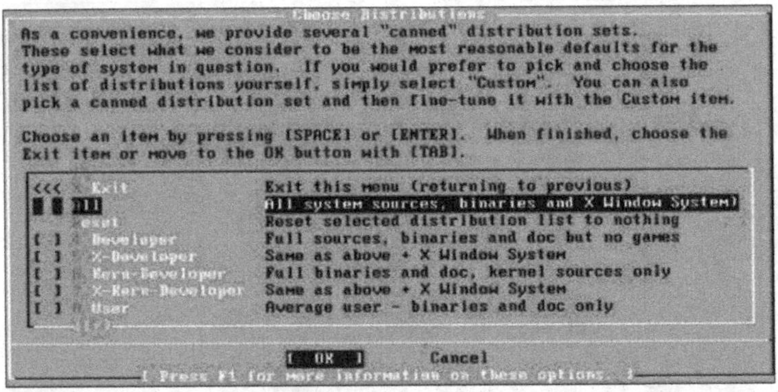

Figure 4–23. Screen shot: Select 'All' using arrow keys.

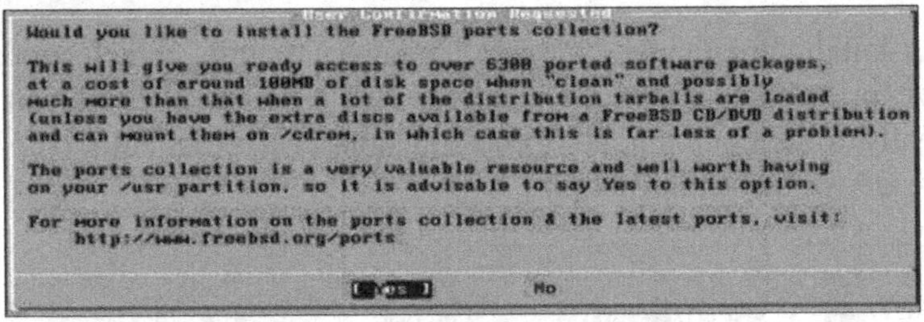

Figure 4–24. Screen shot: User confirmation requested

Ports collection is really powerful and enabled the users to automatically download and install the default ports if click 'Yes'.

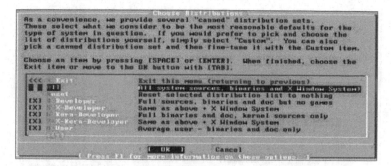

Figure 4–25. Screen shot: Canned distribution sets

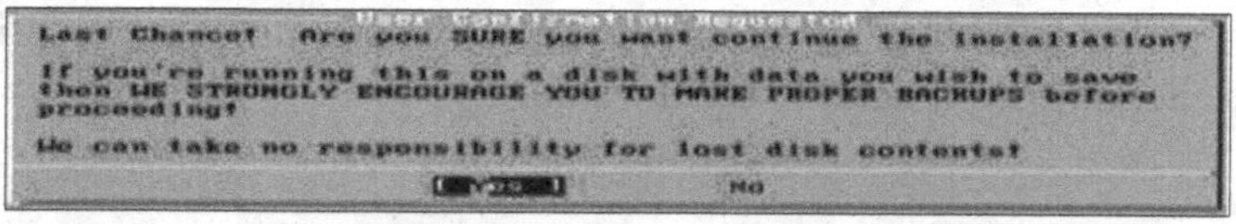

Figure 4–26. Screen shot: Notification message for lost disk contents

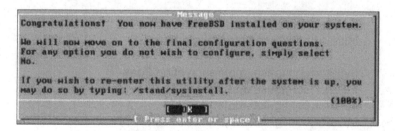

Figure 4–27. Screen shot: Notification message for extracting sshare command

Figure 4–28. Screen shot: Notification message for completing installation

There are so many screens that were shown during installation, which are information disseminating only and also it is difficult to capture all the screens passing by. But when the final screen appears, it signifies that the installation is done!

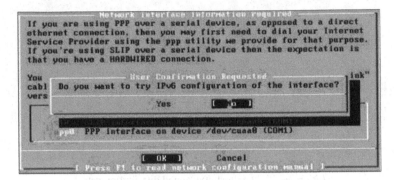

Figure 4–29. Screen shot: Network interface information required

The IPv6 is available in all *BSD platforms by default; it can be verified by using the 'ifconfig' command to see the status.

8. CISCO IOS IPSEC CONFIGURATION OVERVIEW

The security requirements should be based on the organisation's network security policy. The Cisco IOS configuration initiator and responder routers are detailed in Figures 4–30 and 4–31, and configuration steps for the IPSec in VPNs are presented below:

```
Initiator(config)#hostname Initiator
Initiator(config)#crypto isakmp policy 1

Initiator(config-isakmp)#encryption 3des
Initiator(config-isakmp)#group 2
Initiator(config-isakmp)#hash sha
Initiator(config-isakmp)#authentication pre-share
Initiator(config)#crypto isakmp key MyKey address xxx.xx.xxx.xx
Initiator(config)#crypto ipsec transform-set myset esp-3des
    esp-md5-hmac
Initiator(config)#crypto map vpn 10 ipsec-isakmp
Initiator(config-crypto-map)#set peer xxx.xx.xxx.xx
Initiator(config-crypto-map)#set transform-set myset
Initiator(config-crypto-map)#match address 101
! Initiator(config)#interface ethernet1/0
Initiator(config)#crypto map vpn
! Initiator(config)#access-list 101 permit ip 10.1.1.0 0.0.0.255
    10.1.2.0 0.0.0.255
```

Figure 4–30. IOS Configuration at Initiator Router

- Determine security requirements for the IPSec implementation. As the process of IPSec implementation is complicated, a clear and concise understanding of the security requirements and a subsequent planning greatly reduces the risk of mis-configurations.
- Configure the IKE and create IKE/ISAKMP policies in order to establish SAs for the IPSec.
- Configure transform sets to specify the encryption suites that will be used by the IPSec to protect the data, e.g. AH, ESP, etc.
- Configure crypto access lists use the IP extended access lists to specify, which traffic will be encrypted.
- Configure crypto maps are used to consolidate the different policy details.
- The crypto maps are applied to the desired interfaces.
- Testing and verifying the IPSec in VPN debug commands are available within the Cisco IOS.

It is necessary to consider the following as part of the steps that should be taken before implementing Cisco IOS IPSec:

- Each router's name and IP address
- Source host or subnet from which packets should be encrypted

```
Responder(config)#hostname Responder
Responder(config)#crypto isakmp policy 1

Responder(config-isakmp)#encryption 3des
Responder(config-isakmp)#group 2
Responder(config-isakmp)#hash sha
Responder(config-isakmp)#authentication pre-share
Responder(config)#crypto isakmp key MyKey address
    xxx.xx.xxx.xx
Responder(config)#crypto ipsec transform-set myset esp-3des
    esp-md5-hmac
Responder(config)#crypto map vpn 10 ipsec-isakmp
Responder(config-crypto-map)#set peer xxx.xx.xxx.xx
Responder(config-crypto-map)#set transform-set myset
Responder(config-crypto-map)#match address 101
!
Responder(config)#interface ethernet1/0
Responder(config)#crypto map vpn
!
Responder(config)#access-list 101 permit ip 10.1.2.0 0.0.0.255
    10.1.1.0 0.0.0.255
```

Figure 4–31. IOS Configuration at Responder Router

- The packet types that need to be encrypted (TCP, UDP, IP, etc)
- Router interfaces through which encrypted packets must be sent and received
- Ensuring that any configured access lists are compatible with the IPSec
- Encryption algorithms to use between peer encrypting routers (DES, 3DES, etc.)

The overall IPSec process is divided into two main phases. When testing and verifying the IPSec in VPN, the relevant commands available in the IOS are also categorised into the two phases. The commands available for testing and verifying phase 1 and phase 2 are expressed in syntax 4.35 to 4.43

Router#show crypto isakmp policy   (4.35)

To view the configured IKE/ISAKMP policy at a peer.

Router#show crypto isakmp sa   (4.36)

To view information about the IKE SAs at a peer.

Router#clear crypto isakmp   (4.37)

To clear active IKE/ISAKMP SAs.

Router#debug crypto isakmp   (4.38)

To display debug messages about the IKE/ISAKMP negotiations.

Router#show crypto ipsec transform-set   (4.39)

To view the configured transform sets.

Router#show crypto map.   (4.40)

To view the crypto map configuration and the settings used by current SAs.

Router#show crypto ipsec sa (4.41)

To view information about the IPSec SAs at a peer.

Router#clear crypto sa (4.42)

Delete the IPSec SAs from the SA database.

Router#debug crypto ipsec (4.43)

To display debug messages about all the IPSec actions.

Other important considerations are determined by the specific details relating to the IPSec peers. For example the number of routers and the particular IPSec features to be implemented.

8.1   Other OS

It is unlikely that useful IPv6 support for Windows 98 or NT4 will be forthcoming from Microsoft. But the third party support is available via products such as Trumpet Winsock and Hitachi's Toonet6. The MacOS X is BSD running in the Darwin kernel. Furthermore, the version 10.2 Apple is fully supported by the IPv6 and the configurable graphical user interface for network options.

9.   ROUTERS

There are many IPv6 supported routers from different vendors; the results of the questionnaire survey that was conducted revealed that Cisco and Juniper routers are most commonly used. Although with Cisco, it is not easy to say which platforms contain the IPv6 functionality and to what extend, as there are so many different releases of their software. Although Cisco detail support for the IPv6 across their various routers and documented how to configure the different features. However, configuring the IPv6 in Cisco is typically straightforward, if one is already familiar with the procedure in IPv4. The IOS commands are derivable from the names of their predecessors (Cisco, 05).

The Juniper has been offering IPv6 support since the 5.1 releases of JunOS. This support covers the core parts of the IPv6; the protocol itself, forwarding, the IPv6 over various media, and all-routing protocols. The hardware support has been extended to all Juniper's platforms and interface cards. The commands are fairly similar to their IPv4 equivalents. To configure an IPv6 address on an interface, one substitutes family inet6 for family inet.

9.1   Enabling and Testing

The boot time behaviour in most platforms is to perform auto-configuration, unless they are explicitly configured otherwise. The Table 4–3 shows a summary of how to enabled the IPv6 at boot time on various operating systems.

Table 4–3. Enabling IPv6 on various operating systems

OS	Enabling IPv6
Solaris	Create an empty /etc/hostnme6.interfacename
WinXP	ipv6 install
Win 2003	netsh interface ipv6 install
FreeBSD	Add ipv6_enable="YES" to /etc/tc.conf
Linux(Red hat)	Add networking_ipv6="yes" to /etc/sysconfig/network

Table 4–4. Displaying IPv6 interface information

OS	Showing Configured addresses
MacOS X	ifconfig –a
Solaris	ls –l /etc/hostname.*
winXP	Ipv6 if

Table 4–5. Basic IPv6 command

OS	Ping	Trace route
Solaris	ping –A inet6 –I if	traceroute –A inet6
Linux	ping6 –I if	tracetoute6
winXP	ping6	tracert6
Win2003	ping	tracert
FreeBSD	ping6 –I if	traceroute6
Mac OS X	ping6 –I if	traceroute6

*Note: IPv6 is specifically written in small letters within the commands

To ping link-local addresses, the installer may need to specify the interface to use during implementation. The IPSec configured addresses for MacOSx, Solaris, and WinXP is presented in Table 4–4. The most useful test is to check the ping local host. The configuration of the pings and the trace route (link-local addresses) is presented in Table 4–5.

10.   LIMITATIONS OF THE IPSEC

Unfortunately, there is a tendency amongst many organisations to regard IPSec as an all-inclusive security solution. As a result of this misconception, the IPSec is considered as a solution to all security concerns. There is an old adage that says 'if your most familiar tool is a hammer, the whole world starts to look like a nail'. The essence of security is finding the right balance between protecting the business interests and resources, and letting people get their work done (Harrison, 2003).

> 'It has become appallingly obvious that our technology has exceeded our humanity.'
> —Albert Einstein (1879– 1955)

Network security is best implemented as part of a comprehensive corporate policy and quite often involves the deployment of a variety of security solutions. Although the IPSec is a robust and versatile framework for securing IP communications, it is not a complete solution for all deployments. As with any other protocol or standard, the IPSec has its shortcomings.

10.1   IPSec Peer/Key Management

In an environment where the IPSec is largely deployed, the administrative overhead of maintaining the IPSec peers and managing the keys becomes a nightmare. However, in this circumstance the IPSec does not provide any mechanism for automating the configuration process of hundreds of networks wishing to establish the IPSec VPNs with each other, and each peer needs to be configured individually. The implementation and maintenance of a large IPSec network is very resource intensive, with large corporations often forced to employ dedicated IT staff to manage the network.

10.2   Interaction With Multicast Traffic

In multicast data transmissions, there are multiple receivers of a single packet. The SPI protocol field uniquely identifies the IPSec SA and the destination unicast IP address. Although it is possible to use the multicast IP address, but the SPI pose a problem (Doraswamy and Harkins, 2003). In a normal IPSec operation, it is the destination peer that chooses the SPI. However, in multicast communications, there is no single destination for a given address. This clearly poses implementation issues and the streaming of multimedia applications cannot be ignored. Furthermore, the IPSec selection of outgoing IPSec policy parameters is based on the examination of IP addresses, the upper layer protocol ID and port numbers. This works well with protocols that use stable port numbers. However, some application using streaming multimedia utilises UDP and RTP. The source and destination port numbers used for RTP are dynamically assigned, making it very difficult to define the IPSec policies to select the appropriate UDP streams to protect.

10.3   Quality Of Service (QoS)

The end-to-end encryption performed by the IPSec does not allow any intermediary routing devices to check and process flags contained within the original IP headers. The ability to look up certain fields such as the Type of Service (ToS) and IP Precedence fields within IP packet headers is essential to the operation of QoS mechanisms. As a result of the restriction posed by the IPSec, encryption is not possible to secure communications such as IP Telephony data that rely heavily on QoS.

10.4   Resource Consumption

The VPN encryption and decryption processes performed by the IPSec are highly processor intensive. Some vendors offer hardware accelerators for non purpose-built security devices to offload tasks from the main processor. However the purpose built devices tend to have specialised design to handle the demands of the security tasks. An example of such a solution is the VPN Accelerator Card (VAC) from Cisco Systems. This hardware-based VPN accelerator is optimised for repetitive mathematical functions required by the IPSec.

10.5   Configuration Complexity

The configuration process for the IPSec is quite complex. The IPSec has a modular architecture that facilitates great deal of flexibility in bringing together various standards and protocols to create a cohesive security framework. This can be considered a disadvantage. An example of this 'unnecessary flexibility' would be the transport or tunnel mode with either AH or ESP protocols. These additional options do not seem to offer any performance or functionality advantage. There are a number of efforts underway by the IEFT to simplify the policy mechanism for the IPSec but yet none has proposed the SIPSec approach (see chapter 5 for detail discussion).

10.6   Multi-Vendor Interoperability Problems

Due to the complexity of the IKE and the IPSec protocols, it has been difficult to achieve interoperability in a multi-vendor implementation environment. The ICSA Labs have attempted to address this issue by establishing the IPSec Product Developers Consortium and the IPSec Product Certification Testing Program with multi-vendor interoperability as the primary focus. Since it's inception in 1998, the ICSA Labs analysts have identified numerous interoperability problems and have highlighted product configuration issues and genuine flaws in the IPSec architecture. The efforts of ICSA Labs have resulted in the creation of a systematic troubleshooting methodology that many VPN experts now rely on.

10.7 Lack of end-to-end protection

The IPSec secures the communication path; it is rarely used for end-to-end protection of application protocols. It can be used to protect one or more paths between a pair of hosts, between a pair of security gateways, or between a security gateway and a host [see RFC 2401 documentation for further details]. This implies that there is no mechanism in place to secure the communication endpoints, such as the end user machines or applications. This is rather unfortunate, as the original goal of the IPSec was to enable the protection of all types of IP communications. If the communication endpoint becomes compromised, it would be very difficult to analyse the data traversing the VPN tunnel since this data would be encrypted (Jayawickrama, 2003). The IETF is currently working on the integration of common API into the IPSec. This will allow applications to take greater advantage of the IPSec by being able to request appropriate security services from the Network Layer.

10.8 Interaction With Firewalls

The firewall is the first line of most systems defence, when it comes to blocking unwanted traffic passing in or out of network. The Figure 4–32 illustrates the basic concept of a firewall. The three basic design goal of a firewall are as follow:

- The firewalls is the only point of entrance and exist, both incoming and outgoing traffic should pass through the firewall.
- It should only allow authorised traffic that has been defined in the security policy.
- The firewall should be secure and possibly immune to any kind of penetration.

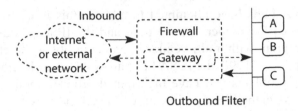

Figure 4–32. Basic concept of a firewall

The filtering of incoming and outgoing traffic is based on a security policy enforced by the network administrator. A set of rules is defined in the security policy that determines how vulnerable the contents are to be considered. The three different kinds of firewalls commonly used in networks are briefly describes below:

i. Packet-filtering router (PFR) applies set of rules to all traffic flowing in or out of the network. The rules are embedded into the TCP/IP header, which includes source and destination addresses, protocol fields and TCP/UDP port numbers.

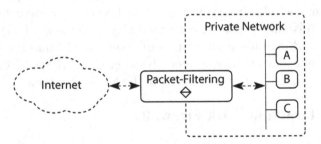

Figure 4–33. Packet-filtering router

If no matching rule is found, the default rule is applied. The default rule can be configured to allow or discard all traffic, which does not match any defined filtering rule. It can forward or discard packets (see Figure 4–33 for diagrammatic illustration).

ii. The Application level gateway (ALG) is commonly referred to as a proxy server and relays on application layer traffic. The user connects to the ALG using a TCP/IP application (Telnet, FTP…). The ALG asks the user for the address of the remote host to be accessed and then authenticates the user by means of a username and password. If the username and password are both correct, then the firewall contacts the application on the remote host and relays on the TCP segments between the two end points (see Figure 4–34 for diagrammatic illustration).

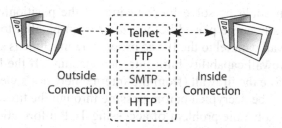

Figure 4–34. ALG connections to the application layer

The ALG is more secure than the PFR as it allows only traffic for specific applications, which are within the proxies. However, one major disadvantage of ALG is the processing overhead in examining traffic for each connection.

iii. The circuit-level gateway (CLG) deals with the virtual circuits that the TCP provides and only use for TCP based application protocols such as Telnet or FTP. The CLG doe not permit end-to-end TCP connection rather it establishes two connections:
   - The CLG and the internal network (TCP user)
   - The CLG and the outer host relays on the TCP segments between the two established connections without examining the contents.

iv. The security policy of the CLG is based on determining which connections would be allowed and which one is to be discarded (see Figure 4–35 for diagrammatic illustration).

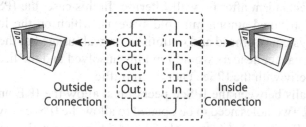

Figure 4–35. CLG connections

The CLG can be configured to support application level or proxy on inbound connections and circuit-level function on outbound connections. In this case the firewall would incurred the processing overhead in examining incoming traffic but not outgoing. However, this configuration should only be deployed if the internal users can be trusted.

No matter what configuration of firewall is used, access to transport layer headers is necessary. When the IPSec is used the TCP information is encrypted and thus the information required by the firewall to enforce the filtering rules is inaccessible. The firewall and the IPSec software vendors have suggested that the problem could be solve by focusing on the positioning of the two devices. A firewall can be placed before, after or in parallel to the gateway. Placing the firewall parallel to the IPSec processing machine is similar to having the IPSec/firewall capability built into one machine. If the IPSec process is performed before the firewall (from the internal network's view) all incoming packets would be decrypted before passing through the firewall. This case would definitely solve the problem of accessing TCP information but creates other serious threats:

i.   If the IPSec processed before the firewall, it implies that an open door is created for attackers to get the entire key to encrypt the traffic outside the firewall.
ii. If the IPSec and firewall is provided within a system i.e. capability is provided to decrypts the packets and then applies the filtering rules, a serious risk of a denial of service attack will still exist. An attacker can capture a legitimate packet and replay it continuously. However, since decryption is a CPU intensive operation, it would be easy to overload the IPSec/firewall system and thereby denying service to legitimate packets.
iii. A bottleneck might be created and legitimate links would not be fully utilised, because of firewall single point of entry and also if system handles the IPSec processing overheads.

With regards to the above problems, it is more effective to put the IPSec processing mechanism after firewall filtering. In this case, the IPSec processing can be distributed among multiple systems, which on the long run will reduced the system overhead and optimised firewall usage but the problem of accessing the packet headers would remains unsolved and the firewall cannot be used correctly with the IPSec encrypted traffic.

The firewalls between the IPSec peers must allow the IKE and the IPSec traffic to pass. Two holes need to be opened to allow the IPSec to work through a firewall (ESP or/and AH (protocols 50 and 51, respectively) and UDP port 500 (for ISAKMP)). In case the firewall is configured on the router terminating the IPSec tunnel itself, the router needs to be opened for ESP or/and AH and ISAKMP traffic. Although this may seem like a potential concern, in reality it should not represent a security hole. This is due to the fact that the IPSec routine drops any packets arriving at the incoming interface without the IP addresses matching the IPSec traffic access list. This is considered an additional configuration overhead.

10.9   Incompatibilities between NAT and the IPSec

The RFC 3715 documentation describes the incompatibilities between Network Address Translation (NAT) and the IPSec. The IPSec does not interoperate with most firewalls and gateways that implement NAT. This is one of the major limitations of the IPSec. Before we can discuss the problems encountered when deploying the IPSec with NAT, it would be useful to provide a brief overview of how NAT works. The NAT was originally developed as a temporary solution to combat IP v4 address depletion and defined in the RFC 1631 documentation as a method of mapping IP addresses from one address realm to another and in turn providing transparent routing to the end hosts.

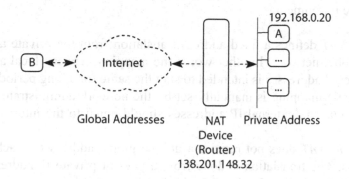

Figure 4–36. NAT implementation

The conceptual understanding of the NAT implementation is diagrammatically illustrated in Figure 4–36. The host on the private network assigned to the private address and the segment are connected to the Internet using a router, which serves as a NAT device. The router is assigned to a global address by the ISP, if host A on the private network segment wants to communicate with host B, which has the globally assigned IP address, the IP header of the outgoing packet must be changed to reflect the router's IP address which is globally assigned. In this case the NAT device (router) will change the IP address from 192.168.0.20 to 138.201.148.32. Once the IP address is changed, it would appear to host B. Thus it would send all the replies destined for host B to the latter address. The router does the translation transparently. For every communication session between the internal and external hosts the NAT device has to maintain a translation table, in order to correctly route packets to the right hosts on either side. The translation table generated from the above example is shown in Figure 4–37.

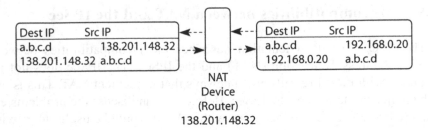

Dest IP	Src IP
a.b.c.d	138.201.148.32
138.201.148.32	a.b.c.d

NAT
Device
(Router)
138.201.148.32

Dest IP	Src IP
a.b.c.d	192.168.0.20
192.168.0.20	a.b.c.d

Figure 4–37. Translation table

The types of NAT that are available are defined in the RFC 2663 documentation; however, the following three NATs are the most commonly used in networks environment:

i. *Static NAT* defines a fixed address translation from the private addresses and global network. In other words the mapping between local addresses and global addresses is intended to stay the same for a long period of time. The static mapping is manually set by the network administrator and requires that the external IP addresses should equal to the internal private addresses.

ii. *Dynamic NAT* does not require a unique global address for each private address. The translation is done from a pool of private IP addresses to a pool of global ones. The NAT device handles the address assignment automatically and user has no influence what so ever over which IP address is picked from the pool.

iii. *Network Address Port Translation* (NAPT) can be classified as a sub category of dynamic NAT, which is most commonly used in networks environment. The NAPT popularity depends on the fact that many hosts on the private networks can share one global IP address. It uses port numbers as the basics for address translation and the number connections per IP address is limited by the number of ports available. This means 65536 (216 = 65536). This is a theoretical value as many ports are assigned for special services like FTP, which uses port 23 and HTTP that uses port 80. The RFC 1700 documentation contains the complete list of ports assigned to specific services.

Besides the conservation of the IP addresses, the NAT can also be used in load balancing servers and networks. It can be used to create a virtual server in order to provide the clients with a single server address and then the requests can be routed to the least loaded replicated server. Similarly the NAT can be used to transparently route traffic through a less congested network. Unfortunately, the need to conserve IPv4 addresses has caused many to overlook the inherent limitations of the NAT. The NAT maps private IP addresses to public routable addresses, when communicating between a privately addressed host and the Internet; the address translation is required (Phifer, 2000a). The NAT routers sit on the border between private and public networks and translate private addresses in each of the IP packet into registered public addresses [see RFC 1631 documentation for further details].

The IPSec AH runs the entire IP packet, including header fields such as source and destination IP address, through a message digest algorithm to produce a hash. The hash is sent to the recipient along with the original packet in order to authenticate the packet. The recipient recalculates the same hash on the received packet and if any field in the original IP packet is modified the authentication fails. As described above, the NAT translates private IP addresses into public IP addresses in each packet header. It is clear that if the NAT is performed on a packet that has been processed by the IPSec AH, the packet will simply be discarded by the destination. The IPSec ESP also performs a message digest for packet authentication. However, unlike AH, the hash created by ESP does not include the outer packet header fields and therefore it can work with NAT (Phifer, 2000a). One of the ways in which the IPSec and NAT (especially AH protocol) can be combined is to locate the IPSec endpoints in public address space. In other words, the NAT should be performed before the IPSec processing (Phifer, 2000b). It can either be perform on a device located behind the IPSec or use a device that can perform both the NAT and the IPSec. However, many routers, firewalls and security appliances implement NAT and the IPSec in the same box; the devices perform outbound NAT before applying the IPSec security policies. The process is reversed for inbound packets. Although the IETF is currently looking into ways to resolve the incompatibility between NAT and the IPSec, the problem is unlikely to disappear in the very near future.

10.10 Traffic analysis

Changing traffic patterns and the evolution of voice and video conferencing has presented network engineers with a whole new set of challenges. Even maintaining an agreed quality of service (QoS) is quite complicated and requires the use of Network monitoring tools. The network analysis tools (Snoop, Sniffer, Ethereal...) perform traffic analysis by accessing the header inside the IP packet. The traffic analysis is a passive attack; unauthorised or unwanted party observes message or other information. The passive attack is very difficult to detect because they do not involve any alteration of data, instead the message traffic is sent and received in a normal way and neither the sender nor receiver is aware that a third party has read the message or observed the traffic pattern.

The IPSec itself does not defend against traffic analysis, but the encryption provides at least partial protection. The analysis is based on things that are visible in the unencrypted headers of encrypted packets such as source and destination gateway addresses, packet size, etc. The IPSec was designed to prevent any type of traffic analysis because of network attackers that might tries to monitor traffic but the current IPSec standard for end-to-end security prevents the use of Network Analysis tools.

10.11   Denial of service

The denial of service is an active attack that prevents legitimate users from getting whatever the system supposed to provide. This attack may have a specific target, for example, an entity may suppress all messages directed to a particular destination. Another form of denial of service is the disruption of an entire network, either by disabling the network or by overloading it with messages so as to degrade performance. It aims at causing:

* Disrupt connections or system crash
* Overload or flood a network

The denial of service does not really constitute a direct intrusion to a system but the impacts of the attacks can be quite dramatic depending on whom the attack is directed against. The SYN attacks the computers and never send the final ACK message; the victim computer will wait for a certain period of time before the half open TCP connection time out. The attacking computer will issue many ACK messages in order to use up the memory of the victim computer. The latter attack is often performed by spoofed IP addresses so that the sender real IP address is not revealed. This IP address will not respond to the ACK-SYN message. Other types of denial of service attacks can involve overloading the network connections bandwidth and the distributed denial of service (DDOS). The DDOS attacks can be sinister in nature and involves coordinated attacks from more than one machine, which consume the victims' network bandwidth. The unusual thing about the DDOS attacks is that the user of the system under attack may not even know that his or her system is involved in the denial of service attacks. On a serious note, the IPSec does not eliminate the possibility of DDOS attacks.

10.12   Cut-and-paste attack

The cut-and-paste attack is initiated when two routers used the IPSec as a tunnel that link the network, which causes message modification. Modification of messages simply means that some portion of legitimate messages is altered, or that messages are delayed or reordered, to produce an unauthorised effect (Singh and Sofat, 2005). The network unobservability or 'client challenges10' can minimise the cut-and-paste attack for real-time interactive communications but not a total solution.

10.13 Session hijacking

The session hijacking authentication mechanisms and long random passwords that resist network sniffing and dictionary attacks. The attackers uses session hijacking to capture a session after the regular user has been authenticated and authorised, which enabled the attacker to use a regular user's privileges to access or modify a database, or possibly to install software for further penetration, even without obtaining the regular user's credentials. The simplest way to perform session hijacking is to first attempt to place the attacker's computer somewhere in the connection path by using a specialized hacking tool. The attacker will observe the exchange and at some point take over by stand in the middle of the exchange, to terminate one side of the TCP connection while using the correct TCP/IP parameters with sequence numbers. The sequence number in the AH header is unprotected, which makes the digest replay possible.

10.14 Non repudiation

Repudiation threats involve users who deny that they performed an action, and other parties have no way to prove otherwise. The AH or ESP do not provide non-repudiation when used with the default algorithms. Use of certain algorithm with appropriate transformation provides non-repudiation.

10.15 Client software

The IPSec requires special-purpose client software, which in most cases replaces or arguments the client system TCP/IP stack. In many systems this introduces the risk of compatibility issues with other system software as well as the security risk of Trojan Horses being loaded. If the client software is downloaded through the Internet and not installed by an expert, the risk of malicious software is very high.

10.16 ESP weaknesses

The initialisation of the vectors are chosen in a predictable manner in the ESP, which opens up the adaptive plaintext vulnerability that enabled the attackers to break through the low entropy plaintext blocks using brute force, as well as verifying strongly suspected plaintext. Furthermore, there are conflicting issues between the ESP and TCP performance enhancement proxy (PEP) deployed in IP wireless networks.

10.17 ICMP message

The design of ICMP reveal segments of the header and payload of the inner datagram in clear text, so an attacker can intercept the ICMP messages to retrieve plaintext data. The attacker can modify sections of the IPSec packet, causing either the clear text inner packet to be redirected or a network host to generate an error message. In the latter case, these errors are relayed via the ICMP.

10.18 Internet key exchange (IKE) problem

In IKE Aggressive mode, the authentication hash is based on pre-shared key-password or shared-secret (PSK). Because the hash is not encrypted, it is possible to capture these packets using a sniffer. For example the TCP dump and start dictionary or brute force attack can recover PSK. It is also possible for an attacker to execute code. The attack only works in the IKE aggressive mode because in the IKE 'Main Mode' the hash is already encrypted. Based on this fact the IKE aggressive mode is not very secure.

Table 4–6. Vendors that are currently aware of affected products

Vendors	Affected Products
Cisco	Cisco IOS, Cisco PIX Firewall, Cisco Firewall Services Module, Cisco VPN 3000 Series Concentrators and the Cisco MDS Series SanOS
Juniper Networks	All Juniper Networks M/T/J/E-series routers JUNOS and JUNOSe Security platforms
Openswan Project	De facto IPSec software used on many Linux distributions
Stonesoft Corp.'s	StoneGate Firewall and VPN products
Secgo Software Oy	Some versions of Secgo Software Oy Crypto IP gateway and client versions

The security researchers from University of Oulu in Finland have discovered a serious security flaw in the Internet Security Association and Key Management Protocol, which expose vulnerable products to denial of service. These flaws could cause denial-of-service attacks and they are vulnerable to the following products (see Table 4–6).

11.   SUMMARY OF CHAPTER FOUR

The details of how to do the basic configuration of IPv6 for a variety of devices when introducing IPv6 into IPv4 environment have been discussed. It has also been proved that when configuring the IPSec on Windows 2000 systems with Service Packs 1 (SP1) and 2 (SP2), they do not properly process the IPSec ESP packets that are fragmented across IP packets. The Windows 2000 system dropped the packets. The symptoms vary according to how the applications handle the dropped packets. The applications that use TCP may hang and eventually time out. The problem appears to be caused by a defect in the Windows 2000 SP1 and SP2 software and also reproduced the ESP packets in Windows 2000 base systems and Windows 2000 system. The IPSec is not a panacea for all network security, which includes the Internet. The best thing to do is to anticipate all the tricky installations, and revise detailed documentation from vendor.

Without doubt both the IPv4 and IPv6 have many limitations but the most incomprehensible limitation of all is the NAT. The NAT rewrites the IP header and also modifies TCP/UDP entire IP packet. The next chapter focuses on synchronising Internet protocol security (SIPSec) model.

REFERENCES

Bragg, R., (2001), IPsec Rules, http://redmondmag.com/columns/article.asp?Editorials ID=56 (28 January, 2007).

Cisco, (2005), Implementing Basic Connectivity for IPv6, http://www.cisco.com/univercd/cc/td/doc/product/software/ios123/123cgcr/ipv6_c/sa_bconn.htm (January 27, 2007).

Doraswamy, N. and Harkins, D., 2003, IPSec: The New Security Standard for the Internet, Intranets, and Virtual Private Networks, 2nd Edition, Prentice Hall USA.

Harrison, J. 2003, VPN Technologies —A COMPARISON, http://vnu.bitpi pe.com/detail/RES/1046358922_393.html (February 7, 2007)

Jayawickrama, W., (2003), Demystifying IPSec Protocol, Implementations and Limitations; www.bridgepoint.com.au/Documents/ipsecpaper.pdf (January 15, 2007).

Matkovich, E., (2003), IP Tunneling: All About Tunnels, PACKET, Vol. 15, No. 3, Third Quarter 2003

Microsoft Corp, (2003), How IPsec works, Microsoft Corporation, http://technet2.microsoft.com/WindowsServer/en/Library/8fbd7659-ca23-4320-a350-6890049086bc1033.mspx (12 January, 2007).

Murphy, N., and Malone, D., (2005), IPv6 Network Administration, First Edition, Published by Oreilly, March,

Phifer, L.J., (2000a), The Trouble with NAT, The Internet Protocol Journal, Volume 3, Number 4, December.

Phifer, L.J., (2000b), IP Security and NAT: Oil and Water?, 'ISP-Planet' http://www.isp planet.com/technology/nat_ipsec.html (January 29, 2007).

Roland, J.F., and Newcomb, M.J., 2003, CSVPN Certificate Guide, Cisco Press.

Sandsmark, F., (2004), 'What You Need To Know About Network Security', iQ Magazine, First Quarter.

Singh, B., and Sofat, S., (2005), Future of Internet Security – IPSec, Security white papers, http://www.securitydocs.com/library/2926 (February 27, 2007).

Weber, C., 2002. Using IPsec in Windows 2000 and XP, http://www.securityfocus.com/i nfocus/1528 (13 February, 2007).

Chapter 5

SYNCHRONISING INTERNET PROTOCOL SECURITY (SIPSEC) MODEL

1.   INTRODUCTION

In 1976 Diffie and Hellman published a paper titled 'New Directions in Cryptography', suggested solution for the key generation and distribution problem. The paper details the groundwork for public key cryptography and suggests that each user would be provided with two different keys, one known to the public and one kept private. With the evolution of cryptography technology and the availabilities of tools that can be used to breach both the public and private key, the secrecy of any Internet transaction cannot be 100 per cent guarantee.

> 'What fortutude the sole contains, that it can so endure...'
> —Emily Dickinson (1830–1886)

The main idea behind SIPSec is to provide maximum security to all out going and in coming transactions using user's biometrics profile and the policy combination for generating public and private key values.

2.   ANALYSIS OF QUESTIONNAIRE SURVEY

The respondents' success factors for implementing IPSec and their experiences conveyed multiple perspectives. The preliminary questionnaire survey of 21 organisations (9 international and 12 trans-national organisations) was conducted to show the current adoption of IPSec and their organisational security policy support (OSPS). The analysis presented in Table 5–1, shows that 12 out of the 21 organisations are still using IPv4, 3 organisations uses IPv6 and other 6 uses both.

Furthermore, 4 organisations have fully migrated from the IPv4 to v6, 11 are still using the IPv4 while 3 are considering migrating to IPv6 All the organisation that were involved believed that IPSec is not 100 per cent secured.

The responses from 15 organisations out of the 21 shows that the OSPS is at the forefront of their strategic planning, it was also revealed that the other 6 are considering adopting the OSPS. The OSPS helped to create security awareness of online transactions (not specific to the IPSec alone) within the organisation.

The questionnaire survey also revealed that the 21 organisations are using combinatory security measures to protect their networks and Internet transactions. This view is supported by Huston (2002) that security in the modern world relies completely on layers of defence, referred to in the military as "defence in depth". The defence in depth goes beyond platforms, products, and patches and the protection of assets can no longer be left to simple single-point solutions.

Table 5–1. Organisational Adoption of IPSec

Survey Factors	Organisational Responds (n=21)		
	Yes	No	Under consideration
i. Version of IPSec			
• IPv4	12	—	—
• IPv6	3		
• Both	6		
ii. Fully migrating from the IPv4 to IPv6	4	11	3
iii. IPSec is 100 per cent secured	—	21	—
iv. Organisational security policy support IPSec	15	—	6
v. Combination of security tools	21	—	—

The firewall security systems was considered nothing more than a little speed bump unless it forms an integral part of an overall security solution integrated with components that enhance and support its position. Huston's view strongly supports the 'Hypothesis 2' that 'absolute security is unattainable on IPSec'.

3.   CASE STUDIES

The term case study has multiple meanings, it can be used to describe a unit of analysis (a case study of a particular organisation or business), or to describe a method. The case studies approach was considered valid for this research. Yin (1994) and Benbasat et al., (1987) discusses the merits of using multiple case studies as away of providing replication logic and rich descriptions of emergent research areas. Multiple case study analysis has been justified and validated by Zikmund (1997), who investigated inter organisation systems. For the purpose of brevity, twenty-one organisations case studies were exploited. These case studies observations (participatory research) were used to identify the current security breaches encountered by using the IPSec. The outcome of the case studies became the cornerstone on which the limitations of IPSec are based (see chapter 4 for further discussion).

4. LABORATORY EXPERIMENTS

Laboratory experiments were performed to test the reliability of both IPv4 and v6 using sniffer packet and other hacking tools that are privately developed. The test were carried out was at a random among selected 21 organisations (9 international12 and trans-national) with prior knowledge of the test, but without specifying when it would be carried out or else the test might create bias. The test was performed 9 times on a specific organisation (see Table 5–2).

Table 5–2. IPv4 and v6 Test results

Number of participants	Type of organisation	Number of tests	Total tests	Test failed	Successful penetration
9	International	9	81	17	61
12	Trans-national	9	108	8	100
21		**18**	**189**	**25**	**161**

The packet sniffer and other hacking tools demonstrated the lack of security in IPv4 and v6, so there is an urgent need for the IPSec security enhancement. The test also showed the lack of privacy/confidentiality in the IPSec operations.

5. CURRENT IPSEC SOLUTIONS

The IPSec models are well established and widely used standard for providing security between systems within and outside the networks. So far the question of which model is best suited to provide secured solution depends on the organisational network security policy. Most of the models are similar in terms of security solution they provide as well as cryptographic algorithms and techniques they use, they vary fundamentally in the manner in which they provide the security services. The most commonly adopted IPSec solutions are discussed below:

5.1   Splitting IPSec end-point

To overcoming the problem presented by the end to end security model, will involve split up the encryption points, apart from having the end hosts or security gateways performing the encryption and decryption, the intermediate systems (router, switches…) should also be provided with keys to decrypt and re-encrypt IP packets. For example, host A on LAN 1 sending a packet to host B on LAN 2. In this case the packet has to travel through the Internet. Traditionally the security gateways would encrypt and decrypt the packet (end-to-end) and the intermediate nodes do not have access the information other than the IP header. This solution enabled the link between each intermediate node to be (see Figure 5–1 for diagrammatic illustration).

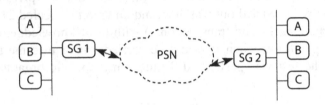

Figure 5–1. Link-to-link encryption

When the packet from host A destined for B leaves the security gateway SG1, it is decrypted at the first packet-switching node (PSN). The PSN analyses the packet to determine the correct route and re-encrypts it before forwarding it to the second PSN. The packet is therefore decrypted every time it reaches the PSN any intermediate device till it reaches its destination.

The link-to-link encryption does not require any modifications to the IPSec architecture. It maintains the end-to-end security concept, as long as each segment in the overall IPSec connection is valid end-to-end encrypted link. However, the intermediate systems should now be trusted and provided with the encryption keys via secured key distribution mechanism. The only advantage of splitting IPSec end point is that it does not require any modifications to the current IPSec specification.

5.1.1   Weaknesses of splitting IPSec end-point

Splitting IPSec end-point is vulnerable to any intelligent switch running management software because it can analyse the traffic. Since it possesses the key for the encrypted algorithm, it is essential for the intermediate systems to implement the IPSec alongside other services. The key distribution mechanism for a wide scale distribution is too expensive and very complicated. Delay in arrival of packets is a major concern and not cost effective.

5.2   Modifying the IPSec specification

The modification of the IPSec is possible using two solutions that will be briefly discuss in this section. The first modification to the IPSec focuses on revealing the required TCP information and encrypted to the intermediate systems (see Figure 5–2 for diagrammatic illustration). The TCP information is behind the ESP header and is encrypted. This solution aims at copying the TCP information and making is available to the intermediate system by putting it before the ESP in the form of a new header as shown in Figure 5–3. For example, host A on LAN 1 generates a packet destined for host B on LAN 2. The packet reaches the security gateway SG1 that performs the IPSec processing and also copies the TCP information before encrypting the packet to new header and the ESP header (see Figure 5–4 for diagrammatic illustration).

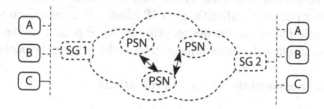

Figure 5–2. Modified packet flow

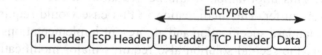

Figure 5–3. IPSec tunnel mode protected packet

The modified IPSec packet flows through the public network where routers and other intermediate systems can access the TCP information required, as it is not encrypted. The packet is decrypted at SG2 and the new header is removed. The packet is then forwarded to host B. It is important to note that both hosts are not aware of the modification made by the security gateway. The major advantage of this first solution is that the packet overhead at the intermediate gateways would be minimal due to unencrypted information.

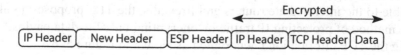

Figure 5–4. Modified IPSec packets

Encrypted

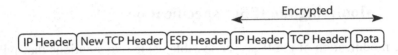

Figure 5–5. IPSec inside the TLC packet

The second solution is quite similar to the first solution explained above. It modifies the IPSec packet by placing a new IP header and a new TCP header. However, the new TCP header may or may not contain the same information as the inner TCP header (the IPSec packet is encapsulated in a TCP packet). In Figures 5–4, when the packet destined for host B reaches security gateway SG1 the gateway opens new TCP connection withSG2 and places the entire encrypted packet into the data payload of the new packet (see Figures 5–5 for diagrammatic illustration). The packet format of the new modified packet is similar to the packet generated by the ESP in tunnel mode except for the new TCP header placement after the new IP header. In comparison to the first solution, this solution maintains the security of the IP packet, as the new TCP header may not contain the same information as the original IP packet.

5.2.1   Weaknesses of the IPSec Modifications

The main weaknesses of implementing the first solution described above are that it copies the TCP information that the IPSec encrypts into unencrypted header. This information would be available to everyone with an access to a packet sniffer. The modification in this case would require changes to the IPSec standard specification and all present implementations. As with the first solution, the second solution also requires major modifications to the IPSec specification. The security gateways would require modifications, as a new TCP connection needs to be established for each packet flow and the encapsulation of the IPSec packets into the new TCP packets. The security gateways incurred significant overheads due to extra encapsulation.

5.3   Transport Layer Security (TLS) specification

The Transport Layer Security (TLS) is defined in the RFC 2246 documentations. The TLS is not a modification to the IPSec architecture nor does it suggest changing the IPSec implementation. Since TCP information is always available to the intermediate routers and firewalls, the TLS proposes an alternative method of protecting IP traffic by encrypting only the data payload and leaving the TCP information unencrypted as shown in Figure 5–6.

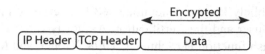

Figure 5–6. TLC protected packet

The TLS specification dictates the data encryption payload and provides security between two applications. It works on connection oriented reliable protocol such as TCP but not UDP. For example, when the packet originated by host A reaches security gateway SG1, this completed the TLS process. The intermediate systems can correctly perform their functions, as the TCP information is not encrypted and hence available to them. The reverse process is performed at the receiving gateway and the packet is forwarded to its final destination.

5.3.1   Weaknesses of TLS

Due to the dependence on transport protocol such as TCP, TLS cannot be used for video conferencing, and voice over IP, which uses UDP. The security of the IP packets is significantly reduced even if the data is encrypted. The venerable TCP headers are left on protected and open to many kinds of attacks. Since TLS cannot work with UDP, security cannot be implement in applicants with multicast requirements. It worth noting, that TLS is not amendable to hardware implementation and the proposal to replace the IPSec with the TCP security or TLS is not acceptable.

6.   PUBLIC KEY ALGORITHMS

The four protocols that relies on the strength of different public key algorithms, are briefly discussed as follows:

i.   *Discrete Logarithm Problem* is based on the original Diffie-Hellman idea, on the difficulty of finding an integer y, given a large prime p, an integer g between 2 and p-1 and the value of g y (mod p). The input values to this algorithm are as follows:
   - L — the length in bits of a seed to be generated;
   - J — the bit length of the prime number that guarantees the security of this method. (The size of J must be considered infeasible for an attacker to solve the corresponding discrete logarithm problem);
   - p0 — a publicly known prime number of the length at least J bits;

- g — a publicly known generator used to secure communications between the user and the Certification Authority (CA) using the cryptographic hash function H (Schneier, 1998, Ylonen and Moffat, 2003).

The user randomly generates an integer x between 1 and 2L -1, computes y=gx (mod p0) and sends y to the CA. The CA generates non-secret uniform random integer z between 0 and 2L -1, computes w=H(y*gz (mod p0)) and signs the private key (SKCA). This signed value is called Sigw. The CA track the number of times this user asked for assistance. This can be done per user or for the entire CA. If the count is more than the threshold for a particular user (or if the CA counters are not kept per user) then the Certification Authority might suspect that a user is attempting a first party attack and the CA will send a warning to a system administrator. The Discrete Logarithm Problem is difficult to audit because only one of the values w1, w2 is correct by making the invalid value available for validation and audit, will lead to inconsistence. There is a probability of this happening.

ii. The *RSA Method* used the following values:

- L — the length in bits of a seed to be generated;
- N — a publicly known composite number of the length L+1 bits (N□pq, where p and q are large unknown primes. The secret parameters p and q are generated by the user and are certified by a trusted third party);
- e — an RSA public exponent and also H, PKca and Skca that are defined as in the previous section.

The auditing requires the user to prove that the proper procedure was followed and compute w=H((Xseed)e (mod N)), using Sigw for validation, and the public verification key of the CA, and PKca. To complete the audit the signature must be valid.

iii. Menezes' '*Elliptic Curves*' is based on the security of data exchange between the user and the CA, and the strength of the discrete logarithm problem for a group of points on an elliptic curve over a finite field (Menezes, 1997).

The Elliptic Curves used the following values as an input:
- L — the length in bits of a seed to be generated;
- J — the bit length of the prime number n that guarantees the security of this method. (The size of J must be such that it would be considered infeasible for an attacker to solve the corresponding elliptic curve discrete logarithm problem: J>L+1 assures that x + z < n);

- E — an elliptic curve over a finite field Fq. This is a set of points that satisfy a certain algebraic relationship. The number of points on this curve is nh, where n is a large prime (has at least J bits) and h is a small cofactor.
- G — is a base point. It is a point of order n on E.

Auditing the Elliptic Curves requires the user to compute w1 and w2, the hash values of the x-coordinates the points (Xseed)G and (Xseed+ 2L)G, which correspondingly, on E,

iv. The UNIX system uses the telnet and ftp to access remote machines in order to establish login sessions and transfer files. These commands transmitted user ids and passwords through insecurity networks. The secure shell (SSH) (Barrett and Silverman, 2001, Ylonen and Moffat, 2002, 2003) has emerged as the de facto replacement for these commands. Rather than typing telnet and ftp to reach a remote machine S, the user invokes SSH (using public-key cryptography) to establish authentication and encrypted communications over unsecured channels. The server presents a public key, and the client machine uses standard cryptography to establish a protected channel with the party knowing the private key—presumably, the server. The SSH can even permit the user to authenticate via a key pair instead of a password.

The four protocols described above could be applicable within different situations and the certificate that the CA issues may contain the value w or both w and Sigw. The advantage of the latter algorithm is that the user does not have to store Sigw. The limitation of Sigw is that it might require some changes to the existing standard protocol between the user and the Certification Authority. However, the Discrete Logarithm Problem, RSA Method, Elliptic Curves and SSH has nothing to do with the IPSec policy that the SIPSec will compromises with, therefore the biometric profile is the last verifying user's identification and platform independent.

There are many cases where IPSec has failed to secure legitimate transactions (see chapter 4 for further discussion). The SIPSec is based on both technical and non-Technical methods:

i. Technical:
- Security incidents involving inherited internet architecture problems:
- Vulnerabilities in the TCP/IP protocols services.
- Host configuration and access control that are poorly implemented.
- IP spoofing:
- Creating packets with false IP addresses.
- Exploit applications that use authentication based on IP address.

- Eavesdropping and packet sniffing:
- Read transmitted data including login information or database.
ii. Non-Technical:
  - Ability to trace illegal act.
  - Organisations and Governments are now depending more on the internet for sending sensitive information.
  - Online payment frauds.
  - Availability of Illegal software downloads for cracking legitimate security transactions.
  - Control over the Internet boundary.

If user does not have a trusted system, how does the user establish the connection? The SIPSec enumerate some desired goals:

- Does not enable users to personify clients in untrusted network environments, to establish trusted connections with users' biometric profile.
- Accommodate users in domains where conscientious system administrators can set up trustable and usable CA services independently without access to the user's biometric profile.
- It also accommodate users in domains where no such services exist.
- Does not require a new universal PKI structure (neither single rooted nor multi-rooted) before an access could be established.
- It establishes that the server with whom the use has just established a session is the server to whom he or she is intended to connect to.
- Moreover, the SIPSec does not require a user to memorise their biometrics profile of all servers to interact with.

7.   ANALYSIS OF FINDINGS

The analysis of findings based on he case studies observation, interviews and questionnaires, have help to developing the conceptualisation of IPSec adaptation factors.

vThe questionnaire survey that was conducted revealed that the IPSec have three major factors that impacts its operation. The factors that impacts IPSec are presented in Figure 5–7. The IPSec correlate methods and configuration with successful data transfer. However, it was realised from the analysis of the case studies that one hundred and seventy large organisations had tried four or more IPSec configurations. This makes it difficult to trace or disentangle what causes a particular IPSec method to compromise or failed to have secured data transfer and the effect, where more than one configuration had been used. The interviewees who contributed to the case studies observation described different

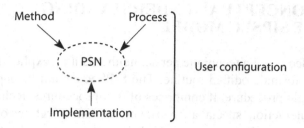

Figure 5–7. IPSec impact factors

methods on how the IPSec worked. It become clear that method was part of the armoury used in the IPSec. The method concerns centred on the IPSec technique. However, the interviewees concerns extend beyond method or technique and the view on effective security of information transfer. The conceptualisation of SIPSec can be thought of as an enhancement to exiting approach.

The implementation of IPSec was a common concern. Even where IPSec was judged to have been successful, the configurations were not always fully implemented. Thus clear directions might be set and commitments made to implement a particular version of IPSec, evidence from the interview conducted suggests that where IPSec were implemented, other concerns arose, including technical and non-technical issues such as quality of services, time and cost effectiveness. Past research has also identified similar concerns and more prescriptive literature has suggested some of the latter concerns. But it is equally arguable that the implementation of IPSec has brought about some believe that data/information can be made secured from one system to the other via the Internet.

It is apparent that process is also a concern in IPSec, which include inadequate user awareness, platform integration and education. The process involved in performing secure operation using IPSec is questionable. The integrity involves in setting up IPSec process for transactions needs further clarification and awareness. The Internet security professionals were particularly vocal about the management and enactment of IPSec methods and procedures; whether it fit the business operations and if not, what is available to secure the Internet transactions.

8.   CONCEPTUAL UNDERSTANDING OF SIPSEC MODEL

The SIPSec is not a technique per se, neither is it an explicit Internet security study or formal codified routine. The SIPSec cannot be captured by one event, or single procedure. It comprises of mix procedures, techniques, user's biometrics interaction, special analysis, and random selections of components within an elements. It also requires both formal actives and informal behaviour.

However, when a user's biometrics information has been stored, to describe how SIPSec decision are initiated and made, a coherent picture is gradually painted to mapped the underpinning philosophy, which makes the elements to stand out. These are the distinguishing features in SIPSec process. The biometric features are place in the method to allow random selections of components within an elements and process focuses on the probability of implementing and integrating the policy. The SIPSec is a process driven. The user's original configured profile will be automatically uploaded for consistence. The Agent should be adaptive but cannot be replicated. Any attempt or instance of replication will require the user's profile redundant and absolute. The SIPSec would enable existing process to be integrated into the user genetic profile, which can be audited and traceable with minimum cost. The SIPSec requires the following:

i.   The factoring involves the implementation of biometrics into the existing IPSec architecture. Since the IPSec are currently in use, it would be unlikely that individuals and organisations will be willing to cease it from operation, as little security is better than none. However, the way forward would be to integrate biometric into IPSec platform and reconfiguring the policy to accept the new SIPSec rules.
ii. Involve agents that cannot be replicated with a limited life span. The life span of the agents would depend on the duration of the transaction.
     The biometrics profiles are unique to each individual. An integrity violation of copy, save, and delete would be applied to all profiles. Updating a profile will requires further identification that can be use to verified the initial registration, the biometrics mapping of current identification elements and components of individuals held in shared biometrics database. The shared biometrics database comprises of the Internet service providers (ISPs), organisations (public and private sectors), governments and international collaborations (see Table 5–3). The Internet Security Event Response Process (ISERP) is the government control body that has the responsibility for maintaining the shared biometrics database and also coordinating updates between participating countries.

Table 5–3. Database integration

Internal integration	External integration
Using system profile / ISPs	Governments (ISERP)
Organisations	International collaboration
Governments	

iii. Replay and auditing approach to trace any operations. After the execution of the IPSec the replay and auditing approach would give creditability to both out going and incoming transaction. The replay will be in a constant loop checking for any violation or interception of the transactions using available system profile.

The cryptographic facilities of authentication and encryption in the IPSec require the use of secret keys known to the participants but not to anyone else. The most obvious and straightforward way to establish these secrets is via manual configuration: one party generates a set of secrets, and conveys them to all the partners. All parties install these secrets in their appropriate Security Associations in the SPD. But the mere act of conveying the secrets of the keys to another site(s) SPD may expose the secret keys that are in transit. In a larger installation with many devices using the same pre-shared key(s), compromise of that key makes for a very disruptive re-deployment of new keys. In the case of SIPSec the biometric profile of an individual is stored in a centralised database with real time update and verification is mapped against primary information (the biometric elements and their components). On the other hand the IKE allows the SA setup, by using the ISAKMP as a framework to support establishment of a SA compatibility with both ends. Although the security architecture of IPSec detailed in the RFC 2401, which has been superseded by RFC 4301 did not mentioned integrating biometric into existing IPSec. Therefore, the RFC 4301 documentation is questionable and requires update. The SIPSec provides multiple and complementary architectures and the approaches to security. It is traversal and encompasses multiple layers security, which is tightly coupled with the existing policies. The SIPSec policies are defined acknowledged and enforced without the individual users being able to circumvent the biometric elements and components stored on the server. The key agent that securely stores the biometrics elements and components that provides the policies exchanges in order to act on the user's behalf are fully dependent on the concept of user involvement (see Figure 5–8 for diagrammatic illustration).

The future of Internet security, therefore, resides in human intervention and innovation. Implementing hardware and software solutions, as well as using human intervention to continually monitor the network, are two of the best

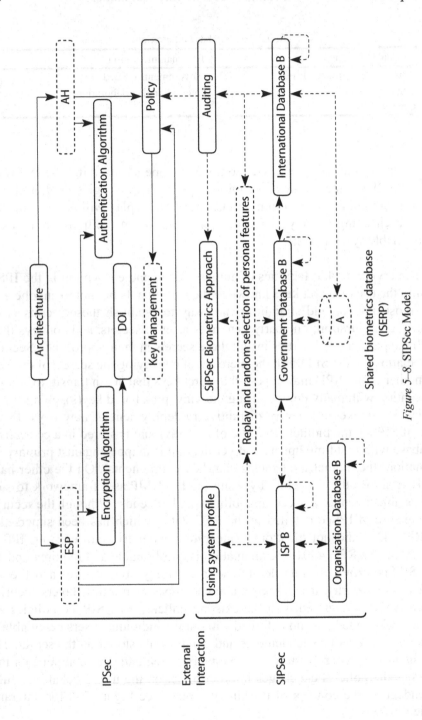

Figure 5–8. SIPSec Model

ways to keep abreast of attacks from the outside. One of the latest technologies in the security market is the adaptive security. This development is a result of Internet Security Systems' (ISS) formation of the Adaptive Network Security Alliance (ANSA) around an application program interface for real secures intrusion detection systems. The technology requires the enlistment of major infrastructure vendors (3Com, Lucent, Compaq, Entrust and Checkpoint) to enable their products to interoperate with ISS's intrusion detection monitors. By communicating between ISS's monitor and the vendor's products, firewalls and switches could be reconfigured in response to perceived break-ins, thereby diminishing the lag time between detection and prevention and ultimately, making the network virtually impossible to penetrate.

The physical biometrics identifications that are deployed in the SIPSec model are palm, finger, face and iris (see Figure 5–9 and sections 10 to 13 for further discussion). Other biometrics identifications includes the following:

- Signature recognition
- Voice
- Sweat
- Gait
- Body odour
- Ear shape
- Salinity

The above list of biometrics identification are not considered for SIPSec user's profile because they are less accurate and also at the early stage of their development.

The Figure 5–9 shows the analytical process of biometric elements and components of an individual SIPSec profile. A SIPSec process circle will start from the checking point of biometric elements, possible combination of identifiers, random selections of identifier and component within elements. If the user's profile is unable to match with appropriate elements and components when requested the agent would automatically generate an error message that terminates the current process. The unsuccessful process will automatically be logged for auditing purpose, the system identification will also be noted and the process will loop to the initial state, requesting for a new start. After 3 unsuccessful attempt the user have to what for another 6 hours before initiating SIPSec. If further attempt were made within the 6 hours, the SIPSec shared biometrics database will lock the user out of any transactions and will request for a new profile registration. The new profile will be used as a secondary profile for validating the existing profile. The sharing of biometric database replica introduces challenging security issues. Very often different user communities do not trust each other. Each user community has its own IPSec to coordinate

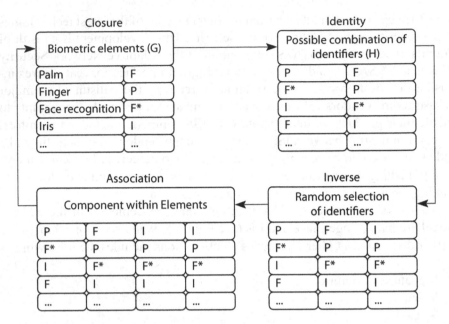

Figure 5–9. SIPSec Biometric Elements and Components

the transactions. The authentication and authorisation methods used in each community are different from each other and the access control mechanism varies too. The problem is how to use a uniform security mechanism to coordinate the IPSec data sharing across those naturally un-trusted user communities while keeping the diverse local security mechanisms intact.

Furthermore, the Jackson Structure Programming (JSP) notation is used to show the processes that are involved and other biometrics profile. The following notations are used in the JSP, 'o' in the right hand corner gives the options and the asterisk '*' is an indication that there would be a continuous loop or number of times, which it has to be repeated until matching set of biometrics components, is found within the elements. If know matching are found within the profile, the process would be terminated (see Figure 5–11 to 5–30 for diagrammatic illustration).

8.1   Mathematic equations and theorem

The mathematical equations and theorem are applicable to the development process of the user's biometrics random selection in SIPSec are briefly discussed below (see Figure 5–9 for diagrammatic illustration):

8.1.1   Groups

The group comprises of a set G (containing the user's biometrics elements of that group) and the operation * have to satisfy the random selection of their properties (see Equations 5.1 to 5.4):

i.   Closure —given three elements g, h, $k \in G$, the operation gives an elements $g * h$, which is required to be an element of G.
ii. Identity —an element $e \in G$ is an identity for *. The element $g \in G$ is presented as:

$$g * e = g * e = g \tag{5.1}$$

iii. Inverse —any elements of $g \in G$, there is an element g^{-1} (the inverse of g), which satisfies:

$$g * g^{-1} = g^{-1} * g = e \tag{5.2}$$

iv. Association —any elements g, h, k, of G

$$g * h\,(h * k) = (g * h) * k \tag{5.3}$$

If the set G and operation $*$ forms a group then:

$$(G,\, *) \text{ is a group} \tag{5.4}$$

In order to show the set of elements and their biometrics operations on set of user's profile the above four properties needs verification with the SIPSec policy.

8.1.2   Isomorphism

The order of an element preserves each transaction, so the isomorphism is used to preserve the order of the elements. The Lagrange's Theorem is adopted to process the order of any user's biometrics subgroup:

- Each coset has exactly $|H|$ elements of G in it.

- The coset in row x consists of all the elements xh as h runs through the various elements of H.
- Different cosets of H in G do not overlap.
- Every element of G occurs in some coset of H in G.
- Therefore G is a factor of the order of G.

8.1.3   Functions

The functions of the elements would be mapped from $\mathbb{R}_2$ to $\mathbb{R}$ (see Figure 5–9 for diagrammatic illustration):

Any element, $\begin{pmatrix} x \\ y \end{pmatrix}$ in $\mathbb{R}_2$ maps to the $(2\ 0)\begin{pmatrix} x \\ y \end{pmatrix}$ in $\mathbb{R}$.

This is written as:

$$f\colon \mathbb{R}_2 \rightarrow \mathbb{R}$$

$$\begin{pmatrix} x \\ y \end{pmatrix} \rightarrow (2\ 0)\begin{pmatrix} x \\ y \end{pmatrix} = 2x$$

- $\mathbb{R}_2$ is the domain of the function
- $\mathbb{R}$ is the co-domain of the function
- $2x$ is the biometrics image of $\begin{pmatrix} x \\ y \end{pmatrix}$
- The set of all the possible value of $2x$ is the image-set.

A function maps a set A (the domain: ISERP) to a set B (the co-domain: ISP servers, organisations, governments, and international databases) in such away that for each element in A there is a unique image in B (see Figure 5–8 for diagrammatic illustration).

9.   POLICY RECONCILIATION

Like the IPSec, the SIPSec establishes set of rules; these rules are carry out by agents that make sure that the rules are applied and adhere to. The SIPSec will have to provide the IPSec policies with some information about the user's biometric profile currently available for verification. This information is dependent on the set of rules that will randomly select the elements and components. Each of the elements in the user's biometric profile is combined together to form a rule. The SIPSec policy is a collection of one or more rules. The SIPSec enhancement is cannot work independently without the appropriate support from the current IPSec implementations. These support lies on the underlying policy management interface, the process of the IP packet that triggers the policy negotiation, and the setup of security rules. The chapters 3 and 4 describe the availability of the support in the current IPSec implementations. The SIPSec model is based on the following policies:

- Provides mechanism for applications to control policies, and allow applications to make authorisation decisions.
- The SIPSec implementations have policy management that interface, whether it is published or not. Since the KAME IPSec implementation for BSD Unix families and the native IPSec implementation for Linux (Kernel 2.6) provide PF KEY extensions for IPSec policy management [see RFC 2367 documentation for further discussion], on other hand the SIPSec build-in policy incorporated in the KAME-like IPSec implementations. These underlying policy management interfaces, create policies that do not allowed user's biometric profile to be copy or deleted. However, this does not imply that SIPSec policy is restricted to the KAME-like IPSec implementations only. The SIPSec can be integrated with other IPSec implementations, as long as they provide the basic policy management interfaces.
- Outgoing IP packet can triggers a policy negotiation, and the IPSec has to hold the IP packet until the completion of the negotiation, rather than to drop it and return an error. This is because the upper-layer protocols usually cannot cope with this kind of error well. Thus SIPSec is capable of providing this kind of support at all time, if there is a mismatch of user's biometric profile.
- The SIPSec allow users to specify the security level in the security policy. As stated earlier the set of rules has been built around SIPSec. The security policy needs to communicate with the server that stored the biometric profile, in order to map the user's biometrics with the database. To cope with probing and mapping of user's biometric profile in a timely fashion, the SIPSec have two levels of security negotiation: the mandatory (organisation or national control user's biometric profile server) indicates that the flows of this policy must be protected and optional (International or central server/database) optional indicates that the establishment of the SIPsec channel is optional for its flows. Once the SIPSec channel has been established as mandatory or optional, the IP flow belonging to this channel must pass through this established channel. Many IPSec implementations do support optional security. For example, the KAME IPSec implementation has three levels: use, require, and unique, and the native IPSec

implementation of Windows 2000/XP also allows users to specify an optional policy.

Since IPSec is at the network layer, it lacks the knowledge of application context and the current IPSec policy is:

- Rigid, coarse-grained
- Lack of expressive power in policy specifications
- Lack of application control over policies and no security protection for different Internet applications
- Lack of support for authorisation, and the inability to link authorisation decisions with security processing

The Figure 5–10 presents the IPSec policy configuration that is associated with two proposals (dynamic-1 and dynamic-2) under consideration to interface SIPISec.

```
[edit security ipsec]
    proposal dynamic-1 {
        protocol esp;
        authentication-algorithm hmac-md5-96;
        encryption-algorithm 3des-cbc;
        lifetime-seconds 6000;
    }
    proposal dynamic-2 {
        protocol esp;
        authentication-algorithm hmac-sha1-96;
        encryption-algorithm 3des-cbc;
        lifetime-seconds 6000;
    }
    policy dynamic-policy-1 {
        perfect-forward-secrecy {
            keys group1;
        }
        proposals [ dynamic-1 dynamic-2 ];
    }
    security-association dynamic-sa1 {
        dynamic {
            replay-window-size 64;
            ipsec-policy dynamic-policy-1;
        }
    }
```

Figure 5–10. IPSec policy configuration

But the SIPSec policy is a flexible middleware that will provides both the Internet applications and network-layer security protection. The SIPSec policy is application-aware, it comprises of socket monitor at the network stack of end hosts, which detects the socket activities of Internet applications, and passes them to the application policy engine. The Figure 5–11 presents the application policy, which consists of two classes of settings, the network and protection settings both classes are use for protecting collaborative biometrics profile.

By transmitting the computation engine instead of data, SIPSec can offers:

- Network bandwidth requirement is reduced, instead of passing large amounts of raw data over the network through several round trips, the agent do all the mappings. This is especially important for real-time applications.
- Better network scalability, the performance of the network is not affected when the biometrics profile is verifying and compromising with the IPSec policy. Agent architectures that support adaptive network load balancing would automatically mapped the user's biometrics profile.

```
application ISP, International, National/Organisation
{
        network xxx.xxx.x.x/xx trusted;
        network xxx.xxx.x.x/xx untrusted;
        network www.xxx.com protected ISP;
        network www.xxx.com protected International;
        network x.x.x.x/x protected National/Organisation;
        protection International {
                localport=XXX
                remoteport=any
                encryption mandatory;
                localport=any
                remoteport=any
                authentication mandatory;
        }
        protection National/Organisation {
                localport=any
                remoteport=any
                authentication optional;
        }
}
```

Figure 5–11. SIPSec application policy

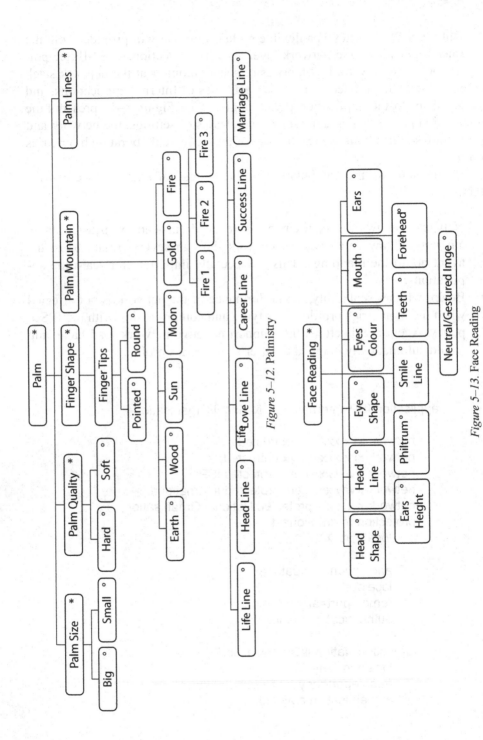

Figure 5–12. Palmistry

Figure 5–13. Face Reading

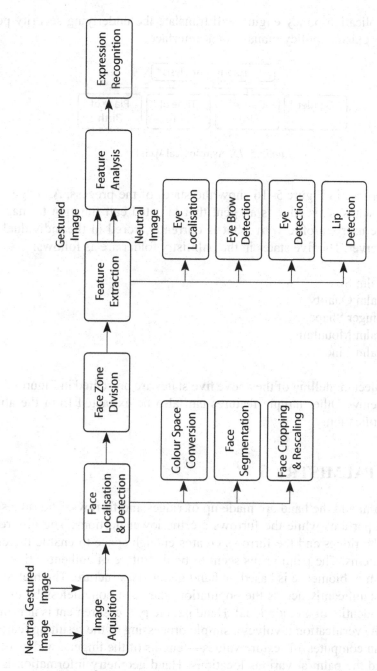

Figure 5–14. Face Feature

The application policy engine will translate the underlying security policies via the existing policy management interface.

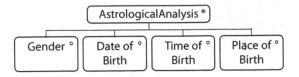

Figure 5–15. Astrological Weight

The vertices in Figure 5–16 show the states of the process. An edge connects two states. This edge is an gent that initiated call function to map the appropriate user's profile with what is currently stored in the individual biometrics server. The five states in the palmistry folder are as follows:

- S1 = Palm Size
- S2 = Palm Quality
- S3 = Finger Shape
- S4 = Palm Mountain
- S5 = Palm Line

The object modelling of the above five states are presented in Figures 5–17 to 5–27 below. Other unique features can also be extracted from the above palm identification.

10.   PALMISTRY

The palm and the hand are made up of ridges and furrows. The ridges are the raised portions while the furrows are the lower portions. The difference between the ridges and the furrows creates enough space to enable the creation of patterns. The palm prints seem to be the future of authentication. The use of palm in biometric is based on hand geometry structure. The metrics do not vary significantly across the population; they can nonetheless be used to verify the identity of an individual. Hand geometry measurement is non-intrusive and the verification involves a simple processing of the resulting features. The system computes 14 feature values—lengths of the fingers, widths of the fingers and the palm at various locations. Hand geometry information is not very distinctive (Ross, 2003, Hong, 1998). The palm will be used in SIPSec validation testing.

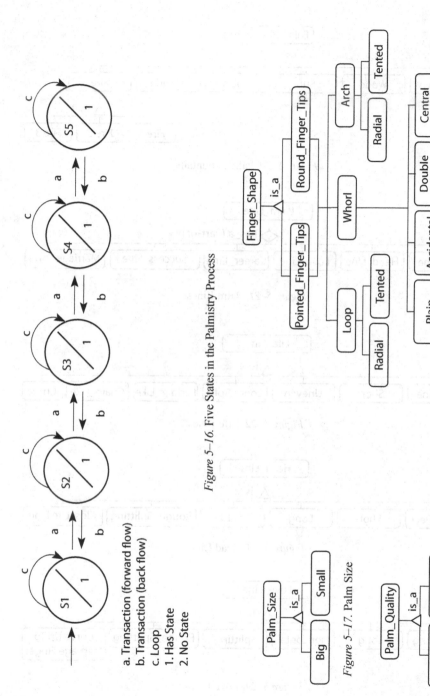

a. Transaction (forward flow)
b. Transaction (back flow)
c. Loop
1. Has State
2. No State

Figure 5–16. Five States in the Palmistry Process

Figure 5–17. Palm Size

Figure 5–18. Palm Quality

Figure 5–19. Finger Shape

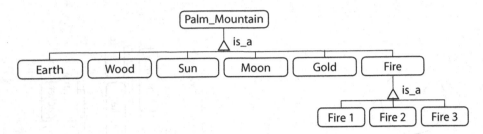

Figure 5–20. Palm Mountain

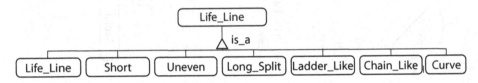

Figure 5–21. Palm Lines

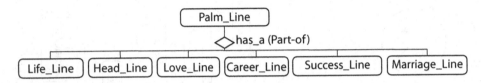

Figure 5–22. Life Lines

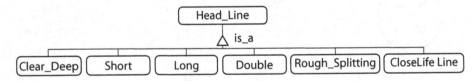

Figure 5–23. Head Lines

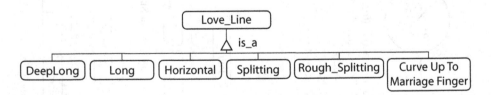

Figure 5–24. Love Lines

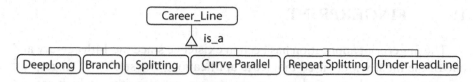

Figure 5–25. Career Lines

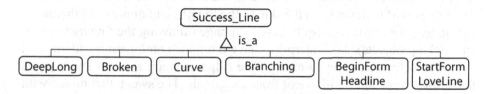

Figure 5–26. Success Lines

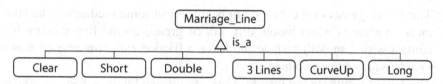

Figure 5–27. Marriage Lines

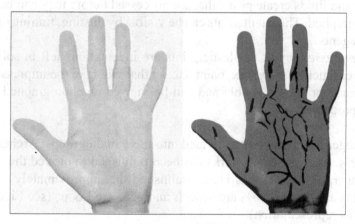

Figure 5–28. Hand and Palm-vein pattern

Joseph Rice developed the vein recognition in 1984. Like fingerprints, the pattern of blood veins in the palm is unique to every individual, and apart from size, this pattern will not vary over the course of a person's lifetime. The palm-vein pattern biometrics is a secure method of verification for SIPSec (see Figures 5–9, 5–28, 5–12 and 5–17 to 5–27)

11.   FINGERPRINT

The fingerprint application has been in existence since the 14th century and one of the most widely used biometric application. The storing of fingerprint information has change and images are store as an algorithm, which are not easily readable (see Figure 5–29 for diagrammatic illustration). The fingerprint ridges are formed between the third and fourth month of fatal development. The ridges start to develop on the skin of the thumbs and fingers. Furthermore, the ridges give a firmer grasp to avoid slippage (allowing the fingers to grasp and pick up objects). All fingerprints have a unique combination patterns and ridge characteristics. The patterns of the ridges contain rows of sweat pores that allow sweat and/or oil to exit from the glands. The sweat, that mixed with other body oils and dirt, produces fingerprints on smooth surfaces. The three main types of fingerprints are briefly discuss below:

i.   The *Visible prints* or the Patent prints are left in some mediums. The common example is when blood, dirt, ink or grease on the finger come into contact with a smooth surface and leave a friction ridge impression that is visible without development.
ii. The *Latent prints* are not visible. They are formed by the sebaceous glands on the body or water, salt, amino acids and oils contained in sweat. The sweat and fluids create prints that are processed before they can be seen or photographed. The latent prints can be visible by dusting, fuming or chemical reagents.
iii. The *Impressed prints* or plastic prints are indentations left in soft pliable surfaces (such as clay, wax, paint, etc…) that will take the impression. The impressed prints are visible and can be viewed or photographed without been processed.

The fingerprint patterns are divided into three main groups: Arches, Loops and Whorls. Many research works has been published to proved the accuracy of the fingerprints and it has been established that approximately 5% of all fingerprints are Arches, 30% are Whorls and 65% are Loops (see Figure 5–29 for patterns representation).

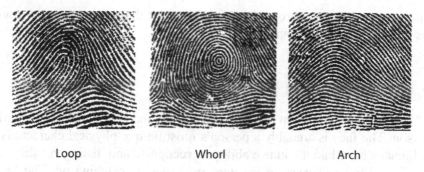

Loop   Whorl   Arch

Figure 5–29. Fingerprint Patterns

The intelligent agent in SIPSec would be able differentiate and recognised the fingerprint patterns of the users based on the most common line-types found in the prints:

i. Rod forms a straight line. It has no re-curve features and tends to be found in the centre of the fingerprint's pattern area.

ii. Ellipse is a circular or oval shaped line-type, which is generally found in the centre of Whorl patterns.

iii. Spiral line-type is generally found in whorl print patterns and. spirals out from the centre of the fingerprint.

iv. Bifurcation is the intersection of two or more line-types that converge or diverge.

v. Tented Arch resembles the tent. The line-type rises and falls at a steep.

vi. Loop is a re-curve line-type. It enters and leaves from the same side of the fingerprint.

vii. Island is a line-type that stands alone and totally contained in the pattern area of interest.

viii. Sweat Gland contains many sweat glands. The moisture and oils allows the fingerprint to be electronically imaged.

ix. Minutiae points are common micro features in a fingerprint. They are the intersection of bifurcations, ending points of islands and the centre point of the sweat glands.

x. Arch can be found in most print patterns. The fingerprints that make up the Arches are sometimes classified as Arch prints.

The fingerprints cannot be altered without creating a new unique fingerprint. Even when the skin tissue is injured or dirty/worn down from abrasion or with rare skin diseases the skin that grows back will have the same print. The prints remain the same throughout life. The print that someone is born with does not change until decomposition.

12.   FACE

The face is an important part of human body and how people can identify a person. The face is arguably a person's most unique physical characteristic and humans have had the innate ability to recognise and distinguish different faces for millions of years, computers are just now catching up. The facial recognition is based on the ability to first recognize faces, which is a technological feat in itself, and then measure the various features of each face (see Figures 5–13 and 5–14 for diagrammatic illustration). It may be far too soon to call the facial biometrics industry 'mature'. Tian and Bolle (2003), proposition of six universal expressions would be adopted to build the SIPSec prototype. The six universal recognised expressions are happy, sad, disgust, fear, surprise and anger in comparison to the neutral face (see Figure 5–30 for diagrammatic illustration).

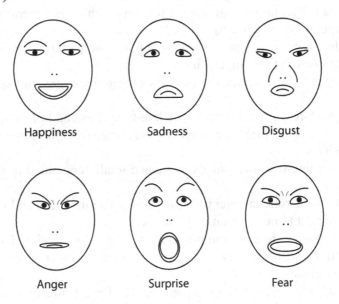

Figure 5–30. Six universal expressions

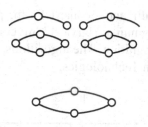

Figure 5–31. Distance Transform

The eyes and nose tip are estimated by visualising the fact that nose tip and centre of both eyes form equilateral triangle. So the eye middle points are estimated and the height is calculated by using formula (see Equation 5.5). Therefore 'α' is the length of side.

$$h = \alpha \sin 60° = \frac{1}{2}\sqrt{3}\alpha \tag{5.5}$$

The control points are required for analysis: eyebrow, eye, middle point of upper, lower eyelid and two extreme corners of eye, four lip control points which are left, right, top and bottom control points of lips (see Figure 5–31 for diagrammatic illustration). The distances d is the Euclidean distances in the control points with reference to neutral face (see Equation 5.6).

$$d = \sqrt{(x_2 - x_1)^2 + (y_2 - y_1)^2} \tag{5.6}$$

The ratio of eyes and lips in gestured image are calculated and its difference with the ratio of eyes and lips of neutral image. Statistical analysis of these distances classifies the gestured image into the corresponding expression. The ability of a computer to detect, analyse and recognised the user's face has many applications in human-computer interaction (HCI), so the automated analysis of faces showing different expressions has been studied to improve mapping quality of user's biometric profile.

13. IRIS

The iris patterns for personal identification were originally proposed by Frank Burch in 1936. By the 1980's the idea had appeared in James Bond films, but it still remained science fiction and conjecture. In 1987 two other ophthalmologists, Aran Safir and Leonard Flom, patented this idea, and in 1989 they asked John Daugman at Harvard University, to try to create the actual algorithms for iris recognition. The algorithms, which Daugman patented in 1994 is owned by Iridian Technologies.

Iris

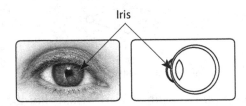

Figure 5–32. Understanding Iris Recognition

The iris features consists of the coloured tissue surrounding the pupil which has more than 200 points that can be used for comparison, including rings, furrows and freckles. It has the ability to create an accurate measurement that can be used for identification purposes, and not just verification. The uniqueness of eyes, even between the left and right eye of the same person, makes iris scanning very powerful for identification purposes. Its relative speed and ease of use make it a great potential biometric. It also takes up a bit more memory for the data to be stored, but with the advances in technology, this is unlikely to cause any major difficulty. The eyeglasses and contact lenses present no problems to the quality of the image and the iris-scan systems test for a live eye by checking for the normal continuous fluctuation in pupil size. The inner edge of the iris is located by an iris-scan algorithm, which maps the iris' distinct patterns and characteristics.

The Iris-scan technology has been piloted in ATM environments in England, the US, Japan and Germany since 1997. In these pilots the customer's iris data became the verification tool for access to the bank account, thereby eliminating the need for the customer to enter a PIN number or password. When the customer presented their eyeball to the ATM machine and the identity verification was positive, access was allowed to the bank account. These applications were very successful, eliminated the concern over forgotten or stolen passwords, and received tremendously high customer approval ratings. Many Airports have begun to use iris-scanning for such diverse functions as employee identification/verification for movement through secure areas and allowing registered frequent airline passengers a system that enables fast and easy identity verification in order to expedite their path through passport control. The false acceptance rate for iris recognition systems is 1 in 1.2 million, statistically better than the average fingerprint recognition system (see Figure 5–32 for diagrammatic illustration).

14.   RESULT SUMMARY OF HYPOTHESESS

The survey questionnaire, case studies, and laboratory experiments (combinatory research methodology) have been carried out in am attempt to prove or reject the hypotheses stated in chapter 1. The total outcome includes other elements that have led the author to prove or reject the three hypotheses (see Table 5–4). The results of the questionnaire survey and the case studies have shown that a staggering number of organisations agreed that absolute security

Table 5–4. Summary of hypotheses tested and results

Hypothesis tested	Reason in favour
Hypothesis 1	(H10) Accepted. Reason for acceptance of (H10) • The IPv4 can work in isolation without IPv6 (see chapter 2 for further discussion). • It is possible to migrate from the IPv4 to v6 (see chapter 3 for further discussion).
Hypothesis 2	(H20) Accepted. Reason for acceptance of (H20) • The limitations of the IPSec as led to the poor security performance (see also ALS, TLS and NLS limitations in chapter 2). • The Internet is a global network with unrestricted boundaries, as a result of this; transactions on the Internet can be intercepted, interrupted, modification, and Disinformation or fabrication. • The IPSec inherited many of the Internet security problems: i. Security in the application layer cannot be 100 per cent guarantee. ii. The TLS, NLS, and NAT are major issues that require further research. • The results of the questionnaire survey and the laboratory experiments have proved that the IPSec is not 100 per cent secured and requires further security enhancement. Security and storage of users biometrics profile is still a major concern.
Hypothesis 3	(H 3A) Accepted. Reason for acceptance of (H 3A) • The biometrics applications can be enabled in some computers and network devices as substitute to typing user's password. • The SIPSec model shows that it is possible to synchronise user's biometrics profile with IPSec policy. Suitable mathematical functions and theorem have been identified, for formulating the interfacing rules between SIPSec and the IPSec.

is unattainable on the Internet transactions. It is also evident that the IPv4 is complementary to IPv6. Previous study has shown that the society is exposed to a plethora of Internet security problems (Shoniregun, 2005) and the current IPSec is not the best security solution. It is believed that the adoption of SIPSec would be away forward to compromise the weaknesses found in the literature review, the questionnaire survey, case studies observations and laboratory experiments.

15.   SUMMARY OF CHAPTER FIVE

The IPSec has an extensive set of parameters within its architecture, and the interaction of those factors is not always intuitively clear. However, the IPSec communications driver follows rules that give the system administrators and developers to utilise the system and interpret security results, even when they are unexpected. The IPSec incorporates all of the most commonly employed security services (authentication, integrity, confidentiality, encryption and non-repudiation) but lack users biometrics integration. The IPSec is very complex with many-associated documentations. It affects network throughput and adds latencies that can disrupt networked applications. The IPSec continuously raising issues and doubts about the efficiency to identify that only the authorised user is using the system. In spite of this the IPSec is believed by many to be one of the best security systems available. The overall impacts of IPSec will be tremendous as the networks migrate from IPv4 to the IPv6. It is hope that the biometrics will become an integral component of the IPSec, which has led to the conceptual think and the proposition of SIPSec model. The SIPSec has the capability of protecting unauthorised interception, interruption, modification, and disinformation or fabrication. The SIPSec is a revolutionary technology that has the capability to combat both the security and identification issues. For smooth operation, the SIPSec requires wide-scale key infrastructures, the management of the security and access policies, and a thorough knowledge of several concepts is necessary to properly administer SIPSec policies. The implementation must conform to standards, to interoperates with multivendor environment. The next chapter critically evaluates the issues relating to this research study.

REFERENCES

Barrett, D. J., and Silverman, R.E., 2001, SSH: The Secure Shell, The Definitive Guide, O'Reilly & Associates.

Benbasat, I., Goldstein, D. K., and Mead, M., 1987, The Case Research Strategy in Studies of Information Systems, MIS Quarterly, Sept, pp 369-386.

Diffie, W. and Hellman, M.E., 1976, New Directions in Cryptography, IEEE Transactions on Information Theory, Vol IT-22, No. 6, November.

Huston. B., 2002, A Higher view of Defense in Depth, www.itworld.comh/nl/securitystrat/02202002/ (February 20, 2002).

Menezes, A.J., 19997, Elliptic Curve Public Key Cryptosystems, Fourth Printing, Kluwer Academic Publishers.

Ross, A.A., (2003), Ph D Thesis: Information Fusion in Fingerprint Authentication, Michigan State University, http://biometrics.cse.msu.edu /publications.html/genbio (9 February 2007).

Schneier, B., 1998, Applied Cryptography, 2nd Edition, John Wiley & Sons Inc.

Shoniregun, C.A. 2005, Impacts and Risk Assessment of Technology for Internet Security Enabled Information Small-Medium Enterprises (TEISMES), Springer-Verlag.

Tian. Y., and Bolle, R, M., 2003, Automatic Detecting Neutral Face for Face Authentication and Facial Expression Analysis, issue24 March.

Yin, R., (1994) 'Case Study Research, Design and Method', London: Sage

Ylonen, T., and Moffat, D., 2002, SSH Authentication Protocol, Network Working group, Internet Draft, September.

Ylonen, T., and Moffat, D., 2003, SSH Protocol Architecture, Network Working group, Internet Draft, October.

Zikmund, 1997, Business Research Methods, 5th Ed, Sydney: The Dryden Press.

Chapter 6

DISCUSSION

1. INTRODUCTION

The past decade has witnessed dramatic changes in IPSec. It is a well-established fact that the traditional security measures such as password and identification cards cannot satisfy every security requirement. Various physiological and behavioural biometrics for the authentication of individuals have broader applications. The number of organisations and individuals that uses IPSec to secured their computer network and the Internet has increase dramatically.

> '...information security is definitely an issue. How and where do we draw the line and how do we ensure that what is behind the line is safe?'
> —Charles A. Shoniregun (2005)

The importance of Internet security has, therefore, become an important aspect as the threat-level of IPSec crime increases. Although current literature has acknowledge the specific weaknesses of IPSec but there is no one best security control measure. The use of the Internet to acquire data has created deep concerns for authenticity and the invasion of privacy by the inadvertent leakage of personal identifiable information (PII) to unauthorised third parties (Azenabor and Shoniregun, 2006). This chapter discusses the issues relating to this study.

2. ISSUES IN IPSEC

As technology advances, systems becomes more sophisticated and the demands that these advanced systems put on networks are totally different as compared to the early 80's when networks were just simple dumb terminals accessing a mainframe. The rise of the Internet has placed new demands on network security, and efficient routing. The Internet communication is no longer an option but has become a necessity for most organisations. It provides organisations and their customers, timely access to valuable information. Employees within an organisation can gain access to services and information on the Internet through their corporate local area network. However, while the Internet provides much benefit it also creates a threat to the organisation because it opens door for the outside world to get into the organisation's local network and interacts with valuable assets (Oppliger, 1997).

The most commonly used alternative encryption technology to IPSec is the Secure Sockets Layer (SSL). The SSL was originally designed by Netscape to secure (HTTP) traffic passing through web browsers and is a session layer protocol. Unlike IPSec, SSL is based on a client/server model and is typically used for host-to-host secure transport. Because IPSec works at the network layer, it can be used to secure subnet-to-subnet, network-to-network, or network-to-host communications. This means that IPSec traffic can be routed, while SSL traffic cannot. While many people see SSL as a technology competitor to IPSec, this view is not entirely accurate. In most cases, IPSec and SSL are used to solve different types of problems. Also, while IPSec based connections require a substantial amount of planning and implementation time, SSL implementations are relatively quick to use, and sometimes require no planning at all, depending on what browser someone might be using and how it is currently configured (Taylor, 2002).

Another point to consider is that TCP/IP is over 20 years old and it remains largely unchanged, whilst hardware and software has advanced considerably and thus the resources at the disposal of the attacker are far greater and with greatly advanced techniques also being available. The TCP/IP is so widely used and forms the basis of the Internet, it therefore has been extensively studied, and hence the strengths and weaknesses of TCP/IP are well known. The problems with security with regards to TCP/IP are generic problems, which are detailed below:

i. *Data-Link-Layer Security* (DLLS): The DLLS consist of the Address Resolution Protocol (ARP), which performs the task of translating hardware or Ethernet addresses on a Local Area Network (LAN) or a Wide Area Network (WAN), into IP addresses not totally secure. This protocol is vulnerable to manipulation. Not all systems will determine or check incoming ARPs for any possible outstanding requests associated with the ARP packet. An example of such a system is the UNIX system. The lack of checking of the ARP packets could result in malicious responses being sent to ARP requests in addition to which, it also makes the ARP table open to unauthorised or invalid updates. The most common or likely effect would be the denial of service. This form of attack will have the attacker manipulating addresses so that traffic routed between two hosts is transmitted through a compromised machine that masquerades as each host to the other.

ii. *Network-Layer Security* (NLS): No matter how reliable the NLS architecture and the sound IP implementation, it can however still be manipulated. The routing of data packets is fairly open, which as a result can lead to data /or information not conforming to configured routing. Packets from the IP protocol can be injected directly onto the network as well. The Internet control message protocol (ICMP) protocol has no authentication, which could permit manipulation of routing (Landwehr, and Goldschlag, 1998). The Internet protocol allows source routing. Source routing specifies the path a packet must take to its destination. Accordingly, an attacker can use source routing to force a device to pass a packet to an intended target. For this reason, source routing must be turned off in firewall routers attached to an Internet. Furthermore, the ICMP is installed with every IP implementation. By its nature, ICMP is inherently insecure. For instance, ICMP redirect messages can tell a host to send its packet to a different router. Falsifying such messages can cause packets to take a path to the attacker's machine, is to limit the scope of change that may be dictated by ICMP. However, old ICMP versions do not use the extra information. Upon arrival of such messages, all connections between same pair of hosts will be affected. For example, if no destination unreachable message is received, stating that some packet was unable to reach the target host, all connections to that host will be turned down. This presents a weakness in ICMP, which is exploited by hackers programs, however exploiting this weakness can be captured. Hackers have used ICMP weaknesses to create new paths to a destination. The hacker can tamper with the knowledge of the proper route to a destination, and is capable of penetrating that host. A user with malicious intent will be able to subvert local routing tables, or ICMP could permit unsolicited mask reply packets or performed what is called a 'Nuke' on a destination system. This works by sending a target machine a packet that its operating system cannot process and potentially crash the machine. In the event that the ISP broadcasts an incorrect routing table to major Internet backbone providers, it would result in huge amounts of traffic to be routed to it, denying large groups of users or communities of their service, as a result, the 'black hole' will be created. Theprotocols managing the network routers are vulnerable enough to cause a further compromise of network security. Poor authentication is provided by Simple network management protocol (SNMP), and unless routers are correctly configured, they remain open to malicious attackers who may reconfigure them with relative ease (Bellowin, 1989).

iii. *IP Security Labels*: The IP security option is one of the security features of IP, it was primarily used by military sites, with commercial variants currently being defined. The data packet is labelled with the level of sensitivity of data or information. The labels used include a hierarchical component, which will state the level of sensitivity (secret, top secret, etc), and also an optional category such as nuclear weapons, cryptography, hammer, and procurements. Within the networks, the main purpose of security labels is to constrain routing decisions. A packet marked "top secret" may not be transmitted over an insecure link cleared only for "bottom secret" traffic.

iv. *IP Origin Forgery*: The forgery of the origin of IP messages does not pose a serious security problem in itself, even though an IP message origin can be forged with relative ease. The seriousness of this problem, however, comes to the forefront when taking into account the fact that most of the high level protocols use the IP origin as a mode of identification. One such example of the use of IP origin as an identification tools, is the example of the "r" commands (r login, rsh). These commands enable access between UNIX systems without the use of authentication, as the IP source is used as the primary authentication method in these instances, opening a doorway for the hacker who may use IP origin forgery.

v. *Transport-Layer Security*: The mechanism for ensuring the consistent use of port numbers is weak within TCP, UNIX systems assume that only privileged processes initiate connections from port numbers less than 1024, however there is no reason to assume that such processes are trustworthy (Landwehr, and Goldschlag, 1998). However, each IP packet must specify the kind of header that follows either a TCP or UDP herder. Since some applications use TCP (such as File Transfer Protocol) and others employ UDP (such as the Simple Network Management Protocol), an attacker can instantly learn the type of the message in the packet. Once the type of packet is known the attacker can look in the TCP or UDP header and discover the exact application to which this packet pertains. This is possible because many applications in the TCP/IP suite are assigned port number. The first 1023 ports numbers are assigned by Internet assigned numbers authority (IANA) and are available to anyone who cares to look. For instance, TELNET15 will request to enter a TELNET server on port 23, SMTP on port 25, and POP3 PC mail service is assigned port 110. Therefore, figuring out the source, destination, and contents of the packet is relatively easy. The TCP segments that follow the IP header also contain sequence numbers. Sequence numbers allow receiving TCP software to detect missing, duplicated, or out-of-order segments. It is possible for a 'spoofer' to guess some of these sequence numbers pretty easily as the numbers often follow a predictable sequence in some UNIX implementations. Using a combination of predictable sequence and knowledge of the target's IP address, it is possible to prosecute an IP spoofing attack against a target. In addition the TCP check summing of IP packets that are not very strong, which can lead to a potential for forgery, injection of information and tailgating of packets. The randomness of TCP initial sequence numbers varies across the UNIX system, resulting in a potential to inject the packets into a connection between two users.

It is very important to have precise plan to deal with incidents, as there is very little time during an incident to plan for managing the threats. When a security incident occurs, the IPSec responsibility for handling Internet security events are faced with various problems. No matter what has happened, before any counteraction is taken, several key questions has to be considered and answered to enhanced SIPSec policy:

i.   Has an incident actually occurred? Something that seems to be the action of an intruder might actually be the result of human error or a software failure.
ii. Was any damage really done? With many incidents, the perpetrator gains unauthorised access but doesn't actually access privileged information or maliciously change the data.
iii. Is it important to collect and protect evidence that might be used in an investigation?
iv. Is it important to get systems back into normal operation as soon as possible? Will rollback and roll forward necessary? The SIPSec is always in consistence state and real time security verification.
v.   Is it acceptable to take the chance to assume that data have been changed or deleted? If not, how can the organisation determine if changes have been made? The SIPSec does not allowed changes to the user's biometric profile with full concessions of both user's and the authorised biometrics database/server administrators (organisations, governments and international bodies).
vi. Does it matter if people inside the organization hear about the incident? If people outside hear about it?
vii. Can the event happen again? The SIPSec socket monitor at the network stack automatically builds a profile of the event.

The answers to some of these questions may be contradictory; such as collecting and protecting evidence may not be possible if the primary goal is to get systems and services back into normal operation immediately. It is very vital to have a well-defined process to help Internet security administrators take appropriate and necessary actions to restore the services, in the event of an incident. The risk analysis and management is a critical factor in finding out appropriate actions to reduce the threat.

Furthermore, the ISERP should carry out by a group of people possessing a variety of skills – not only in the Internet security, but also in non-technical areas such as public relations. This group is referred to as the 'Response Team'. By effectively organising responses to Internet security events, the ISERP allows ISP, organisations, governments and international collaborators to optimally use the technological protection that is provided by the SIPSec (see chapter 5 for further discussion). To harden and secure systems, it is necessary to established secured configurations access to information. If this is done correctly and maintained, many of the common vulnerabilities used by intruders can be eliminated. This can greatly reduce the success of many common recurring attacks. Anything that compromises the security of information stored or held on a computer system or network is viewed as a security attack. There are two main categories of attacks: passive attacks (data interception) and active attacks (data flow interruption, data modification and disinformation) (see chapter 1 for further discussion):

i. *Interception* is used for the replaying messages or part of a message in order to produce an unauthorised access (see Figure 6–1 for diagrammatic illustration).

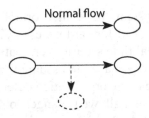

Figure 6–1. Interception

For example, the authentication information of a previously sent message is interrupted to create the denial of service or flooding the data packets. It also includes attack on confidentiality (wire tapping, and copying software).

ii. *Interruptions* violate the confidentiality rules and hardware sabotage but do not delete or modify the transmitted data (see Figure 6–2 for diagrammatic illustration). It uses wire tapping, electromagnetic radiation interception, Fraud network partitioning etc.

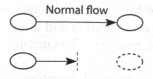

Figure 6–2. Interception

The attack is on file availability (disabled the system management resources, system asset destroyed, made unusable or unavailable.

iii. *Modification attack* modifies (through insertion and/or deletion of characters) a part or all transmitted data (see Figure 6–3 for diagrammatic illustration).

Figure 6–3. Modification

Attack on integrity, modifying message content, and changing software functionality (unauthorised access and tampering).

iv. *Disinformation or fabrication attack*
is an authorised user (see Figure 6–4 for diagrammatic illustration).

Figure 6–4. Disinformation or fabrication

For example, a user tries to substitute another user with the intention to get secret data. A disinformation is accompanied by another active attack for modification or interruption.

The WAN is an un-trusted network with less security while LAN is a close-in system with little secure. The LAN is face with internal threats. These threats may not always be malicious in intent, they are sometimes more damaging than external threats. Preserving the integrity of the data and applications that traverse the wired or wireless LAN is an important part of SIPSec policy. With harden/secure connectivity, organisations benefit from increased user productivity, business efficiencies, and confidentiality of critical information. Therefore the Internet security administrators need to redefine the IPSec configuration to match the SIPSec requirements and policy. This will yield a hardened secure system configuration and an operational environment that protects against transaction integrity. The currently defined mitigating strategies are as following:

i. Install only the minimum essential operating system configuration, that is, only those packages containing files and directories that are needed to operate the computer.

ii. Install patches to correct known deficiencies and vulnerabilities.

iii. Install the most secure and up-to-date versions of system applications. It is essential that all installations be performed before the next step, removing privileges, as any installation performed after privileges are removed can undo such removal and results in, for example, changed mode bits or added accounts.

iv. Remove all privilege and access and then grant (add back in) privilege and access only as needed, following the principle "deny first, and then allow."

v. Enable as much system logging as possible to have access to SIPSec information (user's biometric profile database/server).

Table 6–1. Securing general-purpose network servers

Planning	Address Security Issues in your computer deployment plan (NS, UW)
	Address Security Requirements When Selecting Servers (NS)
Configuration	Keep Operation Systems and Applications Software Up to Date (NS, UW)
	Stick to Essentials on the Server Host System (NS)
	Stick to Essentials on the Workstation Host System (UW)
	Configure Network Service Clients to enhance Security (UW)
	Configure Computers for User Authenticatin (NS, UW)
	Configure Operating Systems with Appropriate Object, Device, and File Access Controls (NS, UW)
Maintainance	Protecting Computers from Viruses and Similar Programmed Threats (NS, UW)
	Congfigure Computers for Secure Remote Administration (NS, UW)
	Allow only Appropriate Physical Access to Computers (NS, UW)
Improving User Awareness	The Development and Rollout an Acceptable Use Policy for Wrokstaions (UW)

The practices for hardening and securing general-purpose network servers (NS) and user workstations (UW) are shown in the Table 6–1. Improvement actions typically occur following a detection or response activity. In addition to those noted under Detect above, improvement actions may includes:

i.   Communication with affected parties
ii. Holding a post mortem meeting to identify lessons learned
iii. Updating policies and procedures
iv. Updating tool configurations and selecting new tools
v.   Collecting measures of resources required to deal with the intrusion and other security business case information

Furthermore, creating a secured posture for information transmitted is not a single event; it is a process, which takes time and must be constantly improved and fine-tuned, to become an integral part of IPSec standard.

3.   IPSEC IS AN APPLICATION SPECIFIC

The IPSec is an application specific that is; they can be used for one purpose only. A positive feature of IPSec is that the various algorithms used for encryption and hashing can be change. For example, if the best security cannot be negotiated, IKE will try to negotiate the second best. This may result in less than the best possible security been used, because one of the peers is set to negotiate to low security. Another problem is increased processor load. Many have argued that the use of IPSec will force users to upgrade their hardware. This as never been the case, as the problem is easily overcomes by using an IPSec compliant network interface card, which has a built-in processor designed for this task only. In this way, the computer's main processor will not have to deal with the IPSec specific work.

The IPsec has many knobs and settings that impede successful connection. It is complex suite of protocols that provides mechanism, instead of strict policy and allows an implementation to provide nearly anything that both ends agree upon. The simplest ways to study IPSec is to simply download and install one of the freeware or shareware programs from the internet. Why is this the case? An indepth understanding of IPSec will comes during installation and the actual logging will enhance user's knowledge of what is going on during an IPSec session. It is therefore very important not to only log onto the session, but to do all the installation from the start. The setting of the IPSec allows who ever involved in the process to do more in terms of experimentation and certainly helps set up a more realistic test and configuration. It is apparent that not everyone can afford to setup the IPSec, but if you work in a big organisation it might be possible to ask the people in the Information Technology (IT) department to run through the setup with you few times before you try to do it on your own. In reality installing IPSec in not very difficult if the person installing it is competent in IT or Information Systems (IS). However, the survey carried out 2006 as part of this study shows that most organisations that run

Cisco gear and have opted for Cisco centric VPN solutions. It is the necessary to ask Why opted for Cisco centric VPN? and Why IPSec VPN? The IPSec VPNs uses the IPSec standards and protocols to ensures the privacy and integrity of all the data that are transmitted and communicated across the Internet or any other public networks. The VPN consists of a collection of hosts that have implemented protocols that secured information exchange. How does VPN works to support businesses? An organisation with large numbers of modems will need to updates to the current commonly supported speeds in order to administer their modems and users. But when the organisation use VPN to support their businesses, a long distance call will be routed to a local access numbers which as been established by the Internet services providers (ISP) (see Figure 6–5 for diagrammatic illustration). This idea is very cost effective. Even though the VPNs and extranets provide some type of security, key management and digital certificates are simply two more locks and keys that could be set in place for peace of mind. Setting up a secured network is a daunting task. It requires careful thought, adequate planning and the perspectives and recommendations of a team of IT staff. The Internet service provider network should be configured so that it is scalable and flexible to handle additional hardware and software as the network grows with combined Internet security technologies and biometrics.

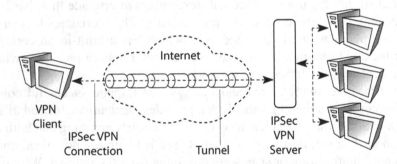

Figure 6–5. VPN Connection

The ISAKMP is responsibility for the creation and maintenance of SAs in IPSec. It is important to note that the use of AH alone does not provide any confidentiality services and the degree of confidentiality provided by ESP depends on the IPSec mode. The AH and ESP are based on the concept of SA. The SA is one way, but two-way connection requires at least two (ESP and AH has there own SA in each direction). The AH and ESP may be use isolation or to gether, however full protection agaist trafficc analysis is not provided. Although the traffic padding and onion routing, and the encryption of data link layer can be use to provide minimal security but only few internet users are concerned with traffic analysis. However, if two endpoints or gateways were going to establish a secure connection, some kind of shared secret would be required. The IPsec key exchange typically takes place over port 500/udp. Three pieces of data that are used to locate the correct SA inside the SAD:

- Partner IP address
- IPsec Protocol (ESP or AH)
- Security Parameters Index

The above three pieces of data are used by IP socket, this uniquely denoted by the remote IP address, protocol, and port number. The open issues of Internet layer security are troubling, so many organisations and users are not comfortable with IPSec status with regards to:

- Properties of the encryption modes used
- Integrity protection in the security transforms
- Host-oriented keying
- Plaintext
- Traffic analysis
- Integrating compression into the Internet layer

Although the transport layer security operates on end-to-end basis, transmitting authenticated and confidential data is not a total solution for the above problems because:

i. It neither addresses nor meets the security requirement of connectionless transport services provided by UDP/IP.
ii. It does not work well with caching and replication of proxy servers.
iii. The question of how and when to secure UDP-based application protocols at the transport layer has not yet been addressed properly. The possible suggestion to these problems is to relay on application specific security enhancement.

There are several extensions to the idea of building an authentication and key distribution system that may serve different applications or use by arbitrary applications to in corporate security services at the application layer but the proliferation of these has been very slow. Security becomes an issue, the moment computers are connected to the Internet and the only way to protect abuse is to use available techniques for secure network connections. The system password file is vulnerable in all systems connected to the internet, allowing the system password file to become compromised would leave the system open to hostile attacks of different kinds. For example, a recent study of Windows XP exposed a vulnerability that allowed a hostile web page to unobtrusively to extract a user's password and transmit it to the page's author. Microsoft sends forth a stream of patches intending to correct what it designates as 'critical' security flaws in it systems, applications, and even its own previous patches. Microsoft certainly is not alone when it comes to software flaws, but as the massively dominant desktop system vendor, its software and support decisions tend to have much more influence on most consumers, and businesses. The network security is also a psychological issue; more people would probably use the Internet if they knew that the IPSec can secure connection properly, and in turn the expected boom in e-commerce may become reality.

There is old adage that, 'if your most familiar tool is a hammer, the whole world starts to look like a nail'. Unfortunately, there is a tendency to regard the IPSec as an all-inclusive security solution. As a result of this misconception, the IPSec is considered as a solution to all security concerns. This is clearly the result of a lack of understanding of the IPSec standard. In a network with hundreds of IPSec Peer or Key Management, all wishing to establish the IPSec VPNs with each other, each peer needs to be configured individually. IPSec does not provide any mechanism for automating the configuration process. The implementation and maintenance of a large IPSec network is very resource intensive, large businesses are often forced to employ dedicated IT staff to manage the network.

In a normal IPSec operation, it is the destination peer that chooses the SPI. However, in multicast communications, there is no single destination for a given address. This clearly poses implementation issues. The IPSec also poses some problems with streaming multimedia. In normal IPSec operation, the selection of outgoing IPSec policy parameters is based on the examination of IP addresses, the upper layer protocol ID and port numbers. This works well with protocols that use stable port numbers for example application using streaming multimedia utilise UDP and RTP (Shoniregun *et al* 2004). The source and destination port numbers used for RTP are dynamically assigned, making it very difficult to define IPSec policies to select the appropriate UDP streams to protect. Due to the end-to-end encryption performed by IPSec, it is not possible for any intermediary routing devices to check and process flags contained within the original IP headers. The ability to look up certain fields such as the Type of Service (ToS) and IP Precedence fields within IP packet headers is essential to the operation of QoS mechanisms. As a result of the restriction posed by the IPSec encryption it is not possible to secure communications such as IP Telephony data that rely heavily on QoS. No mechanism in place to secure the communication endpoints, such as the end user machines or applications. This is rather unfortunate, as the original goal of IPSec was to enable the protection of all types of IP communications. The RFC 3715 describes known incompatibilities between NAT and the IPSec. The IPSec does not interoperate with most firewalls and gateways that implement NAT. This is one of the major limitations of the IPSec. The NAT routers typically sit on the border between private and public networks and translate private addresses in each IP packet into registered public addresses.

4. CURRENT USE OF BIOMETRICS TECHNOLOGY

Over the past years, experts from both the forensic and computer field have expressed their opinions with an insight into the impacts of biometrics on the society and also provided clear understanding of the applicability of biometric technology. According to Arun et.al., (2000), biometric is the process of identifying a person, on the basis of certain characteristics which are physiological or behavioural and the two basic reasons why biometrics is preferred to traditional methods of security (passwords and pins) are as follows:

- The person to be identified is required to be physically present at the point of identification and
- Identification based on biometric techniques replaces the need to remember a password or carry a token.

The biometrics technologies are evolving and widely applied in forensics as (criminal identification and prison security). The advancements made in biometric sensors and matching algorithms have resulted in the deployment of biometric authentication in a large number of civilian applications. Biometrics can now be used to prevent unauthorised access to a number of processes, such as border controls, national ID cards and passport, which are currently been adopted by many countries.

Kaucher (2004) in an inaugural lecture on biometrics held at National Defence University, USA, emphasised the fact that biometrics supplements password collection and is regarded as the latest technology used to enhance security and improve operators' productivity. Biometrics is the ability to use a physical property of the operator (finger print, iris scan, or voice), can be used to reduce operator fatigue and response time. Of all these physical features, Kaucher identified fingerprint verification as drawing the highest attention partly because fingerprint features mark measurable differences between individuals that remain stable over a long period. An interesting part of Kaucher's lecture was a twist on the fact that the full fingerprint image used by the police forces and forensic examiners which have worked for over the years, in terms of finding a match for particular prints from the databases, does not tell the whole story.

Palmgren, (2005) introduced biometric authentication, traced the historical use of usernames and passwords for authenticating systems and compared it to today's evolving use of biometrics, which has otherwise replaced this traditional security method. In his work, he placed more emphasis on the weaknesses of the traditional method, which he dubbed as the worst management headache for IT staff and the biggest network security hole in existence. He went further to buttress his point by stating that many help desks handle more password related calls than any other category.

An article by Danielyan (2004) introduces biometrics and discusses some complex issues associated with the use of biometrics for identification and authentication of individuals including ways it impacts on standalone and networked information systems as well as on physical security. It is now a requirement by the US government to finger print and photographs of all visitors coming to the US this raise a big question on the use of biometrics and associated issues such as privacy and personal data protection which are bound to get unprecedented levels of publicity. Although he went further to state that it's rather too early to judge whether this innovation will actually contribute to the overall security of the United States or increase the general confusion surrounding security procedures, already it has resulted in more questions been asked.

Biometrics is perceives as a technology that can be used to provide a password that cannot be shared. The user passwords have long been a big issue for administrators and users. For administrators, it creates a huge workload to administer passwords and users usually find it difficult to memorize their passwords and this has been discovered to create a big security problem. As a result of this, most times, people make their password easy to remember and this in turn makes their passwords a lot easier to crack. Thus to increase the security level in user authentication systems, identifying a user by biometrics, is a more secure process than 'what he/she knows' because the former method of securing systems cannot be easily hacked and passed to another user (Libov, 2004). The biometric authentication can determine users who genuinely enrolled or an impostor.

5.   COMBINING BIOMETRICS WITH IPSEC

The biometric calculation is based on the unique features of individuals and thus provides security and trust for any transactions. The SIPSec is a combination of existing IPSec and biometrics, it can link user with their biometric profile and timely verification. It becomes difficult to use a stolen biometric profile or for a user to mistakenly repudiate an individual biometric profile. The SIPSec application depend on hardware and an attacker using chip-testing technology can infect the server even though the attacker is unable to download the user biometric profile.

The main obstruction to SIPSec is combination of IPSec and biometrics. The biometric data are noisy and only an estimated match can be predictable to a stored template. The cryptography, on the other hand, requires that keys should be accurately right, or protocols will fail. It is also based on specific hardware devices. It would be better to have a more general protocol-level method that will merge cryptography and biometrics. However, many users are reluctant to have their biometric data stored on central databases. The social acceptance of biometric is significantly important. The fear that the biometric profile will be misuse, makes the users reluctant and this could be especially if there is a large centralised database containing biometrics data. There may be a fear that personal health information will be disclosed and source of information for the terrorist.

Other researchers have tried to map biometric data into a unique and repeatable binary string. Consequently, the binary string would be mapped to an encryption key or direct hashing. The potential of this approach is that storage of biometric profiles would not be desirable; these attempts have endured from several drawbacks. There may be less conflict with biometric technology if users can be credibly guaranteed that there biometric profiles are not stored centrally (or perhaps, at all) but such is not the case with SIPSec. It is a well-established fact that the traditional security measures such as password and identification cards cannot satisfy every security requirement. Various physiological and behavioural biometrics for the authentication of individuals have broader applications such as the control of access to personal computers, private files and information repositories, building access control, and many others. There have been a number of attempts to link the gap between the fuzziness of biometrics and the accuracy of cryptography, by obtaining biometric keys from keystroke patterns, the human voice, handwriting, signature, fingerprints, and facial characteristics (Anderson, 2001). However, in most cases, biometrics systems cannot determine if an individual has established a fraudulent identity, or is posing as another individual during biometrics enrolment process. An individual with a fake passport may be able to use the passport as the basis for enrolment in a biometrics system. The system can only verify that the individual is who he or she claim to be during enrolment, unless a large-scale identification system is built in which all users are matched against all other users to find duplicates or individual attempts to enrol more than once. Although biometrics has been used for years in high-security government and military applications, but the technology is now becoming affordable for use as a network authentication method and general security feature. Biometrics could be a major security system for enhancing IPSec (see Table 6–2).

Table 6–2. Table of biometric technologies

Technology	Applications	Benefits/Barriers
Face Scan	Cheque cashing kiosk, time and attendance verification, ATM access	Facial hair can cause false rejection and this is highly dependent on lighting conditions. In addition, people generally do not like to have this picture taken, which could create resistance by consumers.
Finger Scan	Authentication for bank teller ID, customer ID	An inexpensive technology, although it can be difficult to read some population's fingerprints.
Iris Scan	ATM access	Very accurate under normal circumstances, though there is a high false rejection rate for individuals who wear designer contact lenses. Also iris scanning is quite costly to implement.
Hand Scan (Hand Geometry)	Physical security, time and attendance verification	Easy to use and easily accepted by users as this is not viewed as intrusive. Quite expensive to implement, and physiological changes in the hands can cause false rejection.
Keystroke Dynamics	In beta testing	Can be used with any device that uses a keyboard
Retina Scan	Network access, PCLogin	Extremely accurate and resistant to fraud, but requires the user to stand within six inches of the scanner. Also very expensive to implement.
Signature Scan (Dynamic Signature Verification)	Mortgage pooling application	Not very accurate because handwriting can change over the years.
Voice Scan (Speaker Verification)	Voicemail access, telephone banking	A logical choice for the mobile arena, though the false rejection rate is high

The barrier to biometrics growth is the cost of implementation, cost of connectivity, speed of services, and speed of authentication. For finger scanning, as people become older they lost the fat in their skin, so the fingerprints worn out, which can make difficult for scanner to image it. Research has proved that some biometrics features are expensive and less accurate in result such as hand scan. There could be some false rejection because of external environment like in face scanning lightening can effects the result. External noise can effect the authentication of voice recognition. However, voice changes with the passage of time. The flu, soar throat, or emotional conditions can also affect the voice recognition (Shoniregun, 2005).

6.   UNDERPINING ASSUMPTION OF SIPSEC

The underpinning assumption of SIPSec is that current IPSec requires further security enhancements, therefore SIPSec drive IPSec, the interpretation and further analysis is discussed in chapter 5. It may be difficult to promote the notion of SIPSec as a tighter security option due to many ethical issues and the right to be left alone (individual privacy). But it is important to engage organisations, governments and international bodies in the SIPSec implementation, although some countries may be more forceful in their views and expectations of SIPSec than others. 'How secure is the user's biometrics profile?' This question will reduce the potential contribution of users involvement and participation of other countries; as users may perceive SIPSec as remote, and complain of inadequate involvement. The emphasis here is on privacy and integrity of individual data and the control procedures that are expected to achieve the aims of SIPSec. Since there is a search for the best security model or at least one better than the IPSec or what can be integrated to enhance the IPSec; the IPSec has been found to be deficient for many reasons which are discussed in chapter 4. Therefore, the SIPSec model provides a remedy that is sufficiently robust or comprehensive for enhancing Internet security strategy. Without doubt vendors plays significant role, as challenges unfold, the criteria for SIPSec model evolve round quality and integrity of users biometric profile.

It is difficult to ignore the increasing investment in technology-enabled information (TEI) that has been enhancing Internet business operations (Shoniregun, 2005). The Internet security has appears to be an important area for researchers. It has grown both in size and type of issues that are encountered on a daily basis. The vendors and researchers have developed methodologies and techniques that follow the standard that has been specified by RFC. For many businesses, executive information security personnel, and systems administrations, information security continues to be critical issue. The research conducted prior to written this book shows that the network/Internet security is a major concern and at the sametime it is almost axiomatic that Internet security should be based on only IPSec, so, what is the future of IPSec?

7.   SUMMARY OF CHAPTER SIX

One of the major problems with IPSec today is the compatibility issue. Some large software manufacturers are known for their desire not to comply with existing standards and might instead develop standards of their own. One of the advantages mentioned above, the possibility to change the algorithms, is also considered a disadvantage. This is due to the fact that some of the algorithms used as default have already been broken. Even though new ones are available, it is up to the administrators to make sure that they actually use them.

Furthermore, with common security techniques, if the negotiation fails, there will be no communication at all. In the case of IPSec, if the best security cannot be negotiated, the IKE will try to negotiate the second best and subsequent opportunities. This may result in that less than the best possible security is used, because one of the peers is set to negotiate to low security. Another problem is increased processor load. The encryption and decryption of all information flowing in and out of a computer is pretty hard work. Many have argued that the use of IPSec will force users to upgrade their hardware. This problem is easily overcome by using an IPSec compliant network interface card, which has a built-in processor designed for this task only. In this way, the computer's main processor will not have to deal with the IPSec specific work. The IPSec is a protocol suite consisting of the ESP and AH with the capability of encrypting and authenticating any kind of traffic passing through the TCP/IP stack. The IPSec is equipped with a technique for safe negotiation of encryption keys and the IKE. The SIPSec employs existing IPSec policies and can make use of biometric profile that are proven to be more secure than just using only the IPSec or SSL. The main difference between the SIPSec and existing security techniques is that the SIPSec is not application specific, that is, it can be used in conjunction with all existing applications, without having to modify the application. The use of SIPSec is completely invisible to the users; and does not require any changes to the system requirement. The next chapter concludes this study.

REFERENCES

Anderson, R., 2001, Security Engineering: A Guide to Building Dependable Distributed Systems, John Wiley & Sons, Inc.

Azenabor, C.E., and Shoniregun, C.A., 2006, Electronic Government Security Issues, In Proceedings of the International Conference of Internet Technology and Secured Transactions (ICITST-2006), London, UK.

Bellowin, S.M., 1989, Security Problems in the TCP/IP Protocol Suite, Computer Communications Review, May.

Danielyan, E., 2004, The Lure of Biometrics. Available At: http://www.cisco.com/warp/public/759/ipj_7-1.pdf (24 January 2007)

Kaucher, C., 2004, An Inaugural lecture on biometrics USA, National Defense University, http://www.biometrics.dod.mil/bio101/10.aspx (23 January 2007)

Landwehr, C.E., and Goldschlag, D.M., 1998, Security Issues with Internet Access, In Proceedings of IEEE, Vol. 85, No. 12, December.

Libov, Y., 2004, Biometrics: Technology that Gives You a Password You can't share, http://www.securitydocs.com/library/1032 (31 January 2007)

Oppliger, R., 1997, 'Firewalls and Beyond', Communication of the ACM, May 1997.

Palmgren, K., 2005, Biometric Authentication, An Introduction, http://www.securitydocs.com/library/3003 (3 January 2007)

Shoniregun, C.A., Chochliouros, I.P., Laperche, B., Logvynovskiy, O., and Spiliopoulou-Chochliourou, A., 2004, Questioning The Boundary Issues of Internet Security, e-Centre for Infonomics, London.

Shoniregun, C. A., 2005, Impacts and Risk Assessment of Technology for Internet Security: Enable information Small-medium Enterprises (TEISMEs), Springer New York, USA.

Taylor L., 2002, Understanding IPSec, Intranet Journal

Chapter 7

CONCLUSION

The IP v6 is currently being promoted as a successor to the IP v4. Within the context of network security, the IETF has proposed the addition of extension headers that will allow IPv6 to perform authentication and encryption at the Network Layer; and also have regular IPv6 specifications drafts. It is envisaged that with the IP v6, security will be a property of the network, rather than a special mode as is the case with IPv4 (Carmes, 2002). The wireless networking brings a whole new meaning to network security (Interlink Networks, 2003). With readily available equipment, attacks on wireless networks have never been so easy. Some enterprises have deployed the IPSec solutions to protect their wireless networks. Although the future of the IPSec might depend on the expected transition from the IPv4 to v6 but synchronising the IPSec with biometrics would enhance existing security measures in both IPv4 and v6.

The chapter 1 has set the background for this research, while chapters 2 and 3 discusses the Internet communications protocol and protocol security. These two latter chapters have given the foundation of the study, which are further explored by using combinations of research methods. The methods and methodologies adopted aids in studying the subject matter. Both quantitative and qualitative processes of collecting data were employed which encourages a rich mixture of analysis and conclusive findings. The chapter 4 focuses on the implementations and limitations of IPSec. In the chapter 5, the SIPSec model was presented and chapter 6 is a discussion chapter, which critically evaluates the research area. However, this chapter concludes with recommendation, contribution to knowledge and future work.

1.   DEPENDENCE ON INFORMATION TECHNOLOGY

The short-term focus of IT security is no longer enough for the increasing inter-connective nature of networks, the growing threat from the cyber crimes, requires serious efforts to be devoted into network security. The governments and organisations must consider the possible impact of security problems on other systems. Also, the questionnaire survey that was conducted revealed that majority of network security controls focuses on the perimeter of the external networks; however, this approach leaves internal hosts open to attacks from insiders and other incoming vulnerabilities.

To design and implement an effective security system, the importance of defining the organisational security policy beforehand cannot be underplayed, security must be seen as a property of the system as a whole, not merely of its parts. If sensitive information is disclosed or modified without proper authorisation or by unauthorised parties, or if critical services are denied to, the organisation will be in serious breach of security (Shoniregun, 2006a). When designing the security system that will provide the required level of protection and at an acceptable cost, it requires careful balancing the security issues addressed in the security policy formulated, to determine the hardware, software, firmware, and protocols that would be needed to implement the security policy. The security of the network will also need careful maintenance and constant vigilance by administrators, and system managers, because there are many forms of attack that may prove more difficult to detect, unless the attack is denial of service, the secure system may operate as normal or appear to do so.

Generally speaking, connecting an internal network to the Internet increases the functions that a system provides. An internal network connected to the Internet gives flexibility. In addition, the Internet can also become significantly more complicated. For example individual services and applications have their own settings. Therefore, if an application gateway (firewall) were deployed, an application proxy would be required for every new service or application included into the system. Alternatively, if a packet that filters firewall were deployed, then the filtering rules would need to be changed to permit or disallow any additional or current services. This may result in a considerably more complex system and the combination of security mechanisms can also be unpredictable, particularly if it is poorly designed and installed.

Although, it is impossible to anticipate every possible breach of security, even the best security systems may have unidentified security holes. Thus a well-designed security system would be one that provides maximum security with as little compromise as possible. For example, if an inherently insecure service (Telnet) that is open to abuse is required by an organisation, the organisation will have to compromise with its network security. An organisation may require cryptographic security systems, which provide the fundamental mechanisms for privacy, authentication, and integrity; these services are usually at the heart of most security plans. However, there is no clear-cut answer as to which layer of communications protocol is best suited to provide the encryption security services. The chosen layer should be based on the security requirements of each application. For example, an application that requires non-repudiation services may opt for encryption at the application layer, whereas an application that requires IP tunnelling between mobile station and the organisation firewall may be best served with encryption security at the Internet layer. Moreover, security can be set-up at different layers for different security services. For example, it would be sensible to use SSL to provide confidentiality services to web applications, even though SSL is not 100 per cent secured.

The result of the case studies observations shows that most commonly used combination security techniques, which has led to a possible degrading of QoS and high maintenance cost. Although, the latter does not present much of a problem since the computing power continues to double at an advance rate and cost keep dropping. However, more work need to be done to make sure that the Internet is not crippled through inadequate security.

2.   GLOBAL ISSUES ON INTERNET SECURITY

Generally speaking, many security experts are not willing to consider any compromised to security, and to perform a proper risk analysis. This, in turn, has led some applications developers to shun security. The willingness to think in new ways is required both from application developers and from security experts. The application developers (and even some security experts) need to learn to think in new terms, paying much more attention to authorisation than before. The security experts must accept that often *"-good enough"* security is better than as-strong-as-possible security (Arkko and Nikander 2003). In the digital world, just as everywhere else, humanity has encountered its dark side. Information Age business, government, and culture have led to Information Age crime, Information Age war and even Information Age terror (Shoniregun, 2003, 2005; Liu et al. 2001; Timmers, 2000). If biometrics are the way forward in making sure that IPSec is enhanced with individual biometric profiles, then the questions to ask are: *"How much will it cost to implement such security solution(s)?"*, *"Who should be trust with genetics information?"*, and *"How long will it take the expert hacker to decrypt such human genetic codes?"*

Indeed, the human race has not only brought its business to cyberspace, it has brought its exploration of the psyche there, too. As in the case of IP spoofing, attackers can lie about their identity and location on the network. Information on the Internet is transmitted in packets, which contains information about the origin and destination, but they can lie about it. Most of the Internet is designed merely to forward packets one step closer to their destination with no attempt to make a record of their source. There is not even a *"postmark"* to indicate generally where a packet originated. So it requires close cooperation among sites and up-to-date equipment to trace malicious packets during an attack.

Although, the Internet is designed to allow packets to flow easily across geographical, administrative, and political boundaries but cooperation in tracing a single attack may involve multiple organizations and jurisdictions, most of which are not directly affected by the attack and may have little incentive to invest time and resources in the effort. The attacks against the Internet typically do not require the attacker to be physically present at the site of the attack; the risk of being identified is reduced. In addition, it is not always clear when certain events should be cause for alarm and prevention. What appear to be probes and unsuccessful attacks may actually be the legitimate activity of network managers checking the security of their systems. Even in cases where organizations monitor their systems for illegitimate activity, which occurs in only a small minority of Internet-connected sites, real break-ins often go undetected because it is difficult to identify illegitimate activity. In the case of cross-site scripting, web users trigger malicious code without even knowing they have done so, and web sites can unknowingly pass the code along. Finally, because intruders cross multiple geographical and legal domains, an additional confusion is thrown over the legal issues involved in pursuing and prosecuting them (Cross, 2000).

The security breaches can cause a loss of time and resources as personnel investigate the compromise, determine potential damage, and restore the systems. The systems may provide reduced service or be unavailable for a period of time. Sensitive information can be exposed or altered, and public confidence can be lost. After a successful computer system intrusion, it can be very difficult or impossible to determine precisely what subtle damage, if any, was left by the intruder. Loss of confidence can result even if an intruder leaves no damage because the site cannot prove none was left. Particularly serious for business are denial-of-service attacks and the exposure of sensitive information. Once an explicit DoS attack has been resolved and the service returned, users generally regain trust in the service they receive. But exposure of sensitive information makes an organization highly susceptible to a loss-of-confidence crisis.

3.   ROOT CAUSES OF ATTACKS

The Internet is primarily based on protocols for sharing electronically stored information, and a break-in is not physical. Intruders are easy to get unauthorised access to the sites without knowing to the others, residing in programs, exploding at right time and collecting information. It is true that some attacks require technical knowledge but technically unsophisticated intruders carry out many successful attacks. The technically competent intruders duplicate and share their programs at little cost, thus enabling inexperienced and immature intruders to do the same damage as the experts.

In the 1980s intruders were the system experts. They had a high level of expertise and personally constructed methods for breaking into systems. The intruders are demonstrating increased understanding of network topology, operations, and protocols, resulting in the infrastructure attacks (Allen, et al. 2000) Many attacks consist of large number of hosts, or computers, operating under the control of the attacker. These hosts may be referred to as zombies, agents, slaves, or bots. The huge number of hosts connected to the Internet gives attackers plenty of potential attack agents that are vulnerable to compromise. Root causes include the level of security at individual sites, the nature of attack tools, and vulnerabilities in software products (Householder, 2001). In the late 1980s and early 1990s, the typical intrusion was fairly straightforward. Intruders most often exploited relatively simple weaknesses, such as poor passwords and miss-configured systems that allowed greater access to the system than was intended. There was little need for more sophisticated techniques because the vendors delivered systems with default settings that made it easy to break into systems. Configuring systems in a secure manner was not straightforward, and many system administrators did not have the time, expertise, or tools to monitor their systems adequately. All these activities continue in 1990s; however, more sophisticated intrusions are now common. The CERT Coordination Centre has seen intruders demonstrate increased technical knowledge, develop new ways to exploit system vulnerabilities, and create software tools to automate attacks. At the same time, intruders with little technical knowledge are becoming more effective as the sophisticated intruders share their knowledge and tools.

In the 21st centaury, absolutely anyone can attack a network due to the widespread and easy availability of intrusion tools and exploit scripts that can easily duplicate known methods of attack. Instead of simply exploiting well-known vulnerabilities, intruders examine source code to discover weaknesses in certain programs, such as those used for electronic mail. Much source code is easy to obtain from programmers who make their work freely available on the Internet. Moreover, the targets of many computer intrusions are organizations that maintain copies of proprietary source code. Once intruders gain access, they can examine this code to discover weaknesses. The experienced intruders are getting smarter as demonstrated by the increased sophistication in the types of attacks, and the knowledge required on the part of novice intruders is to copy and launch known methods of attack. A security incident or an intrusion may be a comparatively minor event involving a single site or a major event in which thousands of sites may be affected. A typical attack pattern consists of gaining access to a user's account, gaining privileged access, and using the victim's system as a launch platform for attacks on other sites. A disgruntled former employee or a consultant who gained network information while working with a company may also cause an incident.

Other aspects of the new sophistication of intruders include the targeting of the network infrastructures such as network routers and firewalls and the ability to cloak their behaviour. Intruders use Trojan horses to hide their activity from network administrators; to authenticates and log in without the activity showing up in the system logs. Intruders also encrypt using packet sniffers even if the victim finds the sniffer logs; it is difficult or impossible to determine what information was compromised. In the 1980s and early 1990s, DoS attacks were infrequent and not considered serious. Today, these types of attacks occur more frequently. The tools available to launch an attack have become more effective, easier to use, and more accessible to people without an in-depth knowledge of computer systems. A sophisticated intruder embeds an attack procedure in an email to friends. Thus, people who have the desire but not the technical skill are able to break into systems. Even, there have been instances of intruders breaking into a UNIX system using a relatively sophisticated attack and then attempting to run DOS commands. The SANS Institute and the Federal Bureau of Investigation (FBI) have jointly created the SAN/FBI Twenty Most Critical Security Vulnerabilities list ever produced. The list comprises of the most common threats for Microsoft Windows and UNIX systems. The detail list is available at http://www.sans.org/top20/.

The tool that is available to examine programs for vulnerabilities even in the absence of source code is also use by intruders to find new ways to break into systems. At this point in time a few issues stand out as being under-explored but possibly of considerable interest: Can biometrics be integrated with IPSec? Using biometrics as a means of personal identification is more assuring and comfortable, authentication and authorisation is granted based on a unique feature of an individual. However, a major shortcoming that plagues the use of this system is that accident can lead to loss of biometric identity. (Yeung, 2006). It was emphasised that for biometrics to be publicly accepted, implementations will require cooperation between organizations and individuals, working with developed open standards that meet the demand for security and demonstrates the protection of personal privacy. This idea has been reflected in the proposed model (see chapter 5 for further discussion). In conclusion, biometrics authentication sub-systems should be designed based on the conditions most effective and convenient to suit organization, government or institutions' security activities. Although major controversies relating to the use and applicability of biometrics technology for security purposes have been raised by experts, the expected benefits this method of security could provide to organizations, institutions and the government outweighs the weaknesses of adoption.

4. RECOMMENDATION

The Internet is a worldwide network of insecurely connected networks that are extremely easy to gain access through a host computer. The unauthorised access to information is very easy and is very hard to catch the intruders. The computer connected to the Internet can be a weak link, allowing unauthorised access to both individuals and organisations information irrespective of location. This research recommends that the Internet security vendors, organisations, and governments should targets the following areas:

i. Aligning Internet security with the organisational/business strategy
ii. Exploiting Internet security issues and available tools for competitive advantage
iii. Create efficient and effective way of managing Internet security issues
iv. Continuous improvement of security policies that will be dynamically enhance existing IPSec tool with biometrics (see Chapter 5 for further discussion).

It has been suggested by Shoniregun (2006) that the first two areas above concerned with information security strategy, the third with managing Internet security, and fourth with adopted security policies.

5. CONTRIBUTION TO KNOWLEDGE

The extensive literature research revealed that the IPSec should be combined with other security technologies (hardware or software) to achieve fairly secured operations. The contributions of this research to knowledge are:

i. Conceptual ideology of IPSec
ii. Classification and taxonomy of IPSec.
iii. Impacts of IPSec on operating systems and Internet security.
iv. Synchronising IPSec (SIPSec) with user's biometric profile

This study will help in addressing the critical issues facing Internet users, and Internet security professionals as they endeavour to implement IPSec. It also provides a window on the future understanding of the limitation of IPSec. Moreover, the SIPSec Model has been designed to provide a one-stop shop reference for integrating biometrics into the IPSec operations. Thus the study of the IPSec is not simple but necessary for the users, ISPs, organisations, and the governments all around the world in understanding the limitations and to adopt new strategies of how to secured their transactions. However, security and performance remains to be conflicting opponents!

6.   FUTURE WORK

It is noted that many other factors are relevant to the successful implementation of SIPSec. The immediate future work will investigate the methods of resolving any conflicting policies between the IPSec and SIPSec. A prototype of the SIPSec will be developed based on closure, identity, inverse, and associativity (see chapter 5 for further discussion).

REFERENCES

Allen, J., Alberts, C., Behrens, S., Laswell, B., and Wilson, W., 2000, Improving the Security of Networked Systems, October 2000, Cross Talk, The Journal of Defence Software Engineering.

Arkko, J., and Nikander, P., 2003, Limitations of IPsec Policy Mechanisms Ericsson Research Nomadic Lab, Jorvas, Finland, http://www.arkko.com/publications/SWP03.pdf (30 January 2007).

Carmes, E. June 2002, IP v6: Answers To Your Questions, http://www.ipv6forum.com/navbar/documents/6WIND-IPv6-answers-v2.0.pdf (28 January 2007).

Cross S E., 2000, Cyber Security, 2000, Software Engineering Institute, Carnegie Mellon University, USA.

Householder, A., Manion, A., Pesante, L. and Weaver, G.M., 2001, Managing the Threat of Denial-of-Service Attacks, Research paper v10.0 presented at CERT Annual Conference, Carnegie Mellon University

Interlink Networks, 2003, Link Layer and Network Layer Security for Wireless Networks, http://vnu.bitpipe.com/detail/RES/1055510132_601.html (30 January 2007).

Liu, et al., 2001, E-Commerce Agents, Marketplace Solutions, Security Issues, and Supply and Demand, Springer.

Shoniregun, C. A., 2003, Are existing internet security measures guaranteed to protect user identity in the financial services industry?, International Journal of Services, Technology and Management (IJSTM), Volume 4.

Shoniregun, C. A., 2005, Impacts and Risk Assessment of Technology for Internet Security: Enable information Small-medium Enterprises (TEISMEs), Springer New York, USA.

Shoniregun, C.A., 2006a, Keynote speach: 'Phishing and the Phishers', IEEE International Conference on Digital Information Management (ICDIM-2007), Banalore, India.

Shoniregun, C.A., 2006b, Distinguished Lecture on Synchronising IPSec with Biomterics, Purdue University Calumet, Indiana, USA.

Timmers, P., 2000, Electronic commerce: strategies and models for B-to-B trading, John Wiley.

Yeung, B. (2006). Biometrics Copyrights. Triware Networld System L.L.C, http://www.tns.com/biometrics.asp (18 January 2007).

INDEX

Symbols